John Silvester is Australia's longest-serving crime reporter, covering the beat since 1978. He has won four Walkley Awards, the Graham Perkin Australian Journalist of the Year Award, nine Melbourne Press Club Quills, nine Victorian Law Foundation Awards, a Ned Kelly Award for true crime writing, a Ned Kelly lifetime achievement award, an ASEAN Fellowship to study crime and corruption in South East Asia, and has been elevated to the Australian Media Hall of Fame.

John narrated and co-wrote true crime documentaries produced and directed by Terry Carlyon, including the Logie-winning ABC documentary *Conviction*, on the murder of Jill Meagher. He has written or co-authored over 30 books, including *Naked City*, and the *Chopper* and *Underbelly* series, later adapted to film and television.

John appeared in one *Underbelly* movie as himself but was asked to quietly remove himself from the set for overacting.

He writes the award-winning 'Naked City' column for *The Age*, presents the true crime podcast of the same name, and appears weekly on the top-rating 3AW breakfast program as 'Sly of the Underworld'.

John fought world champion Barry Michael to a draw in a charity boxing match which many experts still refer to as 'The Bloodbath of Blackburn'.

For more on the *Naked City* podcast,
scan the QR code below:

Also by John Silvester

Naked City

DARK CITY

True Stories of Crimes, Cock-ups, Crooks & Cops

JOHN SILVESTER

MACMILLAN
Pan Macmillan Australia

Pan Macmillan acknowledges the Traditional Custodians of Country throughout Australia and their connections to lands, waters and communities. We pay our respect to Elders past and present and extend that respect to all Aboriginal and Torres Strait Islander peoples today. We honour more than sixty thousand years of storytelling, art and culture.

Some of the people in this book have had their names changed to protect their identities.

First published 2024 in Macmillan by Pan Macmillan Australia Pty Ltd
1 Market Street, Sydney, New South Wales, Australia, 2000

NATIONAL LIBRARY OF AUSTRALIA

A catalogue record for this book is available from the National Library of Australia

Typeset in 12/16 pt Adobe Garamond Pro by Midland Typesetters, Australia

Printed by IVE

The author and the publisher have made every effort to contact copyright holders for material used in this book. Any person or organisation that may have been overlooked should contact the publisher.

FSC www.fsc.org MIX Paper | Supporting responsible forestry FSC® C018183

The paper in this book is FSC® certified. FSC® promotes environmentally responsible, socially beneficial and economically viable management of the world's forests.

To the young men and women who patrol in the Divvy Vans.
Sometimes the least experienced have to show the most wisdom.

CONTENTS

WHAT THE CRITICS SAY

'John is the longest serving crime writer in Australia. He's also the funniest person in the world. I like this man, and I like his book.'
Caroline Overington, Literary Editor, The Australian

'His work is witty, engaging and sharp, although the villains wouldn't agree.'
Jason Steger, Book Editor, The Age *and* Sydney Morning Herald

'You wouldn't like it if people caused you or your family grief. Be cautious what you put in your pages and books.'
Tommy Ivanovic, the third inmate in the division when
Matt Johnson attacked and killed drug boss Carl Williams.
Unsurprisingly, Tommy saw nothing.

'A journalist imbued with a desire to promote his own self-interest and publicity will often ignore or disregard the welfare of the community.'
Supreme Court Justice Norman O'Bryan, dismissing Silvester's claim a jury had been nobbled. Justice O'Bryan was unaware the jury he was addressing at the time had been nobbled by the Hells Angels. Oops.

FOREWORD

When I walked into *The Age* as a young investigative reporter in 2006, John 'Sly' Silvester was already a legend. The finest crime reporter in Australia, he knows every cop worth knowing and a good share of Victoria's gangsters, bank robbers, bikies, money cleaners and lawyers, both good and bad. Detectives call him from safe phones, leaving no trace for their superiors as they leak transcripts of phone taps or tips about getaway cars and suspects.

Family members of murder victims respect his commitment to articulating their anguish and pain while pressing for justice, sometimes for years.

Judges nod at Silvester in court, having previously dealt with him as barristers and known him to be fair and scrupulous. Some crims scowl at him, although those with sharper minds also nod, if only because they fear his pen.

Like most with even a passing interest in news and the life of the city, they, too, are consumers of Sly's words: revealing, witty, sage and rich in history and humanity as he transports readers into Australia's underbelly. As with David Simon's portrayal of Baltimore in the seminal series *The Wire*, Silvester can also dissect bad policy and even worse politicians. But it is his ability to capture the true character of those that make up any captivating crime saga that makes his work shine. Hard detectives break down mid interview with Sly. Even harder crooks find that sliver of redemption. Justice is sought. And Sly is there to remind us, as he has done for decades now, that it is only sometimes found.

Nick McKenzie, August 2024

DARK

CITY

INTRODUCTION

From wild-west gunslingers to bushrangers to bootleggers, the law-abiding have always been fascinated by the activities of those on the dark side. We all want to know what makes them tick. And the criminals themselves are equally intrigued. Go to a crook's house and the odds are you will find a framed photo of *Scarface*.

Authors from Shakespeare to Runyon and just about every Hollywood producer knows that a crime yarn told reasonably well brings in the punters. When colleague Andrew Rule and I did a book called *Tough: 101 Gangsters*, we did a proper index in the back with all the page numbers that referred to our selected colourful characters, not to pretend the book had any particular historical merit, but because we knew that if those included flicked to the back and saw their names, they would buy (or steal) 10 copies, which would pay for the print run.

After we published one of our *Underbelly* books, I received a phone call from a gruff-sounding guy who claimed we had put his picture on the cover (he was a pallbearer in a gangland funeral). I expected an earful. Instead, I was given a proposition.

The fellow said that as well as being a mourner at mobsters' funerals, he was a part-time actor and suggested he could be cast in the next *Underbelly* TV series.

I passed on his details. He was not picked. Turned out he was suspected of being a member of one of Australia's best ever armed robbery crews, a case of art imitating life.

Gangsters from the 1950s Freddie Harrison and Normie Bradshaw could always be found on the opening day of a George Raft or Jimmy Cagney gangster flick. Fame can often be judged when someone is recognised by just one name. In Australia, the notorious, such as Roger (Rogerson), Abe (Saffron), Tony (Mokbel) and Carl (Williams), became crime celebrities.

Then there's probably the most famous of all, Mark 'Chopper' Read, who perfectly summed up the public's fascination with crime, observing: 'posh people love gangsters'.

Some of those within these pages have become social media stars and are stopped for autographs and selfies. One once remarked to me: 'Fame is overrated – I had to get shot seven times to become famous.'

Another said he always agreed when asked for a photo because: 'You never know who's going to be on a jury.'

This book, the second volume of *Naked City*, is, I hope, more than just a series of profiles on the bad guys. We look at the crooks, try to go inside the crimes they commit and look at the good guys, those who have made careers out of pursuing the dangerous and others who have simply found themselves in the wrong place at the wrong time.

The feedback from the first volume of *Naked City* has been wonderful. I hope you enjoy this one as much.

PART 1

CRIMINALS & COVER-UPS

A crime is a statistic that covers a tragedy. Behind the crime there is often the most basic of stories: Good v Evil.

We look at the organised crime group who threw up a patsy to take the blame for a homicide. They would have gotten away with it if not for one detective who worked so the innocent man was not convicted, then made sure the right one was.

And the detective handed the cold case gangland murder that no-one expected her to solve. Until she did.

Then there are the cover-ups; from premiers, ministers and the man who would become prime minister – swept under a very expensive carpet.

THE LONG, WINDING ROAD TO THE TRUTH

The star witness was made an offer too good to refuse: plead guilty to a murder he didn't commit or end up on the wrong side of the sort of people who never forget.

The murder and the subsequent trials (including that of an innocent man) were described by Supreme Court judge Kevin Bell as 'unprecedented in the history of the court'.

The case exposed a practice used by an organised crime group to use patsies to confess to crimes they didn't commit to protect the real offenders. It opened a window to a deadly crime feud, the power of gangsters to manipulate the justice system, and three juries, one paralysed with fear and two that saw through a maze of lies to the truth.

*

No one really knows how the feud started. Regardless, participants are prepared to die or be jailed for decades as part of the power struggle for the control of drug markets and protection rackets in Melbourne's west. To them, it is a war and they are the soldiers.

Yet the catalyst for this straight-out execution was not millions in crime assets but a petty dispute over a wedding car. It would be laughable if it wasn't fatal. The influential Mark Malkoun lent his upmarket BMW to the Haddara family as a wedding car but refused a similar request from the Chaouk clan. Malkoun washed his hands of the dispute, suggesting the families work it out themselves.

As they are not the types to head to VCAT for an independent assessment, the dispute was likely to end in violence – although no one could have anticipated a street execution.

On 20 June 2009, the feud between the Chaouks and Haddaras reached another flashpoint in a quiet street in Altona North.

Ali Chaouk had called out Mohammed Haddara. They were to meet one-on-one with no guns, but Ali fibbed and arrived with a .44 Magnum.

As insurance, Mohammed abducted a Chaouk associate, Ahmed Hablas (Ali's cousin by marriage) and forced him into his car. The message was clear: if there was no resolution, Hablas would be bashed.

Mohammed's insurance policy proved useless, as Ali shot his enemy five times, twice in the side and three times in the back, at 7.50 pm in Fifth Avenue.

A neighbour ran out to shield the victim until the ambulance arrived, concerned the gunman would return to finish him off.

The initial head of the investigation, now Superintendent Tim Day, says police expected a likely payback shooting that night. 'The Santiago Taskforce (into Middle Eastern crime) looked after risk mitigation while we investigated the homicide.'

The Homicide Squad went to the Haddaras to promise the murder would be fully investigated. They also went to the Chaouks to make it clear Ali was a suspect and would have to be interviewed, and they wanted to make sure the process was conducted with no risk.

For some context and family history: Ali's brother, Mohammed, was shot dead in April 2005 when police went to arrest him. He pulled a samurai sword on the Special Operations Group, making the classic mistake of bringing a knife to a gunfight. Mohammed Chaouk was wanted in connection with an attempted murder, alleged drug trafficking and a stolen car racket.

His father, Macchour Chaouk, was murdered 14 months after the execution of Mohammed Haddara.

The Chaouk family referred police to their solicitor Alan Swanwick who the next day promised to bring in a person of interest.

Then Homicide detective Barry Gray says: 'We were expecting Ali, and Swanwick arrived with another man saying, "This is Mr Hablas." We knew who he was and we considered him a witness.'

Not only did the lawyer take in Hablas (freshly showered and wearing clothes that couldn't be linked to the crime scene), he advised police to caution him before producing a five-page statement describing how Hablas was abducted, managed to escape, was chased by Mohammed Haddara and then wrestled the gun from his kidnapper and shot him in self-defence.

If the statement was to be believed, Hablas was a hero, not a murderer. The sticking point was that the police did not believe it. Another sticking point was the victim had been shot five times, which included three in the back and one at close range while on the ground.

'It was not consistent with self-defence,' Gray says, attempting to keep a straight face.

Helpfully, Swanwick took in Ali Chaouk the following night to be questioned. The solicitor brushed off Day's concerns that representing both men was a conflict of his clients' interests.

So, there was a man who police believed was innocent confessing he had killed, and another man who police believed was the killer but was denying involvement.

Here was the dilemma: should police charge the wrong man? If they charged the right man, would he be able to use Hablas' confession as the smokescreen to escape a guilty verdict? And Ali Chaouk had two tame relatives who swore he was at home at the time of the killing.

Day says it wasn't a matter for the police, but the courts. 'We are the collectors of the evidence and our subjective views are not relevant. It was a matter for a jury to decide.'

Hablas believed (and was assured by Ali Chaouk) that his concocted self-defence story would hold and must have been surprised that, a year after the shooting, he was charged with murder.

After a couple of months in remand, Hablas recanted his confession, saying he had been intimidated by the real shooter. He was understandably surprised this was not raised at his bail application. His family decided it was time to find independent legal representation and turned to the experienced firm of Stary Norton Halphen.

'They are a decent family that was dragged into this conspiracy,' Gray says.

Police secretly recorded Ali Chaouk telling family members if multiple people confessed to a crime, it could create enough doubt to destroy any police case.

It is part of a pattern several Middle Eastern crime clans follow: treat the police as enemies, refuse to cooperate, try to intimidate local cops by turning up in numbers to deter them from conducting searches, and threaten witnesses.

At Hablas' trial, Gray says everyone in the court knew an innocent man was in the dock. 'We were all on the same page, knowing it would be a travesty of justice if he was convicted.' That included the jury which took just two hours to acquit in October 2011.

Gray could have let the case lapse, but he kept investigating even after he left Homicide, persuading Hablas to give evidence.

Perhaps when the car Hablas was sitting in at a McDonald's car park was peppered with 10 shots from a machine gun, he realised he had backed the wrong horse.

Police traced but did not find the murder weapon, although they located the buried spent shells. Ali Chaouk was charged, but the first jury was disbanded on day six of the trial after some jurors expressed concerns for their safety.

Ali Chaouk's two alibi witnesses were blown out of the water when one admitted to the Office of Special Examiner that while Chaouk had been home on the night of the murder, he had taken a phone call outside then disappeared before the killing. Police believe the call was from Haddara, organising the meeting.

At the second trial, which lasted 22 days in 2018, the jury returned a guilty verdict.

Day says Barry Gray spent more than a decade pursuing justice for the Haddara family.

'Do not underestimate the determination of the quiet man. Without his work the murder would have remained unsolved, and we would have had another gangland war,' Day says.

Had the false confession succeeded, Day says, police would have been swamped by similar cases involving patsies intimidated to take the fall.

Judge Bell sentenced Chaouk to 24 years in prison to serve a minimum of 18.

By the time Ali Chaouk is eligible to apply for parole, he will be 55 and will have spent 29 of the previous 30 years in prison. His son was six when Chaouk was arrested for the murder. The boy will be 24 by the time his father has served his minimum term.

Chaouk himself, having intimidated someone to falsely confess to murder, persuaded witnesses to lie on his behalf and having shot someone dead in cold blood, responded with profound indignation at his sentencing.

'I don't accept the verdict, it's unsafe. I'm appealing the decision. It's a miscarriage of justice.'

Perhaps he should reflect that shooting someone five times in the street is very unsafe.

ROOKIE DRAGGED INTO TRIPLE MURDER

The 12-storey Manchester Unity Building can lay claim to being the most beautiful and innovative structure in Melbourne. Built in 1932 with Depression labour, it was designed to show that even in times of turmoil, the solid insurance company was still a trusted investment.

The Gothic design was a smaller model of the famous Tribune Tower in Chicago. (About 10 years later, the art deco Russell Street Police Headquarters was built as a mini version of New York's Empire State Building.)

The Manchester Unity Building was the first in Victoria to include an escalator, the first with air-conditioning and the first with a high-speed lift. It had a rooftop garden with ponds, and in the basement was a South Pacific-themed restaurant.

But when dairy farmer-turned-policeman Peter Kemp walked from the Elizabeth Street office of Victoria Police's traffic and patrol group to the Manchester Unity Building, his mind was not on history or architecture. The self-confessed 'green-as-grass' cop was assigned to direct traffic in the shadow of the building, at the intersection of

Collins and Swanston streets. Wearing white gloves and the summer-issue pith helmet – and without a gun or even a radio – he was about to step out into the intersection for what he expected would be a routine shift.

Kemp was brought up on the family's Katunga dairy farm and joined the police force almost on a whim. 'I dropped in at the police station at Numurkah and grabbed an application form. That was late in 1976.'

His mission was not to right wrongs or solve cases. He was about to marry and wanted a secure wage. On the farm, he earned $90 a week, at a horticultural centre it was $120, but in the police force, it would be $240.

In February 1977, he was given five days' notice to turn up at the Police Academy for the five-month training course. At 23, he was the oldest of his squad.

On graduation, all but one of his squad (who had relatives in the force who pulled some strings) were sent to traffic and patrol, which is why on that hot afternoon in March 1978, he found himself outside the Manchester Unity Building.

'I was standing by the curb when a man came running down the street yelling for me to come with him because his friends had been killed. I didn't want to leave my post, but he almost dragged me with him.'

Kemp was supposed to have taken the police radio from the cop he was relieving on point-duty, but he had wandered off without handing it over, which meant the young constable couldn't call for back-up. Most days it wouldn't matter but this day it did.

Hidden behind a locked opaque-glass door were the bodies of jeweller Paul Pace and jewel dealers Robert Wartman and Keith Hyman.

Kemp and the unknown tenant who had virtually dragged him to the eighth floor peeked through the slit-style letterbox and could see no activity.

'I wasn't really sure what to do, and it was the citizen who grabbed my pith helmet off my head and started smashing the glass in the door. I took over and smashed it in, then climbed in,' says Kemp.

'I remembered the lessons from the academy to preserve the crime scene.' (It was later described as perfectly preserved.) 'There were two males face down who looked like they had been shot in the back of the head.' In the next room, he saw blood splatter on the wall and the third body.

'I didn't need to try and check a pulse. I had been around farms long enough to know they were dead.'

Hyman and Pace had been putting together a deal involving eight cut diamonds valued at $31,000 for a mystery buyer who was supposed to arrive with the money. Wartman had just wandered in to buy a pair of inexpensive earrings. It is thought he was shot because he could have been a witness.

They were forced to lie face down with their arms outstretched in the surrender pose before being shot in the back of the head.

Kemp went to another office to ring his bosses, who at first thought it was a practical joke. A crime car was sent to confirm the discovery.

The keen but raw Kemp was determined to preserve the scene, so much so that he refused entry to a senior Homicide investigator until he proved his identity. Kemp was told: 'Sit over there and write down what had happened.'

Eventually, he walked back to his office, deposited his kit and took the train home. No debriefing, no stress counselling, not even a pat on the back. On the train: 'I had time to start thinking, and I started to feel a bit wobbly.'

Walking home from the station, delayed shock hit him. 'I froze in the middle of the street and grabbed hold of a traffic pole.' It took minutes for him to compose himself.

The next day, a boss took him aside and said: 'You did good.' Then it was back to directing traffic. Kemp remembers the inquest and seeing the devastated families. 'It was so sad. It's never left me.'

I had been a cadet reporter for 40 days when the news of the Manchester Unity triple murder broke, and I was ordered to get there fast. I ran the four city blocks, gasping like a goldfish not from fatigue but panic – and was unable to find out the most basic information until I was relieved by crime reporters who knew what they were doing.

The murders remain unsolved. The main suspect, Alex Tsakmakis, had a short and violent history on the wrong side of the law. In January 1978, about seven weeks before Manchester Unity, he bound professional runner Bruce Lindsay Walker with ropes, chains and chicken wire before tossing him over the side of a cabin cruiser.

Walker was alive when he went under, and his body was found washed up at Point Lonsdale. Police believe he was killed over a dispute involving payment for a 1935 Plymouth.

While on bail for murder, Tsakmakis, desperate for money to pay legal fees, robbed a Hawthorn Tattslotto agency on 29 June 1979. He forced Ivy and George Kartsounis to lie on the floor in a manner identical to the Manchester Unity crime scene, shooting George twice in the head and his wife three times. Against all odds, they survived.

In 1984, Tsakmakis murdered jail rival Barry Robert Quinn by pouring industrial glue over him then setting him on fire. A fake death notice was put in the paper under Tsakmakis' name saying he and Quinn 'always stuck together'.

Kemp soon left Melbourne to spend nearly 20 years working in country stations in the Shepparton district, enjoying the work but not the pettiness of some administrators.

As a country patrol cop, his cases rarely made headlines, but they left their mark, like the fatal car accidents on lonely roads and the suicides. 'One used a shotgun in front of wife and children. He was still breathing, though he could never have survived. The ambo turned off his lights and sirens.' A local photographer was called to take pictures for the inquest brief. Kemp said the difference was the photographer had attended every fatal crash while police shared the load. 'He was a lovely fellow. He said he was OK with it, but it hit him hard later on.'

For Kemp, the pull of the land never left him. He and his wife, Aileen, bought an orchard filled with pear, peach and apricot trees. He thought he could balance being a cop and an orchardist. He was wrong. One day after being 'jacked up' by a violent offender, he came home to tell Aileen: 'I'm done. It's time for me to go.'

She says: 'He said it was the closest he had come to drawing his gun, and he had not joined to shoot someone.'

Kemp finished on 14 February 1996, serving exactly 19 years.

If he thought he had escaped policing unscathed, he soon found he took mental baggage into retirement. 'It took me two years to debrief,' he says. The petrol fumes from the farm machinery would take him back to fatal accident scenes. 'I could smell the blood.'

It was only the peace of the farm that eventually healed him.

Peter was suffering from terminal cancer when he shared his story with me in 2023. He passed away a few weeks later.

HOW MORSE BROKE THE CODE OF SILENCE

When Detective Sergeant Sara Morse walked into the Purana Taskforce, she didn't expect a soft case to settle into her new job. In fact, she was handed one of the oldest and most difficult murder files – the contract killing of Graham 'The Munster' Kinniburgh, gunned down in leafy Kew on 13 December 2003.

The first problem for Morse was that, after nearly 10 years, many who knew what had happened were gangsters who adhered to the code of silence.

The second was that the man who ordered the hit, drug dealer Carl Williams, had been silenced in 2010, when he was bashed to death in Barwon Prison.

Morse had been part of the Petra Taskforce, set up to investigate the murders of Terence Hodson and his wife Christine, killed in their Kew home in May 2004. (Who would have thought Kew was such a gangsters' nest? You would think the only risk there would be getting skittled by a Range Rover at school pick-up.)

Purana investigators had persuaded Williams to become a prosecution witness, only to see the case die with his murder. To make matters worse, one of the men nominated as part of The Munster's hit team, Terrence Blewitt, hadn't been seen for years. At least six separate underworld sources claimed Blewitt had been killed in a shootout with his gangland partner and buried 'without a headstone'.

Morse went about trying to find the original source of the claim, which proved to be a senior member of the Carlton Crew, Mario Condello, who had been murdered outside his Brighton home (at least it wasn't Kew) in 2006.

Yet there was a tiny flicker of life. There was a statement from one of Carl's hitmen – the man we call the Runner. A former armed robber, he was hired to murder Jason Moran in 2003 for $100,000. (He also killed Pasquale Barbaro, who was sitting next to Jason.)

Williams failed to pay – a very shortsighted financial strategy, as the Runner turned on him and became a police witness. According to the Runner, Williams planned to kill anyone connected with the Moran family.

'Carl had me also do surveillance on Graham Kinniburgh and Steve Collins, who were friends of the Moran camp. Carl told me that if he couldn't kill Jason, he wanted Kinniburgh and Collins dead.'

He would tell police that another hit team was assigned to kill Jason Moran's father, Lewis, and that again Williams nominated Kinniburgh as the alternate target. He said he delivered a $20,000 down payment, two guns and some white powder to the team on behalf of Carl. That team, he said, was Terry Blewitt and Stephen John Asling.

So, who is Asling?

The precise moment the country kid who boarded at Assumption College graduated from a likeable larrikin to gangster may never be known, but even then he had a reputation as a short guy with a short fuse.

In a school where there were two religions – Catholicism and football – he was, according to a fellow student: 'a little forward pocket rover who wasn't frightened to dish out and cop his share [of punishment].

'He was a tough bastard, but what you remembered were his mad eyes. He just looked like he genuinely wanted to hurt you.'

Perhaps Asling's future career path was illuminated after an away game in Bendigo. 'He pissed on the Bendigo courthouse door.' Much later, the judicial system would return the favour.

'We thought we would be reading about him one day,' the schoolmate said. And they were right.

Asling and his close mate Stephen Barci had an inside man in the security business, which meant they were able to pull off several major armed robberies, including one where they netted more than $420,000.

The trouble was that their inside man later became the police's inside man, which meant the Armed Robbery Squad learnt the location of the next target.

On 28 July 1992, Asling, Barci and veteran robber Normie Lee (who was connected with the 1976 Great Bookie Robbery) arrived at Melbourne Airport armed with a .38 revolver, a .357 magnum, a .380 pistol, a .223 self-loading rifle with 26 cartridges, and a .308 rifle. Their target was $1 million in cash held at the Ansett Freight Depot, but when they arrived, 52 police were waiting.

Asling was the keen getaway driver – a touch too keen, as it turned out. Asling reversed the panel van to the depot. Barci and Lee grabbed three large bags with the money, threw them in the back and jumped in.

When Asling saw the Special Operations Group coming to intercept, he planted the foot just before his partners snipped the back doors, which meant they and the cash hit the bitumen. Lee was shot dead by police. Barci was shot three times and Asling stopped when the SOG smashed head-on into his utility.

Asling eventually served ten years for the armed robbery. When he was released, it was the middle of the underworld war. Where he met Williams hardly matters because it was well known that Carl had money and was hiring.

Williams wanted Blewitt and Asling to kill Lewis Moran for $150,000, but as Blewitt knew Lewis and wasn't too keen, Kinniburgh became the target.

Kinniburgh was no fool and began to carry a gun for the first time in years. He managed to fire a shot when he was ambushed outside his home shortly after midnight, but it did him no good. He was shot three times with two guns and died at the scene.

I met Carl the following day, and the man who had started to call himself The Premier ('because I run this town') was remarkably relaxed. Our conversation naturally headed to The Munster's demise.

'I've never met him and I've never heard a bad thing said about him. I have nothing to profit from his death. It's a mystery to me. I haven't done anything. My conscience is clear,' he lied.

As usual, Carl dudded his team of the remaining $120,000, and so Asling and Blewitt planned another job, this time to rob the Yarrawonga & Border Golf Club, in Mulwala, NSW, picking the Tuesday after Easter 2004, in expectation of a huge haul from the holiday crowds.

It was 13 April, four months to the day since the Kinniburgh hit. So optimistic were the raiding party that they lined up wheelie bins to fill with cash once they broke in. That is, until security guards pulled up and the job was aborted.

What happened next is uncertain, but there were harsh words about the failure to radio a warning about the guards, a gun drawn and then Blewitt was dead with a bullet in the back.

Using underworld sources and phone records, Morse's team found Asling rang underworld figure (and, ironically, Kinniburgh associate) Jeff Reading, who ran a scrap/refuse business in Thomastown. Homicide detectives say there is always a link between a killer and the location where the body is hidden. In this case, Asling had worked at Reading's business and knew the property well. Plus, Asling's phone was pinged in the area late on Easter Tuesday.

Morse was convinced the body was buried on the property and went about convincing her bosses to authorise a dig. But there is only one thing senior police hate more than an unsolved murder, and that is spending a truckload of money and still having an unsolved murder.

And they weren't looking in some pristine meadow. Reading, who died in 2009, had turned his leased land in Thomastown into Melbourne's Chernobyl, dumping everything from asbestos to dry-cleaning fluid next to the creek (it would eventually cost more than $2 million to rehabilitate).

Morse decided not to use a sledgehammer to crack a walnut, but a 20-tonne digger to crack a murder. In January 2016, they started to dig. After removing 4000 cubic metres of soil (half the MCG) over three days, they were still without a body. 'I was getting a little nervous when I was being reminded how much it was costing,' Morse says.

Then they found a three-metre-deep trench and human remains. It was Blewitt.

Asling's appeal over his Kinniburgh murder conviction was rejected. Sentenced to a minimum of 27 years, he will be in his 80s before he is eligible for parole. He is expected to be extradited to NSW to stand trial for Blewitt's murder.

Morse's then boss, Inspector Andrew Gustke, says: 'It takes a special type of investigator to take on a protracted case like this with no guarantee you will get there in the end. Sara and her team were able to think outside the square and ultimately remove a very dangerous person from our streets.'

THE DARKNESS OF THE DARK NET

Maybe it was because the detective (a Serbian refugee) had overcome many obstacles in his life that he readily took on the seemingly impossible case. When you grow up with a minefield at the end of your street, you tend to develop a healthy level of resistance to adversity.

The death he was asked to investigate was interstate and the trail to Victoria tenuous at best. The file contained a few screenshots from the computer of a young man who had died of an overdose in Perth. Worse still, the trail disappeared into the Dark Web, the internet version of quicksand.

But Senior Detective Igor Rusmir was prepared to have a go, even though he admits: 'I felt totally out of my depth.'

Henry Phillips, a graduate of Perth's Scotch College and the University of Western Australia, was a happy-go-lucky guy who was also hiding anxiety issues according to his brother, Ryan, who is also the Victorian Corrections and Community Services Deputy Secretary.

'He wouldn't take heroin in a million years and then somehow he ends up taking fentanyl.'

On 9 March 2017, Henry said goodnight to his father, went to bed and didn't wake up.

When the devastated family gathered at the family home, Henry's girlfriend gave Ryan a password to access his brother's computer, which showed a list of Dark Web accounts with purchases made with Bitcoins. 'There was a list of purchases similar to eBay where customers rate products like online shoppers.

'The dealers were given stars according to quickness of delivery, quality of package disguise and the quality of the product.'

The order forms are frightening in their professionalism. Order dates, expected express post delivery dates (free priority shipping!) and itemised billing are included.

Fentanyl can be fatal through accidental contact, and yet it is banging around the country in planes, trucks and posties' motor scooters with no one knowing the danger. One split, one drop and the powder is airborne, creating an immediate hazard.

Ryan saw one of the sellers had a code name that made him suspect a Melbourne link. And that is when he contacted Victoria Police.

Once Rusmir had the file, he realised he needed a crash course in computers. 'I was brand-new to all this and so I went to E-Crimes to learn what I could. They were fantastic and, without them, we wouldn't have been able to go any further.'

Shortly before he died of an overdose, the victim had asked online if 40 milligrams of fentanyl was safe. The drug is so powerful, two can be fatal.

Many were sceptical about Rusmir's investigation. No one was seizing fentanyl in Victoria and the Dark Net was too hard to penetrate.

Fentanyl is 50 times more powerful than heroin, 100 times more powerful than morphine and has caused an epidemic of fatal overdoses in the US and Canada. So what is the attraction? For the dealer, it is cheap and, as only tiny amounts are needed, relatively easy to import. It is often used to mix in with other drugs to increase yields by up to 1000 per cent.

Finally, the computer records showed Henry bought 40 milligrams from a dealer on the Dark Web site Dream Market. They found that after he placed the order, it was sent on 5 March 2017 and arrived two days later. The quick turnaround meant the dealer must be somewhere in Australia. Eventually, with the help of Australia Post, Rusmir found the delivery had come from Victoria.

Slowly, Rusmir identified the Melbourne source's online profile. His customers had given him a five-star rating for delivery and product purity, even though he was selling possibly the deadliest illicit drug ever made. It is also incredibly dangerous for police, but more of that later.

Now, the sting.

In January 2018, E-Crime detectives bought 100 milligrams of fentanyl powder for around $450 in Bitcoins. So dangerous is the drug that when it was tested at the police forensic lab, the wing was cleared.

A second buy was made, this time of 100 millilitres of liquid. It arrived labelled 'Perfume Forever'. Again, it was fentanyl.

This Dark Web dealer is the exact opposite of what you would expect. A respected national manager in an established firm, he was earning around $150,000 from his day job.

'You would never pick him. He looked like just about any other office worker in a suit,' says Rusmir.

The man, who we will call 'Richard', was 45 years old, a loving father of two daughters and a part-time drug dealer. Not that he made a fortune – a long-time drug user, he became addicted to OxyContin to manage pain. In 2012, he decided fentanyl was a cheaper option and began importing. Soon he was selling part of his shipments to pay for his own addiction.

He would prepare his sales on the kitchen bench near his two daughters. 'He seemed unaware of any danger,' says Rusmir.

Then the target disappeared. In May 2018, the site Dream Works banned the sale of fentanyl after multiple deaths in the US. Eventually he resurfaced on another Dark Web platform – complete with his five-star rating.

When police came knocking, it was a little confronting for Richard. Not only had he been pinged as a drug trafficker, but due to the toxicity, his house was declared a biohazard, meaning the place was searched by clandestine lab experts fully kitted in protective suits.

To the man in the suit, it must have seemed like he was being raided by Martians. He had a panic attack and needed ambulance staff to calm him via a triple-0 call.

Here is the hidden danger of fentanyl: investigating police are facing health dangers from the fumes. Many years ago, police found they were getting high when seized cannabis was burned, then drug police couldn't sleep for days from the fumes at speed labs. But fentanyl is on another level. In Pittsburgh, 18 SWAT team members collapsed and were hospitalised during a raid when a table containing the drugs about to be bagged was knocked over. The officers were overcome by the airborne particles.

Such is the risk that police from the Drug Taskforce may need to be equipped with the narcotic antidote Narcan for protection from accidental contact.

Drug dealer Richard cooperated immediately with police, to the point that when another fentanyl shipment arrived at his home, he alerted detectives.

He pleaded guilty to trafficking a drug of dependence and was sentenced to a community corrections order with 300 hours of community work. In the darkest of ironies, he was supervised by Ryan Phillips' staff in the Justice Department.

Richard was no big fish. He didn't make a fortune and he will never do it again. But the drugs he sold resulted in a young man dying. For that family, it is a life sentence.

'Such a tiny amount can kill,' says Ryan.

'The packages were delivered to my parents' Post Office box in Swanbourne. Mum would pick it up just as a normal parcel for her son.'

In the weeks and days before his death, Henry was looking forward to the future. The day before he had a job interview at a major hospital. The morning of the day he overdosed, he met his mentor for coffee, telling him the interview went well. He texted a mate to confirm they were going surfing the next day.

'People are taking this without understanding that this is so toxic. This will get much worse unless people are made aware of the dangers.'

There clearly is a major lag in the law here. The quantity required to be convicted of trafficking a commercial quantity of fentanyl is 50 grams or 50,000 milligrams. A fatal dose can be as low as two milligrams.

When Rusmir started his investigation, he found six dealers selling fentanyl on 10 different platforms. Now there are 106.

LEFT FOR DEAD ON THE SURGERY FLOOR

It is amazing what goes through your mind when you are about to die.

For Dr Andrew Taylor, it was all about preventing the gunman standing over him from pulling the trigger one last time.

In April 1999, Zuber Vukovic walked into the Hastings Clinic angry about his WorkCover and Transport Accident Commission (TAC) injury compensation package. He wasn't looking for treatment but revenge, believing his medical report underplayed his long-term injuries from car and workplace accidents. He had convinced himself he was going to receive $7 million; he was awarded $350,000, having already borrowed more than that from his relatives on the expectation of a massive payout.

Vukovic had been to the clinic more than 100 times in eight years, but Taylor was not his physician and was not the gunman's initial target. He had been to his regular GP's home the previous night – almost certainly armed – but that doctor was overseas on sabbatical. So Vukovic, 46, waited until the following morning to go to the clinic and shoot the first doctor he could find.

Taylor recalls: 'I saw him in the waiting room when he pulled the gun. I thought: "Oh no, he's going to kill himself", then he shot me in the right hip and left knee (mirroring Vukovic's own injuries). He then said: "Now you know how I feel."'

The wounded doctor crawled to a counter to try to find protection, but the gunman cornered him. 'He moved like Usain Bolt – not bad for a man with a permanent disability.'

The gunman shot him a further three times, leaving him with wounds in the legs, shoulder, chest, lower stomach and backside. One bullet travelled through his chest, missing his heart by a millimetre. 'He used solid target ammunition that went through me and that probably saved my life. It didn't shatter through the body.'

Taylor, a father of three, looked up and said: 'Zuber, you've killed me. Can I please phone my family and say goodbye?'

'I was trying to buy just one minute. I wanted to humanise me to him,' he recalled, 22 years after the unprovoked attack.

Instead of giving his victim his last phone call, the gunman lay down beside Taylor and shot himself in the chest.

And this is where it goes from inexplicable to downright weird. When the ambulance officers arrived, they decided Vukovic was in more danger than Taylor, making the call that the gunman would be given priority and taken by medical helicopter to The Alfred Hospital's specialist trauma centre. His victim would be taken by road to the local Frankston Hospital.

That is, until one of the police officers present stepped forward with a second opinion, delivered quite forcefully: 'This is bullshit. He's going in the chopper.' Room was made for both.

Sometimes too much knowledge is counterproductive. As he was loaded in, Taylor looked up and counted the tubes going into his body – there were seven. 'When you have four, you are in serious trouble,' he says.

He blacked out when he reached the hospital heliport and didn't wake for a week. He underwent emergency surgery on his 40th birthday.

Years earlier, Taylor had conducted a review of the NSW ambulance service, concluding that state-of-the-art trauma centres were not a great priority because shootings were a rarity and helicopter ambulances did not make enough difference to justify the costs.

When he arrived at The Alfred, he was given 17 units of blood in 40 minutes using a machine not available at most casualty centres. If he had been taken to the Frankston Hospital in a road ambulance, he would not have survived.

It is fair to say Taylor no longer agrees with his NSW conclusion. When he recovered, he worked some shifts at The Alfred trauma centre 'to see what it was like on the other side'.

Taylor was slugged $3500 for the helicopter flight while Vukovic flew for free. The offender was charged with attempted murder but allowed to plead guilty to intentionally causing serious injury and sentenced to a minimum of four years.

Two decades on, we are still facing this massive hole in the criminal code. Shoot someone repeatedly and, if they die, it is murder; if they live, it is nearly impossible to prove attempted murder. Isn't it time to change the law?

For all Taylor's pain and suffering, agonising rehabilitation, loss of income, nightmares and fears that the offender might come back, he received the same compensation as the patients and receptionist who witnessed the attack.

He shows no obvious hostility to the offender and no apparent mental scars from the attack.

'Getting shot doesn't hurt at all,' he observes.

Asked why he is so matter-of-fact, he replies: 'Because I lived.' The only time his eyes glisten with emotion is when he mentions his niece, Emily, then seven years old and battling a brain tumour. Weeks earlier, her parents, the wonderfully generous Peter and Jenny Schwab (Taylor's sister), had been told there was no hope.

Taylor organised for her to come home for those last few weeks and had already told his practice he would only work mornings, as he wanted to care for Emily every afternoon.

On the day of the shooting, he had planned to go to the Schwabs' for their son, William's, pirate-themed birthday party. (William is now a teacher in country Victoria and an expert on US presidents.) Emily was there enjoying the party and watching *101 Dalmatians* on TV.

Taylor's parents were at a wedding when they received the news that their son had been shot. 'My father said his happiest moment was sitting with Homicide detectives at the hospital when they told him it wasn't going to be their job.'

Emily felt sad her cousins and uncle had missed out on seeing Humphrey B. Bear at the party, so Humphrey turned up at The Alfred to see the still seriously ill doctor. Other patients in intensive care must have thought their medication had been doubled, seeing a giant bear standing next to a heavily sedated shooting victim.

Emily passed away the following month, while Taylor was still in hospital. 'Sometimes there is just no reason,' he says.

Taylor could have taken a risk-free job. Instead, he works in a Frankston clinic which cares for the drug-affected and mentally ill.

The day we visit, he opens the solid sliding door that separates patients from medical staff, speaks gently to an elderly and clearly sick woman to make sure she has some food, then walks purposefully to the busy cafe just up the road.

Outside is a man wearing a ship's captain's cap sitting at a bus stop, a pencil-thin man pacing back and forth yelling into a mobile phone and a woman who, if spitting was an Olympic event, would finish on the podium.

Ordering a coffee, he hands the young pregnant server a large box of free sample maternity vitamins so she doesn't have to pay over the counter and cheerfully answers a medical question from a lunchtime patron. Taylor has a wound on his head from a sailing mishap a few days earlier. Clearly, being shot hasn't slowed him down.

As a shooting survivor and a medical practitioner at the sharp end, his views on crime and addiction deserve to be heard. 'One in three of our patients with drug issues have done jail time and because they can't get a job, they commit more crime. We have 1000 heroin addicts at the clinic and we know opiate substitutes work.'

These addicts can be managed, he says, and are not a threat to the community. 'It is methamphetamines that is driving this craziness. They would be better off in jail, where their violence can be managed and they can detox.'

He suggests drug addicts who commit minor offences should be put in a secure facility for six weeks to break the cycle without a criminal conviction. If they continue to offend, they should be jailed.

Taylor is worried at the growth of illegal firearms in the area. One patient came in and remarked that he had been raided that morning by police looking for firearms. 'He said he had the laser dot on his chest [police aiming a gun at him] and seemed perfectly relaxed about it. I would be a shaking wreck.'

Another patient taught himself to make machine guns from scratch. 'He never said who bought them.'

He says some of these addicts are the victims of big pharmacy companies. 'Pain specialists were using the same six products for chronic conditions as for short-term intense pain. You take opiates for a year and your tolerance grows and you become addicted.

'You have to manage it and learn to live as normally as possible with the pain,' he says. Having been shot five times, he probably knows a bit about that subject.

Three years after this story first appeared, the bureaucracy has nearly done what the gunman couldn't – crush Dr Andrew Taylor.

A clinic that helps thousands of addicts is likely to close because of a bureaucratic decision that has left patients devastated and substance abuse experts bewildered.

Frankston Healthcare is in many ways the last chance for homeless, mentally challenged and addicted patients. The alternative is hopelessly clogged hospital emergency rooms, prisons or death.

There were four doctors. One found the COVID crisis the last straw, another has reached retirement age, a third is looking to move to a quieter practice. The last, Dr Taylor, is about to return his practising certificate after a decision by the Australian Health Practitioner Regulation Agency (AHPRA) to restrict his ability to prescribe drugs.

The decision to put training wheels on Taylor was made without visiting his clinic or interviewing any patients. It was made even though the agency acknowledged Taylor may not be in breach of any Victorian regulations.

If there is one GP entitled to seek a comfortable living working in a comfortable practice treating the comfortably well-off who are in discomfort, it is Taylor.

Instead, when he recovered from the shooting, he chose to work for the needy. He is a trusted and respected member of the local community.

AHPRA have been concerned about the amount of drugs Taylor prescribes, including Valium and the painkiller Tramadol. They have told him he will require permission from a medical mentor to prescribe, a decision he says is unworkable because he prescribes drugs such as methadone 50 to 60 times a day.

He argues the decision doesn't consider the unique nature of the practice. 'My first six patients today were homeless. I deal with 1360 patients with substance dependency that requires high dosage of medications,' he says.

His aim – and the clinic's – is to keep patients functional, then guide them to a path when they want to deal with addictions, something that can take years.

'AHPRA knows nothing about what we do, and I can't fight it. I was not judged by a doctor or a local expert. I can't tell you what sort of trainwreck is coming.

'If the clinic closes, some of our patients will go back on heroin, some to methamphetamines, crime and prisons, and others will kill themselves.'

A local homeless outreach nurse, Claire Lang, wrote to the government in protest.

> I work directly with many of the patients whose lives will be turned upside down as a result of this decision. Dr Andrew Taylor's practice caters for these patients' needs – without his services our patients will go unmedicated, further burdening the already stretched mental health and hospital system.
>
> Many will return to using illegal drugs – mainly opiates – and without a doubt these clients will be at increased risk of overdose and death.
>
> Dr Taylor will consult with a patient in the alleyway behind his surgery, where many of the rough sleepers in the area reside. He will consult in the local community kitchen if a patient is in need.
>
> He provides an amazing service to the most disenfranchised patients every single day. If he is unable to continue, no other doctors in our community will see this type of patient. They will be on their own. [He] provides genuine emotional support and often food for homeless and hungry patients.
>
> I am unable to comprehend how this decision can be made by people who have not spent a single day in his practice or worked a single day with his patients.

She told us: 'He prevents so many admissions to hospital it is amazing. If he is not here it will be carnage for the poor clients.'

In writing to AHPRA to defend himself and deny wrongdoing, Taylor pointed out he had not breached any regulations. 'I deeply value my professional reputation and my standing within the field of my work. It is work of great rewards and of onerous responsibility. I believe

I practise with patient safety and wellbeing as my goal, and I believe that harm minimisation is a cornerstone of addiction medicine.'

AHPRA responded: 'We note your submissions that you are compliant with Victorian regulations, however the Board made no findings in relation to your compliance with these regulations. Regardless of whether you are or are not compliant with Victorian regulations, the information before us indicates that your prescribing is not in accordance with the standards expected by the Board and the public, and that your prescribing and lack of insight into the Board's concerns presents an ongoing risk to the public that requires regulatory control.'

Except his public – the patients – are on his side. Some have headed to the local MP's office to express their concerns in a most colourful manner.

Regulations relating to treating the drug-dependent vary from state to state. Victoria is considered progressive while Tasmania and Queensland are more conservative.

Taylor is a warm and enthusiastic bloke. However, he is often too busy for niceties and may well have put a few noses out of joint (without anaesthetic) by not responding to initial queries in the way some would like.

So is he being punished because he broke the rules (apparently not) or because he ordered red wine with the fish?

Dr Taylor prescribes more drugs because his patients are the drug-dependent and mentally ill who, if not given their medications, will need hospitalisation or will return to illicit substances bought on the street. He is not handing out morphine for ingrown toenails or injecting filler into the lips of wannabe social influencers.

As he says: 'You have to be an idiot to do this sort of work.'

Bagging Taylor for prescribing drugs is a little like criticising the fire brigade for their water bill.

One of Australia's top experts in drug-dependency treatment supports Taylor and the clinic. The doctor, who cannot be named for professional reasons, says: 'Andrew sees patients with complex problems. About 95 per cent of GPs refuse to see them because they are perceived as too much trouble.

'The Victorian treatment system is dependent on doctors like Andrew.'

The issue, the doctor says, is not what Taylor is doing, but that he and his colleagues are doing too much. 'They are probably looking after too many patients, but they won't say no and don't turn anyone away.'

He says instead of restricting Taylor's practice, AHPRA should be looking at ways to support him.

'The evidence is that practices such as Andrew's are extremely cost-effective and rather than closing it there should be an investment to ensure it is run better.

'He is a genuine caring doctor who needs support.'

The doctor says AHPRA should use a local practitioner to evaluate the clinic and allow Taylor a hearing to explain his work. 'I don't think there has been natural justice here.'

In a statement, AHPRA said:

> Dr Andrew Taylor has conditions on his registration. The conditions limit his ability to prescribe Schedule Eight drugs and certain Schedule Four drugs without a supervisor in place. Dr Taylor's ability to practise is not otherwise affected.
>
> Under the National Law, conditions on a practitioner's registration are *only* applied where a National Board believes they are necessary to ensure public safety. Context of practice is one of the issues considered by the Board when making decisions.
>
> A decision by a National Board to impose conditions on a practitioner's registration is a decision that can be appealed to a tribunal. We are working with Dr Taylor to support his review options.

There are plenty of quacks who masquerade as cosmetic surgeons, give questionable evidence in court cases or overprescribe drugs for varying reasons.

Taylor works with our most needy and goes to places most of us try to avoid.

Restricting Taylor rather than supporting him will damage the people AHPRA wants to protect. Perhaps the body should adhere to the first rule of medicine: do no harm.

Postscript

Reporting is about telling a story as close to the truth as you can get. It is not about lobbying or trying to change the world.

But sometimes, just sometimes, the pieces fit together. Hours after we contacted AHPRA, they started to make noises that perhaps there could be a compromise.

When this story first appeared, we were approached by barristers prepared to fight for Taylor for free, patients who wanted to organise a protest and doctors who had concerns about the regulatory body.

Ten days after publication, AHPRA had the good sense to change its mind and the good grace to contact us to say it had reversed the decision to curtail Dr Taylor's medical practice.

A spokesperson for AHPRA said: 'Since conditions were placed on his registration last month, we have continued to work with Dr Taylor regarding his options to seek a review of those restrictions.

'As a result of that further engagement, the Board had sufficient information to be satisfied that the conditions are no longer required, and on 20 December (2022) have removed them. The public register is being updated to reflect this change.'

Taylor says when he was contacted: 'I had my bike on the rack and the surfboard on the roof, but I'm happy to go back into harness because these people are worth saving.

'With AHPRA's change of heart I just hope we can encourage more doctors to safely work in this space.

'The story you published certainly made a big difference.'

THE UNLIKELY WITNESS

At a rough estimate, I have written more than five million words on crime in the last 45 years, but there is one story that reminds me that good can, and does, triumph over evil.

Mersina Halvagis, 25, knew the drive well along Seventh Avenue at Fawkner Cemetery as she headed to the grave of her namesake grandmother in November 1997, who had died 18 months earlier aged 86.

It was All Saints Day, a busy day for the Fawkner Cemetery tearoom catering manager. But she was able to remember the polite young woman who asked for a bunch of the long-stemmed blue-and-white statice flowers and, as an afterthought, two bottles of Sprite. A check of the cash register roll showed the $9.70 sale was made at 3.47 pm.

After buying the flowers and drinks, Mersina drove her boyfriend's red Ford Telstar TX5 to a small car park in the Greek Orthodox section of the cemetery then walked about 50 metres to the family grave. As she was about to put water in the matching stone vase, she was attacked and stabbed to death.

Police profilers say the killer had probably established a beat and wandered the cemetery for weeks or months, looking for the right moment to strike. He probably went through dry runs, following other women, but chose not to attack because he was disturbed or because he was rehearsing his plans until he was ready.

A police reconstruction indicates that Mersina was bending over the grave when she was attacked from behind. She turned and was probably blinded by the sun as she fought for her life. She was struck viciously to the head, and although she was tiny, just 155 centimetres and less than 50 kilograms, she continued to fight and scream for help.

Her attacker stabbed her repeatedly. Her body was later found three graves from where her grandmother was buried, in an empty plot. The killer, who must have been covered in blood, managed to slip out of the cemetery unnoticed using a planned escape route.

On the first weekend of November, Crew One of the Homicide Squad was on call. They worked full-time on the case for more than three months. The seven investigators, aged from 29 to 40, chased down 400 leads and interviewed 1500 people. The government offered a $50,000 reward, then $100,000 and finally $1 million.

Mersina's parents, George and Christina, were immigrants who had built a loving family of two boys and two girls.

George was in the Greek merchant navy when in 1956 he jumped ship at Melbourne's Station Pier. He cut cane in Queensland, picked pears in Shepparton, grapes on the Murray, built railways and bridges and cleared scrub from Hamilton to Edenhope. He drove taxis in Melbourne and taught himself English by listening to his fellow workers.

Christina emigrated to Australia in 1964, met George and married in 1968. The next year, they bought a milk bar in Warracknabeal – the first of several businesses, including a restaurant and a bakery.

Then their daughter died.

I remember visiting their house, with carefully tended flowers and fruit trees in the garden. The formal dining room to the right was now a shrine to Mersina with photographs, teddy bears, a condolence book, the cross from her coffin and paintings of Christ.

George, a strong, self-sufficient man, was standing in the middle of her room, tears rolling down his cheeks. Christina clutched at dresses in her daughter's wardrobe and buried her face in the clothes. 'The bastard, the bastard . . .' she sobbed. 'Why? Why us? What did we ever do to deserve this?'

George taught himself to be a one-man lobbyist, pushing police and politicians not to allow his daughter's case to be archived. He became a regular presence at the Supreme Court, becoming a source of strength to the families of other murder victims.

There was the initial investigation, a second investigation and eventually a taskforce. A suspect emerged: serial sex offender and multiple murderer Peter Norris Dupas. Dupas had already been convicted for the stabbing murders of two women and sentenced to two life sentences with no minimum.

In 2000, he was convicted of killing psychotherapist Nicole Patterson, stabbed to death at her Northcote home. In 2004, he was convicted of the stabbing murder of Margaret Maher, a lost soul who had become a street sex worker, whose body was found in an industrial estate at Somerton in 1997, one month before Mersina's murder.

Dupas was a regular at the pub across the road from the cemetery and was suspected of stalking other women there. The case against Dupas was strong, but not strong enough. The Office of Public Prosecutions would not lay charges.

Then, in 2006, one of the fresh investigators, Paul Scarlett, made a phone call more in hope than expectation. It was to former criminal lawyer Andrew Fraser, who was serving a sentence for drug use and possession.

Fraser was hated by the cops, who had always thought he ran too close to the crims and were delighted when he crashed and burned through a cocaine addiction.

Placed in prison protection, he was stuck with 39 of the most repulsive inmates in Victoria and ended up doing regular gardening duties with Dupas. When Dupas was brought out of prison for a police interview, he refused to comment, leading detectives to believe he had been schooled by Fraser.

Even so, Scarlett rang and asked Fraser if he had information on the Halvagis case. The ex-lawyer responded: 'What took you so long?'

Fraser made a statement that Dupas had mimed the attack on Halvagis, including details never publicly released. With the new information police went back to Director of Public Prosecutions Paul Coghlan (later Supreme Court Justice Coghlan.)

Remember that Dupas was serving life and would never get out of jail. It would have made economic sense to refer the matter to the coroner to seek a finding that Dupas was the killer.

Instead, Coghlan authorised the prosecution. His sense of justice to the community and sense of compassion to the Halvagis family demanded it.

After Dupas was charged but before his trial, I asked a go-between to see if Fraser would meet with me. It is fair to say we were not fans of our respective work. I thought he was captive to his clients, didn't act as an officer of the court, was so competitive he had lost perspective and would do just about anything to win. Long before he was charged and convicted over drugs, I knew he was spiralling out of control from cocaine use. He no doubt thought I was too close to the cops and didn't give his clients a fair shake.

He would later tell me that gangster Jason Moran was in Fraser's office when he spotted me wandering on the footpath below. According to Andrew, Jason said: 'That's Silvester, I'm going to go down there and bite his nose off.'

'As his lawyer, I advised him against that,' Fraser said. According to Andrew, he did front me, but he must have had second thoughts as we had an amicable chat before we went our separate ways.

But when in 2001 Fraser was sentenced to five years, I thought it was unfair. He was a user, not a big wheel, and he got a big whack because the judge thought he had let the profession down.

There was another thing; Fraser was doing the gear with plenty of his colleagues (up to $1000 a day) and a handful of judges. He could have done a deal if he gave them up. Instead, he took his punishment and took responsibility for his actions.

He should never have been in maximum security, with the most dangerous men in the state. I have no doubt a cop with a grudge submitted a report that Fraser needed to be in the protection unit to make sure he did his time hard.

After his release, we met in a coffee shop in Clarendon Street, South Melbourne. He greeted me with: 'I don't know whether to buy you a coffee or punch you in the mouth.'

I said: 'Let's start with a coffee and see how we go.'

Fraser was honest and energetic, telling me the story of Dupas confessing. I asked him if he would participate in a video interview, embargoed until after the trial. He agreed, telling his story and mimicking Dupas and his stabbing action.

It was a generous act. Out of prison, he had lost his savings, his profession and many of his friends. He could have sold his story to several media outlets but stuck with our deal. Much later, he would rightly receive a large part of the million-dollar reward. He rebuilt his life and died in 2023 after a long and brave battle with cancer.

In 2007, Dupas was convicted of the murder of Mersina Halvagis. He appealed, and the conviction was overturned. Coghlan authorised a second prosecution; in 2010, Dupas was convicted again.

The Halvagis family was there to see justice was done.

HOW TWO UNDERCOVER COPS INFILTRATED A BIKIE GANG

He was used to his new life, almost relaxed in his new persona. He had successfully turned himself into an outlaw, riding beyond the realms of society with the worst of the bikie gangs.

But now the undercover cop said a silent prayer. He turned his head and ducked down behind the bowser at the country petrol station. It was a moment that could end the operation; one that could end his life.

As he filled his Harley-Davidson, he looked up to see the family sedan pull up on the other side. He held his breath. The man removed the petrol cap and fiddled with the nozzle. He hardly gave the dirty biker a second glance. Their worlds would never cross; what could they possibly have in common?

Little did he know that it was his next-door neighbour, far away from the serenity of his suburban life, in the middle of a carefully contrived operation to infiltrate the Bandidos.

This was the final strategy in a police campaign to prevent a bikie gang war.

It had begun months earlier in bleak, damp Ballarat, the first morning of winter only hours away. Two angry and suspicious men and two detectives meet in a desolate car park.

Out of sight, armed police watch, ready to move if things turn ugly. Trouble has been fermenting for more than a year and they know that if nothing is done, killings will follow.

The police want to get representatives of two warring bikie groups together: the Vikings, for years the tough gang that controlled Ballarat; and the Bandidos, the predators with a worldwide reputation for violence and drugs.

Their world is always filled with tensions, but usually there is a balance between the bravado of drug-enhanced aggression and the basic instinct of self-preservation.

But that balance was destroyed in Victoria when the two main biker groups agreed to divide the state, leaving other gangs exposed.

According to police intelligence, the Hells Angels, long the biker power in south-east Australia, agreed to allow the Bandidos to expand into regional Victoria on the condition the Angels' power remained unchallenged in Melbourne.

The Bandidos had an established expansionist policy. They simply moved into country centres and used their national numbers to take over local biker groups. 'Join us, or get beaten to a pulp' was the general message. The result? An increase in membership and new drug distribution opportunities.

If a major feud is looming, the police often try to broker a peace deal. No headlines or spectacular arrests, but many underworld figures owe their lives to quiet intervention before guns are drawn.

But on that Friday, 31 May 1996, only the Vikings wanted to talk to Detective Senior Sergeant Graham Larchin and Detective Sergeant Rob Sodomaco from the Organised Crime Squad. The two Vikings office bearers told the Melbourne detectives they just wanted to exist in their own right and would respond with violence if attacked.

Police phoned the Bandidos the following day, still trying to negotiate a peace. The Bandidos responded with their own demands:

guarantees that police would not attend or monitor national bike runs or fundraising concerts. A peace deal with the Vikings was not an option.

Detectives reported back to senior officers that the Bandidos wanted to deal drugs without police resistance. At that point the police decided conciliation had failed and turned to old-fashioned detective work.

The target committee of the state crime squads met and declared Bandidos a major organised crime target and a priority investigation.

But over the previous 30 years, target policing had most often failed against bikie gangs. Police success against bikers had involved opportunistic investigations into individual crimes, not long-term exposure of the organisations themselves.

Outlaw motorcycle gangs around the world have proven to be virtually impossible to infiltrate. In one US case, an undercover policeman accepted into a bikie group turned and became worse than the criminals he was sent to pursue.

But, despite concerns over their chances of success, police set up Operation Barkly, the secret investigation into the Bandidos. In mid-1996, the Covert Investigation Unit briefed two of its best undercovers with instructions to do what seemed impossible: get inside the gang, be accepted as brothers and provide evidence that would stand up in court.

Wes and Alby were born, created to go deeper undercover than any police in Australia had ever been before. They were two unemployed men in their late 20s on the fringes of the criminal world. Wes was to have a criminal record involving drugs. They were then set up in a rented house in Ballarat. Both were keen to make money and were happy to go outside the law to do it.

The carefully sculpted image of the Bandidos – as a group of renegades who dropped out of society to share an interest in bikes, booze and broads – is anything but true. The biker world actually mimics mainstream society, where money and power open doors and those who do not obey the rules are eventually shunned.

At a struggling chapter like Ballarat, the fee for members was $105 a month plus $1000 to join, putting it just under exclusive clubs such as the Royal Melbourne Golf Club.

According to police, the fees for members at the Prospect chapter in Sydney were $600 a month – not bad, when most of the members were supposed to be battlers on the dole. Most of each month's dues were divided between the national defence fund, local legal fees, the central chapter and clubhouse rent. Members leaving the club were also expected to donate their Harley-Davidsons to the Bandidos. This was no glee club.

One young member without a job said he had just bought a top-of-the-range Landcruiser for $60,000 and a Harley for $30,000. 'Paid cash,' he bragged.

The gang had set up chapters in Geelong, Ballarat, Perth, Brisbane Hinterland, Griffith, Hunter Valley, Sydney, Prospect (Sydney), Inner City (Sydney), Hunter Valley, Mid North Coast (NSW), Brisbane City and Cairns.

With nearly 300 members in Australia and connections with overseas organisations, the Bandidos had the power to intimidate and an apparent unlimited arsenal to back up their threats. Police say the Bandidos used a shoulder-fired anti-tank rocket launcher to kill two and injure 17 at a Copenhagen Hells Angels party in 1996. One of the suspects later travelled to Australia for a national bike run and complained that he couldn't hear for two weeks after firing the rocket.

The Bandido motorcycle gang was formed in Texas in 1966 by Donald Eugene Chambers, who was later convicted for killing two men. According to the FBI, the first Australian chapter was established in Sydney in 1983, to give the gang access to chemicals banned in the US that could be used in the production of amphetamines.

US authorities pinpoint the Bandidos as one of 'The Big Four' international biker-organised crime groups. It has one of the best counter-intelligence systems and is considered the hardest to crack.

So Alby and Wes kept a low profile when they moved to Ballarat. Being too keen would have ruined their chances. They had to develop trust with a gang of men who claimed to trust nobody. The Bandidos say they are no longer part of society. 'This is why we look repulsive. We're saying we don't want to be like you or look like you,' according to their code. Their motto is 'God forgives, Bandidos don't.'

But bikie gangs can't live in isolation, they need cannon fodder: men who want to be near the tough guys and bask in dubious reflected glory. These are the people seen to be disposable. They are used to guard buildings and run errands. In return, they attend parties and buy drugs at a cheaper rate.

Over months Wes and Alby ran into the Bandidos at pubs and drinking holes in the area and the relationships slowly warmed. To the bikers, the two seemed ideal; men who were prepared to look the other way at the right time and weren't too concerned about the subtleties of the criminal code. In November 1996, Wes and Alby were invited to the clubhouse at 4 Greenbank Court, Delacombe for a party.

If it was a test, they passed. It was the first step in a 13-month journey that would lead the two undercover police to give up their professional and personal lives to become hard-drinking, foul-mouthed bikers.

They remained on the periphery before finally being invited to become 'hangarounds'. They were welcome at any Bandidos chapter in Australia. They were in.

Alby arrived as a would-be biker. He already had a Harley-Davidson – borrowed by the force for the job. Wes bought his from the Ballarat president, Peter Skrokov, with $17,000 provided by the police department. 'We got ripped off,' a police bean-counter observed later.

They were living on the edge – one slip could result in exposure and death. They had to remember every lie and stick strictly to the script.

And they had to avoid anyone who might recognise them.

Wes and Alby were to report what they learnt, including the Bandidos greeting – right handshake, left arm embrace and kiss on the lips.

Ironically, the police agents may have done the bikers a huge favour in the long-term. Senior police say the undercover officers not only gathered evidence to use in prosecutions but saved lives with several early warnings of planned attacks on opposition biker groups. More than once they slipped away to warn of major biker ambushes that loomed and police set up blitzes, roadblocks and other apparently random operations to stop the violence. Each time, it was made to look as though bad luck had thwarted the Bandidos' attacks.

Detective Superintendent Ian Thomas, the head of the Organised Crime and taskforce division, said: 'There is no doubt the two undercover police were at grave risk. Their work helped us move in and stop incidents with the potential to turn violent.'

But it was not one-way traffic. The club rule enforcer, Ballarat sergeant-at-arms Andrew Michlin, approached Wes and Alby and asked if they would grow hydroponic marijuana in their home. It was an offer too good to refuse.

Their rented home in Lydiard Street, Ballarat, was filled with state-of-the-art recording equipment. Michlin set up one of the bedrooms as an indoor nursery, complete with lights, watering systems and tubs. It was all recorded.

Wes and Alby were promoted to prospects in August 1997 and on 21 October they were promoted to full members on 12 months' probation. It was personally ratified by the national president of the Bandidos, Michael Kulakowski.

The power and charisma of Kulakowski was undisputed. He was internationally respected in the biker world, so much so that he flew to the US in July 1996 to be part of peace negotiations to stop a war between the Hells Angels and the Bandidos in Europe that had claimed 11 lives.

A former soldier and rodeo rider, 'Mick K' or 'Kaos' as he was known by his biker mates, opted out of mainstream society at 40, but he still enjoyed the trappings of success. He drove a Mercedes, owned a $300,000 home and a top-of-the-range Harley-Davidson.

The Bandidos already had a strong grip on the amphetamines market and a healthy sideline in marijuana, but under Kulakowski, they were moving into the lucrative club drugs of ecstasy and LSD.

According to police, the Bandidos needed distribution points and began to set up techno discos where they could cultivate thousands of new clients. Senior Victorian Bandidos were observed in Sydney discussing plans to open techno discos in Ballarat and Geelong as fronts to sell ecstasy and LSD as part of the national expansion.

Wes and Alby were able to buy LSD from the Ballarat Bandidos for $5 a tab. Later they were able to buy it for $3.50 from the Sydney chapter. Brothers were prepared to undercut brothers. They transferred money to a Bandido-controlled bank account in NSW and the drugs were moved by express post to a designated postbox.

The profits were massive, with each tab selling for $7 retail. Each sheet contained 200 tabs and the Bandidos bragged their courier was walking in through Sydney Airport carrying a bundle of LSD sheets 25 centimetres thick on every smuggling run. The tabs carried a variety of stamps: the Sydney Olympic logo, a Smiley design, love hearts, and Beavis and Butthead stamps.

While they were undercover, Alby and Wes were involved in more than 30 deals buying marijuana, amphetamines, LSD and ecstasy from Bandidos in three states. They were so trusted that Alby became the secretary-elect for the Ballarat chapter, giving him access to the club's financial records.

Meanwhile, the Bandidos continued their plans to expand. The next target was Wangaratta and that meant an attack on the local biker club, the Tramps. In February 1996, its president got a letter saying the Tramps, their friends and children would be in danger if the gang did not disband and leave town.

The power of the group over the individual was all-consuming. When a member of the Griffith chapter, Dean Francis Corboy, said a member of the Tramps looked the wrong way at him on 3 October 1997, he called in 60 members from Geelong, Ballarat and Griffith to come to Wangaratta for a confrontation.

According to the Bandidos code, members were expected to just walk out of their jobs and drive. When a brother needs help, whether he is right or wrong, you must support him. But one of the undercovers managed to get the message to police and when the Bandido strike force turned up, there 'just happened' to be a major police blitz on in Wangaratta. Wherever the bikers went, they were pulled over. Also unexplained was why no members of the Tramps were anywhere to be seen that night.

Just to show their strength, the Bandidos started their 1997 national run in Wangaratta on 23 October, with more than 250 bikers from Australia and around the world present in full colours. To make matters worse for a country town with limited police resources, it was the break-up day for VCE students. The town would be filled with drunken bikers and drunken teenage girls.

Police had a meeting with Kulakowski and explained the situation. He agreed to keep control and sent out the message to his troops – stay cool. The night passed without incident. 'That was his power,' a senior policeman said.

On 24 October 1997, some of the gang, including a few international Bandidos, went out to test fire their illegal firearms. One of the overseas-based bikers had to be dissuaded from opening fire on a passing Geelong–Melbourne train.

You need more than charisma and power to stop a bullet. On 9 November Kulakowski, sergeant-at-arms Bruce Harrison and fellow member Rick De Stoop were shot dead in the basement of a Sydney dance club. Another Bandido was shot in the head but survived.

Bandidos from around Australia, including the two undercover police, drove to Sydney for the funeral. In a ritual fit for royalty, more than 200 bikers filed past for a brief moment with their dead leader.

One of the undercover officers bent over to embrace the deceased leader and allegedly whispered into the casket: 'I'm a copper, you know.' Dead men tell no tales.

But while the bikers were grieving, life went on. Wes and Alby were able to buy 1000 LSD tabs from one of the Sydney leaders of the Bandidos straight after the funeral.

With the real possibility of revenge killings, police had to move – and quickly.

Wes and Alby were called back. On 11 December, more than 100 police in four states conducted coordinated raids that resulted in 19 arrests and the seizure of drugs with a street value of more than $1 million. They also found chemicals capable of being used to make amphetamines worth $6 million and seized firearms, including an AK-47 rifle and pen pistols.

The head of Operation Barkly, Detective Inspector Andrew Allen, said: 'Some outlaw motorcycle gangs seem to think that the law does not relate to them. I think we have shown that no one is beyond policing.'

Wes and Alby had gathered so much evidence that most of the bikers charged decided to plead guilty. But the main players, such as Peter Skrokov and Andrew Michlin, were destined to spend about six months in jail, less than half the time the two policemen spent risking their lives to infiltrate the group.

In 2004, the final biker, Dean Corboy, pleaded guilty in the Wangaratta Magistrates Court to trafficking amphetamines. He was sentenced to eight months, with six months suspended – an effective jail term of two months.

But justice sometimes moves in mysterious ways. Another court has also passed judgement. According to police intelligence, the national chapter of the Bandidos sentenced the bikers who embraced Wes and Alby to be flogged when released from jail. There would be no appeal.

Police say Wes and Alby received professional counselling to re-enter mainstream policing but it was a long road back.

Both gave a large part of their personal and professional lives to the operation. It was a success but came at a cost many would not be prepared to pay.

SIX WOMEN MURDERED BUT STILL NO CONVICTION

Long before kids collected hundreds of fake friends through Facebook, Vicki Reid had a handful she thought would remain her mates forever.

In the days when Berwick was more country than outer Melbourne, the kids from the local high school spent their spare time together, gossiping, listening to music on their parents' record players and watching *Countdown* every Sunday night.

'We would just hang out really, go to the movies, sit around, talk, that sort of thing,' Vicki, now a mother of three, recalls. Sometimes they would head to nearby Akoonah Park with that generation's version of Spotify – a giant battery-operated 'boom-box' that played their home-recorded cassettes.

But like most school friends, they eventually drifted apart. Some left the area while others developed new social circles.

Except one: a lively 14-year-old named Catherine Linda Headland, who remains frozen in time. More than 40 years ago, somebody stole her future and stole from her friends their last shred of innocence.

It was about 2 pm on 6 December 1980, when a man dumping

animal remains saw what he thought was a human body, and then another. He called police, who discovered the bodies of Catherine Headland, Ann-Marie Sargent, 18, and Bertha Miller, 73.

It would take a further two years to find a fourth body on the other side of Brew Road – Narumol Stephenson, 34, a woman abducted from Northcote in November 1980.

The killer, or killers, have never been found and the cause of the deaths never established, which is why Tynong North remains one of Australia's most chilling mysteries.

Catherine lived with her parents and older brother. She was devoted to her friends but also to her horse, Prince, which she rode every chance she had. The family emigrated from Lancashire in 1966 when Catherine was one and had lived in Allan Street, Berwick, for five years. Catherine was popular at school and loved competing with her pony in local gymkhanas.

Her mother, Hazel, was adamant that she had to contribute to the upkeep of the horse and to do so she had to take on some part-time work.

For three weeks, she had worked part-time at the Fountain Gate Coles supermarket and Thursday, 28 August 1980 was to be her first midweek shift, from noon until 4 pm. Hazel was employed at the same supermarket and arranged for her to work extra shifts during the August school holidays – not that the teenager was grateful. She would rather hang around with her mates than work on the supermarket register.

That day Hazel left home at 8.30 am, leaving her daughter 70¢ for the bus fare.

During the morning, the friends met at the home of Catherine's boyfriend, John McManus, who had been ill. She told her mates that she didn't feel like going to work that afternoon and that she wanted to give up the job because it was stifling her social life.

They watched morning television and played records before McManus walked her to the gate as she headed off to catch the bus. Before she left, she said: 'Goodbye, I'll see you after work.'

She saw the bus go past towards Beaconsfield at 11.10 am and knew she had five minutes to get to her stop at the corner of Manuka Road and the Princes Highway.

There were many alleged sightings of Catherine, which would later confuse the initial investigation. A bus driver told police he picked up a girl fitting Catherine's description and a blonde girl at the Peel Street bus stop, 800 metres from Manuka Road. But police found 'there is no evidence that she caught the bus'.

Friends claimed to have seen her and the blonde girl at Narre Warren about 2.30 pm that day, but the blonde associate was never identified and police were to treat the Narre Warren sighting as unlikely.

If she had gone to Narre Warren and had only 70¢, she might have decided to hitchhike home, a common practice at the time. The regular bus driver in the area told police he believed he had seen Catherine hitchhiking along the Princes Highway on previous occasions.

What probably happened is that she accepted a lift from a stranger who had already decided to use the Tynong North scrub as his dumping ground. He knew it well, as he had left Bertha Miller there 18 days earlier after he had abducted her near her Glen Iris home as she waited for a tram to take her to church.

When Catherine Headland reluctantly left her friends, she was wearing a thin leather strap on her ankle. The girls from Berwick High wore the straps from one of their fathers' leather bootlaces as a sign of friendship. Vicki remembers wearing hers on her wrist.

Police used that friendship strap to help identify the body when she was found at Tynong North more than three months after she went missing.

'When she disappeared, we were just shattered. We knew she hadn't run away, it wasn't in her nature,' Vicki says.

'We knew someone had taken her away, but we couldn't really comprehend what had happened.'

When police found her: 'We were just so angry, we wanted to find out who did this.'

But no one has.

There was an old man who remains a suspect. Harold Janman, 88, died in 2020, maintaining his innocence. Devoutly religious, there are intriguing links between him and at least six unsolved murders – the four at Tynong North and two in Frankston.

Allison Rooke, 59, disappeared near her Frankston home on 30 May 1980 and Carmel Summers, 55, went missing in the same suburb on 9 October 1981. Both bodies were found in Frankston North bushland.

Janman once lived in North Frankston, and also lived and worked near Tynong North. He agreed to two polygraph tests and was found to be lying when asked questions about the Tynong North and Frankston murders.

But he is not the only suspect and after interviewing 2000 people and taking 11,400 pages of notes, police remain split. They may be searching for one killer or as many as three.

It is possible that it is a coincidence that Stephenson was found in the same area and the Frankston women may have been taken by another man. What appears certain is that Miller, Headland and Sargent were all the victims of a serial killer.

A detailed analysis by the Bureau of Criminal Intelligence indicated the three bodies found together at Tynong North had been placed there by the one killer. It also showed a series of marked differences with the other three murders: 'The person(s) who placed the bodies near the sand quarry off Brew Road, Tynong North, took care in the way he/they placed the bodies . . . Such care was not shown in the placement of the bodies of the other three victims.'

The report concluded that the offender(s) 'had given some thought to how and where they might dispose of a body and suggests that he/they may have planned to commit a particular offence if and when the opportunity arose'.

The Frankston victims and Stephenson were left within 50 metres of busy roads. 'This suggests that the three were placed at the first available suitable location known by the offender(s).'

What is certain is there will be a link between the old sand quarry where the bodies were found and the killer. He knew the remote area well and suspected the bodies would never be found. In one case, he sawed off branches to use as cover.

This shows he was in no hurry and was confident the area was so remote that he would not be interrupted. He knew the location and planned his moves well before he took his first victim.

Covering the case back then, it was clear from the beginning this was no random drop. Well off a road and 200 metres down a hidden track, it had been carefully selected. And the police were up against it. The killer had months' head start, there were no forensic clues and no sightings of the women being abducted. And one was an elderly woman while the other two were teenagers.

What we still don't know is why did he start and why did he stop?

Did he learn he was a suspect? Was he interviewed and not charged, or was he jailed for another offence?

One name often mentioned is Raymond Edmunds, known as 'Mr Stinky', who murdered Shepparton teenagers Abina Madill and Garry Heywood in 1966 but was not arrested for the murders until 1985. Police believe he committed at least 32 rapes and remains a suspect in several murders spread over nearly two decades.

Edmunds has refused to speak to police but confided to a fellow sex offender that he had killed 'dozens' of women. 'If I told them everything I've done, they'd neck me,' he said.

Bandali Debs is a four-time killer, a violent, vicious, callous man with no compassion and no conscience. A prodigious armed robber, he was convicted of the 1998 murders of Sergeant Gary Silk and Senior Constable Rod Miller. He was also an opportunistic and homicidal sex offender.

In 1995, he killed Sydney sex worker Donna Hicks, dumping her body near a sand quarry in Minchinbury. Two years later, he killed Melbourne sex worker Kristy Hart, also concealing her body in bushland.

During the Silk–Miller investigation, he was bugged, bragging about how to kill a woman. 'If you put the rod in the mouth and blew her brains away, when you put the rod in their mouth and close their mouth there's no noise . . . I've seen it. I've done it.'

There are geographic reasons to put Debs on the suspect list. He lived in Narre Warren, not far from the Princes Highway where Headland and Sargent were last seen. Even Bertha Miller was likely to have been taken from a tram stop that was a few hundred metres from the same road.

Debs' two known victims were taken from highways and dumped just off main roads. The two Frankston women were taken from the busy Frankston–Dandenong Road. However, there is no direct evidence to link him to the cases. He remains on the list but not at the top.

A 1990 re-examination by the same agency rejected the 'three killers' theory. 'On the balance of probabilities, the same person or persons were responsible for the murders of Allison Rooke, Bertha Miller, Catherine Linda Headland, Ann-Marie Sargent and Joy Carmel Summers.'

It did not have enough facts to draw conclusions regarding Stephenson's murder.

The review examined several suspects but declared the 'best nominated' was Harold John Janman, a former projectionist with a propensity for offering women lifts in his car and with links to both Tynong North and Frankston.

So, what do we know about Janman?

The religious family man presented as a prude who would turn 'girlie' photos to the wall in the small city projection room where he worked. Yet he had been charged with soliciting for the purposes of prostitution the year before the murders commenced.

It was also around that time, he would later tell police, that 'my wife was going to leave me'.

He freely admitted that he often offered women lifts on the Frankston–Dandenong Road. He agreed to drive with police down the busy road and identify where he invited women into his van. He indicated nine stops, including the two where Rooke and Summers would have been waiting for a bus.

But he was less forthcoming on every other question.

Detective: 'Do you know where Skye Road is?'

Janman: 'Where sir?'

Detective: 'Skye Road.'

Janman: 'No sir, I have never heard of it.'

And yet for years he had worked as a projectionist at the local drive-in just off Skye Road, near where the bodies were found.

Police took him to where the bodies were found. '[He] became nervous and sweated a lot. He walked around the sites as asked, but at no time did he walk in the immediate vicinity of where the bodies had been lying.

'Extensive areas around the sites had been cleared of bush and scrub by the police crime scene searchers and the investigators stated that without some prior knowledge it would not have been possible to tell exactly where the two bodies had been lying,' according to a police analysis.

In other words, detectives concluded he knew where the bodies had been left and didn't want to step on the dumping ground.

Three days after the interview and on the anniversary of the discovery of the first body at Tynong, Janman turned up unannounced at the Frankston Police Station to ask Senior Constable Michael White: 'You know I was brought in about two murders in Frankston, well why haven't I been asked about five murders instead of two?'

White: 'Which other ones are you talking about?'

Janman: 'The ones in Tynong . . . I'm just saying, why haven't they asked about that?'

The trouble was no one, at least publicly, had at that time linked the two murder scenes. No one, that is, except Janman.

According to FBI crime profiler Robert Ressler, serial killers often reach out to investigators. 'Some offenders attempt to inject themselves into the investigation of the murder, or otherwise keep in touch with the crime in order to continue the fantasy that started it.'

It is a matter of fact that after Janman was interviewed on 3 December 1981, the murders stopped – a fact that may, of course, be entirely coincidental.

Fifteen years after the last body was found, Janman was nabbed in St Kilda when he approached an undercover policewoman and asked for sex. He immediately told police he was 'the prime suspect in the Tynong North killings'.

Homicide investigators try to find links between where bodies are discovered and the offender, as in most cases killers return to areas they know.

Janman had lived in Garfield, the area adjoining the killer's dumping ground. He had worked at a nearby hotel and was a truck driver whose route took him to the Brew Road sand quarry where three of the victims' bodies were dumped.

The Headlands kept to themselves after Catherine's body was found, preferring to grieve in private. Eventually it became too much and they sold up and moved.

Vicki Reid doesn't drive near Brew Road very often as it always brings back so many sad memories. Even so, she thinks about her teenage friend nearly every week.

A few years ago, her friends put up a little plaque for her in nearby Akoonah Park – the same park where she loved to hang out with her closest mates.

Vicki's eldest child is Catherine, named after the friend she lost more than 40 years ago.

'I just wanted her to live on.'

USING THE NET TO CATCH CRIME'S BIG FISH

Senior police are usually good at three things: calling for extra powers to fight crime, ordering steaks and red wine at long lunches and holding press conferences to declare victory over organised crime.

More than 30 years ago, I took one to Florentino, the swish Melbourne restaurant, to discuss secret stuff. He asked just one question: 'Who's paying?'

When assured it wouldn't be him, he ordered a pasta the size of the Hindenburg, a shank so large it must have been from a woolly mammoth and a gelato big enough to give him an ice-cream headache for a week.

Politicians are usually good at three things. Failing to give a straight answer to Leigh Sales on *The 7.30 Report*, failing to remember who was responsible for the latest stuff-up and standing next to police at press conferences to win the law-and-order vote.

And so when Australian Federal Police Commissioner Reece Kershaw, Prime Minister Scott Morrison, Home Affairs Minister Karen Andrews and FBI legal attaché Anthony Russo took to the microphone, you knew this was serious stuff.

Police had pulled off an international sting, codenamed 'Ironside', providing around 12,000 encrypted phones to gangsters connected to 300 criminal syndicates in 100 countries. There were about 1100 phones operating in Australia. In three years, they monitored 27 million messages from crooks who thought their conversations were secure.

Let's put this into perspective with totally irrelevant facts. If each message was the size of one jigsaw piece (a standard 2000-piece puzzle comes in at around 75 centimetres by 50), a 27-million-piece jigsaw would be about 90 metres by 60. If each monitored message was a Lego two-by-four brick, stacked end to end they would reach from Melbourne to Sydney.

Kershaw said the poisoned An0m app made up only five per cent of organised crime messages, meaning that all the Lego pieces would stretch from Melbourne to London, with 12 million or so left over to build giant dinosaurs. (The jigsaw, by the way, would be nine hectares – or four and a half times the size of the MCG playing surface – enough space to snugly park 432 double-decker buses.)*

The beauty of the Ironside intercept is the police have captured the 'golden thread' – the crooks' own words to be used in court. The crooks were so confident in the system that they used direct language to discuss criminal conspiracies. Juries love that stuff. Defence lawyers don't.

Police say they have mined only two per cent of the material, like prospectors who have picked up glittering nuggets without even breaking the surface. Ironside gives us a rare and sobering insight into organised crime and how police must respond – a model that has taken four decades for many in authority to accept.

While cracking the encrypted code is a high-tech solution, the method of intercepting crooks' communications is not. Drug dealer Tony Mokbel and his team that ran a $400 million syndicate were

* Figures compiled by idiot journalist.

nabbed after an informer managed to provide the key players with phones monitored by the Purana Taskforce.

The An0m material shows organised crime is multicultural, with Triads, Russian Mafia, bikies and Middle Eastern crime gangs all cooperating, because money speaks all languages.

US court documents list 17 key figures in the distribution of the An0m device. The seven Australians listed are based in Colombia, Asia, Europe and Australia.

So how did it work?

When international police disabled Phantom Secure, a Canadian encrypted service that let crooks destroy messages remotely, the FBI recruited one of the system's former operatives, who was building An0m.

In exchange for a reduced sentence and $US120,000 ($156,000), he gave the FBI control and built in a back door. Three international gangsters (two connected to Australia) became enthusiastic controllers, spreading it across the world, unaware they were disseminating a police-inspired virus. It was marketed as 'made by criminals for criminals', with users paying around $1700 for a six-month lease. With about 12,000 devices it was bringing in more than $40 million a year. The app was designed to be wiped remotely if a unit fell into police hands, concealing the user's location – or so they thought.

At the time police announced the breakthrough, Kershaw said it had resulted in 224 arrests, 525 charges, raids on six clandestine laboratories and thwarted 21 threats to kill. Police seized 104 firearms and weapons and almost $45 million in cash. There have been nearly 1000 arrests worldwide. Considering the FBI paid the informer just $120,000, it was a better investment than Bitcoin.

That's all big-picture stuff, but what does it mean on the street? Plenty. Much of this intelligence will not make sense on a national level, but as it trickles down, it will provide keys to hundreds of local crimes.

One recent Friday night, the feds contacted Victoria with an urgent message: a shooting had been ordered by a bikie boss to be carried out at a Melbourne fight night.

The planning was so detailed, police moved in to seize two stolen cars to be used by the hit team, cloned numberplates and guns. Someone is walking around today unaware they are alive because cops unscrambled the encrypted message.

The bikie model is to have chapters in drug source countries, with many of the bosses living in countries without extradition deals with Australia. A key promoter of An0m, the Facebook gangster Hakan Ayik, fled Sydney more than 10 years ago but remains influential with the Comancheros.

The real damage to the crime syndicates will not be the arrest of soldiers or even their generals but the doormen – the enablers who work in legitimate positions and open doors for the crooks. These lawyers, accountants, baggage handlers, officials and cargo controllers assist in the distribution of tonnes of drugs and the laundering of millions in funds. So far, six police and one lawyer have been charged in the international raids.

On the docks, an agent who organises an illicit container to piggyback on legitimate imports is paid $600,000 and a controller who warns when a drug container has been diverted to be examined receives $50,000.

When cops brag that they have seized a container of drugs but don't mention arrests, you know the syndicate has been tipped off and have cut their losses.

If enablers are caught on An0m, their loss will be catastrophic to syndicates. Meatballs with meat cleavers can be replaced overnight; sleepers in positions of authority can't.

Ironside acts as a template for future investigations, for without total, enthusiastic and committed cooperation between state, federal and international law enforcement, we are just kidding ourselves.

The crooks are multinational, with 70 per cent of Australian organised crime assets held offshore. One division, one police force or one country cannot deal with crime that doesn't respect national boundaries. This is not a new thought, but generations of blinkered, bent or blindingly stupid cops more determined to protect their patch than do their job have sabotaged collaboration.

When Victoria Police had key information to solve the 1977 murder of Griffith anti-drugs campaigner Donald Mackay, the head of the NSW investigation, Joe Parrington, came to Melbourne for a visit.

When detectives tried to brief him, he put up his hand and said: 'I don't talk to monkeys, I talk to the organ grinder.' They should have stuffed a banana in his ear and sent him back to Sydney.

The best cop of his generation, or any generation for that matter, was Victoria's Chief Commissioner Mick Miller, who argued for a national intelligence scheme way back in 1980. He made sure the first director of the Australian Bureau of Criminal Intelligence was someone he could trust: Fred Silvester, my father.

Time and again, Fred briefed the commissioners on what was needed. And time and again, they knocked him back. He wanted accountants, lawyers, and tax and money-laundering experts embedded in law enforcement, plus international agreements on intelligence sharing. The commissioners wanted schnitzel sandwiches for lunch.

Little wonder they obstructed: one ended up in jail and another was lucky not to find himself in the same place.

With Ironside, the penny has finally dropped. It shows no one is above the law, as long as you have people with the courage and the drive to enforce it.

WHEN PEOPLE FALL OFF THE RADAR

As a law-abiding family man, Roger Wilson would have had no idea there was a contract out on his life. Which is why the honest and successful businessman immediately pulled over as he was heading to his Narre Warren home in his luxury Porsche when flagged to do so by what he thought were police.

It was alleged by the prosecution in court that the plainclothes police were the hit team Christopher Dale Flannery and Kevin 'Weary' Williams, who were paid $35,000 by a business rival to kill Wilson.

It was 1 February 1980 and Wilson's body was never found. Eventually Williams, Flannery and a third man were charged with the murder. But in those days, without a body and a cause of death, the prosecution was always pushing their case uphill.

They weren't helped when the defence raised unconfirmed sightings of Wilson from Lakes Entrance to the Greek isles. There appeared to be enough reasonable doubt for the jury to acquit.

Not that it did Flannery any good. A few years later he was abducted and murdered in Sydney. His body was never found.

Then there was Deborah Boundy, Williams' one-time girlfriend, who was also murdered. Again, she simply disappeared after drinking at a Richmond pub on Christmas Day 1980.

Three murders, no bodies and not one conviction. That's how it was back then because we didn't leave an electronic footprint. There was virtually no CCTV, credit cards were a novelty and mobile phones were considered as likely as Maxwell Smart's shoe phone.

Today, Boundy would have been recorded arriving, drinking and leaving the pub. Police would have known who she was with on the night she disappeared, and she probably would have used social media that would have left a breadcrumb-like evidentiary trail. Wilson would have been recorded on the toll road, his mobile phone would have pinged on his way home and he may have been recorded on dash cams on the way.

The use of CCTV has become so important in criminal investigations that London Police have a hugely successful 'super-recogniser unit' staffed by police who have been scientifically tested to have an abnormal ability to recognise faces in a crowd. In three years, the unit has identified thousands of offenders from grainy footage, solving murders, sex offences and identifying members of robbery gangs and street rioters, often when the perpetrators have most of their faces hidden from plain view.

They were drafted in to check 5000 hours of CCTV as part of the investigation into the March 2018 Salisbury chemical attack on a Russian double agent and his daughter. Two Russian agents have since been charged in absentia, though the chances of them ever standing trial are about the same as Winx being beaten by a Shetland pony.

Traditionally police have been slow to move a case from a missing persons investigation to a homicide investigation, and often by that time, the trail has gone cold.

On 6 October 1983, Edwina Boyle vanished from her Dandenong home. Her disappearance remained unreported for months until her sister in England raised the alarm. Although she was devoted to her daughters, police at first accepted husband Fred's claim she had run off with a truck driver named Ray.

They were apparently unaware that Fred's mistress had moved into the family home the day after Edwina disappeared. Eventually the case made its way to Homicide and although Fred was the one and only suspect, without a body the case was considered too weak to take to court.

That is until her remains were found in a barrel at Fred's home 23 years later. He was finally convicted of murder and sentenced to a minimum of 17 years.

(Fred was a smart arse. As a carpet layer he turned up at Homicide to quote for the job of replacing the floor coverings – the same office where he had been questioned over his wife's murder. He didn't get the job.)

Victoria Police now has a specialist Missing Persons Squad that takes on cases that are really homicides without a body. The head of the squad, Detective Inspector Andrew Stamper, says the first step is the 'proof of life' test, which involves checking bank, telephone, medical and taxation records.

Most of us 'check in' daily, taking money from an ATM for a slap-up dinner, buying shoes we don't need with a maxed-out credit card, being captured on CCTV walking down laneways, using mobile phones, driving on toll roads, or posting the most mundane events to Facebook friends we have never met.

Or, as Stamper says: 'Some people can just fall off the radar.'

Such as the inner-city man who disappeared without trace. 'His flatmate sold his five-year-old car for peanuts as scrap, which created suspicions. It was looking pretty bad for a while.'

'The one thing we couldn't find was his iPad. Then one day it was activated on the internet. It turned out he had decided he had enough of his life and wanted to live on the streets. We found him living on the banks of the Yarra, so we shook his hand and said see you later. It is not an offence to go missing.'

More often, there is no happy ending, just resolution. The 15-strong Missing Persons Squad initiates about six new investigations a year, and while some generate headlines (such as Jill Meagher, who was attacked as she walked home from the pub in September 2012), most are people who live on the periphery.

No one will ever know why Simone Quinlan's life took her down the path of drug abuse and homelessness. By 2015, at the age of 33, she was homeless and was deemed unable to care for her two sons.

She was living under a bridge when she met builder Brendan Neil and she eventually moved in with him in Melton. Far from being a new start, it quickly fell into a pattern of vicious domestic violence that would end in her murder.

In June, Simone went to the local hospital with head wounds, telling staff she had hit her head on rocks when she slipped jumping a fence. Later, she told a friend Neil had hit her with a baseball bat.

She moved out of the house but later returned. In August, she told a friend Neil had again attacked her with a bat. The friend said she was covered in bruises. Neil turned up at the friend's house where Simone was staying and threw a rock through the front window. When she told the police she had been badly beaten by Neil, they began the process of taking out an intervention order.

Just over a week later, outraged that she was a 'snitch', Neil tortured her for hours, binding her with cable ties and duct tape, hitting and kicking her before repeatedly smashing her head with a hammer.

It will never be known if she was dead when Neil and his friend Wayne Marmo wrapped her motionless body in a sheet and bundled her into the back of a Toyota HiLux. Marmo then drove to Kangaroo Flat, stopping on the way to shoot her five times in the head. Her body, doused in petrol, was thrown down a disused mine shaft and set on fire.

Neil started a disinformation trail, texting and telling friends Quinlan had left him and was back on the drugs. It was likely the conclusion would have been that she had drifted back to her homeless life and the murder would have gone unreported. Except, three weeks later, someone with a conscience connected with Marmo walked into the Werribee Police Station to express her concerns.

The Missing Persons Squad soon concluded Simone was dead and became interested to find out why, around the same time, Neil had hired a floor sander. (It was to remove his victim's blood.)

Just over a month after she disappeared, police found Simone Quinlan's remains in the mineshaft. Neil pleaded guilty and Marmo was later convicted of the murder.

For the Missing Persons Squad, the Quinlan case was a relatively quick investigation. Others can take years. The squad also has about 100 historical murder cases dating back to the 1960s where the victim just disappeared.

(One crime gang had access to an industrial pet food grinder while another preferred to use a dim sim factory under the waste-not-want-not principle. In the 1960s crooks connected with the Painters and Dockers ended up in freeway constructions, building foundations or in unofficial sea burials. In Sydney, when it was decided that law clerk Brian Alexander knew too much, he was thrown in the harbour attached to a gas cooker.)

Missing Persons Squad detectives often work exactly the opposite to orthodox investigation. In most cases, detectives look at what is there while the missing persons detectives look at what is not. In effect, they are the Sherlock Holmes Squad, working on the process of elimination.

The historical cases include gangster Laurie Prendergast, who went missing in August 1985. Prendergast was part of a three-man murder squad who killed standover man and gunman Les Kane in 1978. And, you guessed it, Kane's body has never been found.

Or Sarah MacDiarmid, 23, who disappeared from the Kananook railway station in July 1990, almost certainly killed in the car park during a robbery.

'We are constantly reviewing these cases,' Stamper says.

While police can use new techniques, there is another asset that is as old as time – a guilty conscience.

'People with information can come forward years later to tell the truth,' Stamper says. 'They simply can't take it anymore.'

CONSCIENCE OR CASH CAN CRACK A CASE

It was an innocent slip that simultaneously ruptured a young sports-woman's right cruciate ligament and her dreams.

Michele Brown had been a champion netballer in a sports-mad family. Suddenly, she was an ex-champion. A member of the Victoria under-17 side, she was in the squad to be selected for the Australian Institute of Sport. The knee injury robbed her of her sporting ambitions and also her drive and direction. Her bright future grew bleak.

'It changed her life,' says her sister, Simone Kapiteyn. It was at a time when knee operations were more of a gamble, and she chose not to undergo surgery.

Michele was one of four sisters who all played netball. Eventually, her mother, Jeanette, father Bert and brother David joined in to form their own family team. Now 79, Jeanette plays walking netball.

Weekends were spent piling into two family cars and heading from game to game. If Michele had spare time, she spent it in the ocean chasing her other passion, surfing.

With a bung knee, Michele drifted from her sporty social group to the wrong side of town, associating with Frankston locals who lived on the fringe, dabbling in drugs and small-time crime.

By this time, Simone had joined the police force and was stationed at Frankston. She knew some of Michele's new 'friends' professionally, but her sister, 18 months older than her and now in her 20s, was entitled to make her own life choices.

The family did what good families do. They hung in, believing Michele, who remained loyal, loving and caring, would come through this rough spot and stabilise her life. Sadly, she was robbed of that chance.

On 1 March 1992, she went missing. It was her 25th birthday. Her body was found on 14 March in a disused shed at the back of a gun shop in Playne Street, Frankston.

There are more than 200 unsolved murders on the Victoria Police books. At any one time, six are selected to be reinvestigated by the Cold Case Homicide Unit. It is labour-intensive work; a new investigation can take years. Most police departments don't bother, and if a case can't be solved in days, they park it unless a breakthrough presents itself.

The head of the unit, Detective Senior Sergeant Paul Scarlett, says the unsolved cases are examined and those selected for a deep-dive reinvestigation are the ones considered solvable because of new information or the potential for modern forensics to unearth new clues.

There is another key component. People change, alibis break down and old loyalties crumble. Such as in the case of James Russouw, 24, murdered in an East Burwood reserve in 2008. Eight years later, in what was considered the last roll of the dice, police announced a $1 million reward and released a short clip of CCTV footage that showed a man in a public phone box, who phoned Russouw from the East Burwood Kmart, about a kilometre from the murder scene.

The quality was so poor it wasn't considered vital, but within two days, a caller to Crime Stoppers claimed the man walking from the phone box was Christopher John Lavery, who – like Russouw – was a former Whitefriars College student.

The caller, who also went to the same school, recognised Lavery's gait and his habit of wearing ill-fitting pants. A check of the file showed Lavery had an alibi claiming he had been at a movie with a mate. When police re-interviewed the mate, he admitted he had been lying.

In 2017, Lavery was convicted of Russouw's murder.

The murder of Michelle Buckingham, 16, who disappeared in October 1983 seemed one of those cases destined to remain unsolved – until the Shepparton News partnered with Cold Case detectives to re-open the file.

Blanket publicity from the local paper in 2012 led to a series of tips from the public. One caller came forward after his conscience was pricked by the photo of Michelle's mother, Elvira, in the paper.

According to the informer, Norman Gribble, the day after Michelle was murdered, his brother-in-law Steven Bradley confessed he had killed her.

In May 2014, Bradley was charged, extradited from Brisbane, and eventually convicted and sentenced to 27 years' jail with a minimum of 21.

Cold Case detectives have to develop a mindset different from that of the present-day Homicide investigator. In the modern era, the detectives usually have a crime scene, phone records, CCTV data, modern DNA technology and credit card footprints.

In a cold case, the detectives have a musty file, police and coronial records and often not much else. It is a little like a modern Formula One driver racing against a Jack Brabham special.

This is gumshoe work. Strip the case back, hit the files and find the witnesses. Talk to them again and again. Is there anything they forgot? Is there anything on their minds they now wish to share?

Senior detective Jodie Stoll has been in Homicide for four years, and is now investigating the Michele Brown case. 'It is a different process,' she says. 'You have to be prepared to be patient.'

First, the facts.

On 1 March 1992, Michele Brown left her family home in Baxter about midday and went to Frankston North to visit a friend. After 7 pm, the pair walked to the FoodPlus store on the Frankston–Dandenong Road to buy cigarettes.

Brown borrowed 30¢ from her friend to ring home to ask her mother for a lift from the agreed spot behind the railway station. Her brother answered the phone and later told police she sounded intoxicated. When her mother arrived, Michele was not there. This was unusual, although she would stay away from home for days at a time.

Jeanette began to make enquiries with her daughter's friends. When they told her they had not heard from Michele, and as she had not been in contact asking for money, she reported her missing.

On 14 March, a worker at the gun shop noticed an odd smell at the shed and discovered the body. The shed was on the Frankston railway line, about 300 metres from where Michele had wanted to be picked up. She had previously gone to the shed to use drugs, which is one of the reasons police believe she was killed by a person, or people, she knew.

The group of people who associated with Michele Brown were unable or unwilling to help the initial Homicide investigation, which was hardly surprising as many of them saw the police as enemies. But many of them would now be in their mid-50s and would have left that world behind.

Police believe that more than one person knows what happened in that shed 30 years ago. They have announced a $1 million reward and the possibility of immunity for a co-offender who comes forward with the truth. The brutal reality is someone in the know could clear their conscience and their debts in one go.

Scarlett says cold cases can be solved by just one phone call.

'Anyone with any information, no matter how small, should contact us,' he says.

'There are now one million reasons to come forward.'

Michele Brown's sister, Simone Kapiteyn, spent 24 years in the Victoria and WA police forces dealing with criminals and victims. She saw people spinning out of control and people who came through dark times.

'[My sister] fell in with the wrong crowd, made some poor choices and dabbled in drugs but should never have been forced to pay the ultimate price,' Kapiteyn says.

'We have always believed this is solvable and there are people who know what happened. No parents should have to live without knowing what happened to one of their children.

'If there were answers 30 years later, it would give them some level of peace.'

POLICE BUNGLES THAT LED TO WALSH STREET

The case was doomed from the start.

What should have been the high watermark of investigations ended in recriminations, acquittals and no justice for two police constables murdered on duty. From the crime scene to the offices of senior police, a series of mistakes compounded by a raft of decisions that were plainly bizarre left the detectives handling the case hopelessly handicapped.

This is not rear-view wisdom – many of those in the middle saw the slow-motion collapse, like the implosion of a building being demolished.

Yet from within the rubble was a gold nugget – a criminal informer who left a tip that, years later, would lead to solving an unrelated professional hit. But more on that later.

First, the original crime. On 12 October 1988, on Walsh Street, South Yarra, two Prahran police constables, Steven Tynan and Damian Eyre, were checking an abandoned stolen car when they were ambushed and shot dead.

On 26 March 1991, 895 days after the murders, four men –

Victor Peirce, Peter McEvoy, Anthony Farrell and Trevor Pettingill – were acquitted by a Supreme Court jury. They maintained their innocence.

It began at the crime scene. In a confidential review, taskforce leader Detective Inspector John Noonan wrote: 'Crime scene was cordoned off by crime scene tape. However, this was disregarded by most police members and by members of the public.

'The crime scene was severely contaminated, understandably by police and ambulance in assisting injured members, but later by persons disregarding general crime scene instructions.'

When emotions run high, mistakes can be made, but there was a school of thought among some senior police that would underpin a series of decisions that were silly then and remain stupid now.

Noonan believes the initial view was that the murder of two police officers should be treated as any other double murder, failing to acknowledge that such an ambush was an attack on law and order and, by extension, on society itself. Does anyone seriously think the assassination of a prime minister would be assigned the same resources as any other murder?

It was a full two weeks before the Ty-Eyre Taskforce was established, and when it was, it was sent to the 13th floor of the St Kilda Road police building, where there were no phones, desks or cupboards.

For a period, calls relating to the investigation were sent to Homicide. 'Information was lost because of this move,' the review states.

This was not a logistical problem but an exercise in bloody-mindedness by senior police who initially failed to act with the urgency the investigation required. When the taskforce requested basic office equipment, detectives were told to find it themselves, resulting in them travelling to police stations begging for spare desks and chairs.

They were provided with one computer terminal without software. Police were forced to use pirated software to start inputting information.

Melbourne business tycoon Lindsay Fox, upon learning the taskforce was hopelessly underequipped, donated $50,000 for IT.

The police accepted the donation but had a policy that benefactors could not specify how the money was spent. Noonan says it was not used to support the taskforce.

Eventually, they were given the new ISYS system for evaluation. Pause here: this was the most important investigation in Australia, and it was provided with an untested computer system. It was down for seven days and eventually crashed without a backup, resulting in the loss of 300 statements.

In August 1989 – 10 months after the murders – a new system, valued at $12,000, was purchased.

The taskforce was also short on cars. They had a great relationship with a hire car manager that became strained when the police force didn't pay the $40,000 account – until the company threatened to repossess the vehicles. They had to engage a cheaper, inferior provider.

The listening devices used by police proved to be cheap and nasty, constantly breaking down and easy to detect. This meant police had to break into crooks' homes and cars to replace or fix them. Time and again police chose the cheap option rather than the right one.

One of the alleged shooters at Walsh Street was Jedd Houghton, who was often armed with four guns (two shoulder and two ankle holsters). He had told friends if he was confronted by police, he intended to shoot it out.

Despite the likelihood of a fatal confrontation, in a decision that defies common sense, the use of the experts – the Special Operations Group (SOG) – was initially refused to arrest him.

At the last minute, that decision was revoked, and on 17 November 1988, the SOG went to arrest Houghton in a cabin at the Ascot Vale Lodge caravan park at Bendigo. Houghton pointed a gun at police and was shot dead. A search found five loaded guns near Houghton – four revolvers and one pistol. 'I have no doubt that if we rather than the SOG had done that raid, we would have lost members who would have been shot dead,' says Noonan.

After the suspects were arrested, the taskforce was told it would be disbanded and its office closed. Noonan mutinied and changed the locks. Investigators were sent to new duties, even though the massive brief of evidence for the trial was incomplete.

Despite it being one of the most complex cases involving forensics, difficult criminal informers who had become police witnesses, and listening device material, four police – three with little experience in court hearings – were assigned the preparation. The case involved 960 statements, 11,945 bugged telephone calls, 230 witnesses, 1700 listening device tapes and 700 physical exhibits.

By that stage, Noonan's relationship with his superior officer had broken down to the extent that they needed a go-between to communicate. It created multiple delays.

Noonan says: 'We worked seven-day weeks and 12-hour days to get it ready. It was only finished on the day of the committal. It was a disgrace.'

The key witness was Wendy Peirce, the wife of one of the accused, Victor Peirce. But by the time of the trial, Wendy had changed sides and her testimony was lost. She would later be convicted of perjury and sentenced to jail.

Multiple police sources say the delay between charging the suspects and commencing the trial led their star witness to have second thoughts.

Years later, Wendy told me: '[Walsh Street] was spur of the moment, we were on the run. Victor was the organiser. He just said: "They deserved their whack. It could have been me." Jedd was the trigger man, he had the shotgun.'

Many of Noonan's recommendations after Walsh Street, ignored at the time, have been implemented – including a taskforce/disaster room ready to go and improved bugging capacity and training.

But long before the litany of Walsh Street mistakes, an informer came forward with information that, if acted on, may have prevented the ambush murders.

It began when an inmate (we'll call him 'Mr Jones') contacted a respected country copper wanting a deal. The inmate was facing five armed-robbery charges, and while he admitted he was guilty of two, claimed he had been stitched up on the remaining three, with witnesses shown his picture before an identification parade.

'I asked why he was telling this to me and was told he knew I was an honest cop,' Sergeant Russell Anderson said in a scathing report that has been hidden for 36 years.

Jones first contacted Anderson at the Benalla Police Station on 1 October 1987. Tynan and Eyre were murdered on 12 October 1988.

Anderson, who would go on to become a trusted member of the Internal Affairs branch, went to a superior officer who told him to contact the Armed Robbery Squad with the information. 'I was told not to see [Mr Jones].'

Not satisfied, he jumped the chain of command, and a senior officer gave him permission to visit the inmate in Beechworth Prison on 27 June 1988.

'I found [him] to be a person with a wealth of information regarding a number of serious crimes [that] included murder, conspiracy to murder, armed robberies and a plan to use explosives against the Richmond Police Station,' said Anderson.

Jones provided information on six armed robberies that had been carried out by a team of gunmen known as the Flemington Crew, responsible for a series of raids on banks. He provided information that could only be known by an insider, including where they swapped cars, cut holes in cyclone fences, jobs where shots were fired at police, and where guards were injured.

Jones said the gang was run by a team of four. Police would later find Jones was accurate, and the crew was led by Victor Peirce, Graeme Jensen, Peter McEvoy and Jedd Houghton. The second-tier soldiers included Victor's half-brother Trevor Pettingill, Anthony Farrell and car thief Gary Abdallah.

But there was another gang pulling jobs – led by NSW prison

escapee Russell Cox – that included Mark Moran, later gunned down in Melbourne's underworld war, and the little-known Santo Mercuri.

While Anderson was convinced Jones could help crack multiple crimes and destroy a prodigious armed-robbery gang, he was thwarted from above. He discussed the case with a colleague. 'We believed a taskforce should be set up to investigate the matter further.'

Three days after his first visit, Anderson returned to prison with a senior officer. Despite inside details provided by the informer from handwritten notes, the senior officer 'was not impressed by [Jones] and he believed a lot of what [he] had to say could be jail talk'.

At that meeting, Jones identified future targets, including the State Bank in Preston and a raid on the Armaguard van at the Coles store at Barkly Square, Brunswick. Less than two weeks later, and nine months after Jones first offered to inform on the gang, a member of the Armed Robbery Squad finally went to Beechworth Prison to interview him. It was too late. That same day, three armed robbers pulled the Barkly Square job.

A source inside Armaguard had already – for 10 per cent of the takings – provided information on six robberies worth $500,000. The details were exaggerated; it was supposed to be worth $200,000 and easy pickings. Instead, the 11 July job netted only $33,000 and went horribly wrong when security guard Dominik Hefti refused to give up the cash tin.

Hefti, 31, was fatally shot in the chest and leg but managed to return fire, shooting one of the robbers through the hand. The injured gunman ran to the car park, where he dragged a woman from her Nissan Pulsar and drove off. The other two escaped in their own getaway car.

The Armed Robbery Squad concluded (wrongly) that Jensen was the gang member who killed Hefti. On 11 October, they attempted to arrest him at Narre Warren. Three cars with eight detectives attempted a box intercept. It failed, and when Jensen attempted to drive away, he was shot dead.

Police had already killed two associates of the Flemington Crew – Mark Militano in January 1987, and Frank Valastro five months later. The crew had discussed a two-for-one revenge plot, where they would kill two members of the Armed Robbery Squad. But after Jensen's death, they decided on a random attack on police. They stole a Holden Commodore and planted it in the middle of a quiet South Yarra road – Walsh Street – knowing residents would call the police.

When the night shift Prahran van heard the call, Steven Tynan and Damian Eyre volunteered to attend the scene, where they were ambushed and shot dead. It was 13 hours after Jensen was shot by police.

It would be years later that police – using DNA technology – would establish that Hefti's killer was Mercuri, a sausage maker-turned-gunman. It was Cox's group, not the Flemington Crew, who did Barkly Square.

Police received credible information that a professional hitman planned to kill Anderson. The SOG began preparing to raid the hitman's Euroa property and Victor Peirce in Richmond. The date was set for 25 August. On 23 August, Anderson was told the raids would not go ahead because a senior officer 'would not authorise the SOG for the Euroa property or Peirce's address in Richmond'.

Peirce was the driving force behind Walsh Street. If he is in custody, it doesn't happen.

With more insight, perhaps they would have also used the SOG for the Jensen arrest, which almost certainly would have avoided the fatal shooting.

Nearly five years after the Hefti murder, when police went to arrest the dangerous Mercuri, the same senior officers stubbornly refused to authorise the use of the SOG until Assistant Commissioner Frank Green intervened, saying: 'That's what they are there for.' Mercuri was arrested without incident.

Two months after Walsh Street, Anderson wrote a report about the failure to efficiently use Jones, saying he believed it could have thwarted Walsh Street.

'I have felt very sad at this great loss and wonder if this tragedy may have been prevented by more effective and expedient handling of this inquiry.

'I felt that from the onset of this inquiry there was a lack of direction. A taskforce would have been efficient and had the support of all officers, who would have allowed the SOG to be used when required. All the offenders would have been arrested (before Walsh Street).'

Two Walsh Street suspects, Jedd Houghton and Gary Abdallah, were shot dead by police in separate incidents.

One Walsh Street weapon was a Japanese KTG shotgun, the same gun used by Houghton in a Flemington Crew armed robbery. The weapon was found, buried and wrapped in plastic, near the Melbourne Zoo.

John Noonan said the revelations in the Anderson report was 'further evidence of incompetence and just more proof that there needs to be an inquest'. The families of Tynan and Eyre have previously requested the coroner hold an inquest into Walsh Street.

Noonan has backed the push. 'There are many facts that were not revealed at the trial that would be admissible at an inquest. The truth needs to be finally told. Steven and Damian and their families deserve nothing less.'

Here's the twist: the underworld informer, Mr Jones, also told police he was offered a contract to kill a chemist's wife in Essendon. He refused the job but handed it to another gunman – the same one who threatened to kill Anderson – who took the job.

On 6 May 1988, Anne Louise Crawford, former primary school teacher and mother of two, was found dead under her 1983 brown Ford Fairlane. The hitman had arranged the crime scene to look as if the car had slipped off the jack as she reached underneath for a wheel nut while trying to change the driver's side front tyre.

Police fell for the ruse, even though the jack did not match the car, the victim was wearing smart clothes, she hadn't bothered to put down a protective rug and both tyres, the one to be replaced and the spare, were obviously flat.

No one seemed concerned that if she was reaching for the nut, why would she be found on her back, why a fingernail was missing, and why there were four bruises on her left bicep that seemed to show she had been roughly grabbed?

Homicide Squad detectives, if notified, would have wondered why two framed photographs on the wall had been displaced in her home as if there was a struggle. But they weren't notified. The crime scene was cleaned and the case treated as an accident, despite Mr Jones' claim it was a hit.

That is until a phone call 15 years later from the ex-wife of the gunman known as PS who rang Crime Stoppers with a tip. A cold case investigation led to PS confessing and agreeing to plead guilty if he could serve his time interstate.

He was sentenced to 12 years' jail. Anne's husband, chemist Ron Crawford, was charged with murder. At his trial, his legal team argued PS killed Anne when she found him burgling the family home. Ron was acquitted by a Supreme Court jury.

OF CRIMES, CRASHES AND COVER-UPS

When politicians get themselves in a twist, they should look to Victoria's long-time premier Sir Henry Bolte, who lived and nearly died under the creed 'deny everything'.

Bolte was a law-and-order man (he succeeded in hanging Ronald Ryan, the last man executed in Australia) although in his own case, he thought the law should bend to his orders.

While his government had introduced compulsory front-seat safety belts, Bolte was a man of habit and driving home full of scotch was one of them. Which is why he makes the list of this reporter's top five unresolved scandals.

Bolte's bolt of luck

Twelve years after his 1972 retirement as Victoria's longest-serving premier, Sir Henry had a head-on crash near his farm. While logic suggested he should be sent to the Geelong Hospital, rat cunning required him to go to the Ballarat Hospital, where he had many friends.

Despite his initial protest, blood was taken to be tested for alcohol and, as usual, split into three samples: one to be tested at the spot, a second to be sent to forensics for a test to be used in court and a third to be given to the injured driver.

The first sample was said to be nearly three times the limit, but the two remaining samples were substituted and the evidence box left unlocked, meaning Sir Henry got away with it, unlike the driver of the other car, who suffered life-altering injuries.

Bolte always said he was not involved in any conspiracy. 'Of course I know nothing, I was unconscious.'

The offside offsider

Back in the 1950s, before legal off-course betting, there were thousands of SP bookmakers in back lanes and pubs. Then there were the Big Eight – the illegal bookmakers that set the market and controlled much of the industry.

One of the most enthusiastic punters was deputy premier and chief secretary Sir Arthur Rylah, who had the perfect betting system: if he won, he would be paid; if he lost, he would not be charged.

Perhaps that was why the government wasn't that keen to change the system. Certainly, his bookie (one of the Big Eight) was always welcome to park his car in the Parliament compound. No one knows if it was bravado or he had the unofficial keys to the city. When the bookie died, among his possessions was a note to his partner: *I think we may have lost a customer. Sir Arthur is getting married today.*

It is on Parliament letterhead.

This would be Sir Arthur's second marriage, on 9 October 1969, to his long-term mistress. His first wife, Lady Ann Rylah, author and Girl Guide commissioner, had died seven months earlier. She was found unconscious in the back garden of her Kew home with a head wound. She and Sir Arthur had separated months earlier.

Lady Rylah was a vet who would usually put her work boots on at the back door. This time, she apparently walked several metres past the shoes before collapsing.

Homicide quickly found there were no suspicious circumstances.

A postmortem by pathologist James 'Mac the Knife' McNamara found death was from a brain haemorrhage.

After I wrote about this case in *The Age* newspaper, I was contacted by a long-retired staff member at the Coroner's Court. 'You missed a critical part of the Lady Rylah autopsy. The part where Mac was called in the middle of the night to perform the autopsy and stamp the paperwork.

'The story that was put about was that it was done to avoid unfavourable publicity.'

Yeah? Pull the other one.

'I can't quite recall if there was someone there to hold Mac up. Probably one of the then Homicide Squad.

'No doubt you are aware Jim McNamara was an alcoholic. This played into the hands of the then bent Homicide Squad. There were many murders that went unrecorded, due to the fact Mac was open to suggestions for a cause of death.'

Truth is certainly stranger than fiction.

There are many who believe Lady Rylah's bleed came from a heavy blow from a garden spade. The cremation was held four days later. The Homicide officer assigned was Detective Inspector Jack Ford – also a prodigious punter.

I once asked a Homicide Squad detective of that era about the case. He paused, then said it was handled by Ford's best friend. 'There was not much paperwork.'

At the time there was growing evidence some members of the Homicide Squad were being paid bribes by abortionists. Sir Arthur opposed an inquiry for years, saying he owed the Homicide Squad a debt of gratitude as they were kind to him when he was in need of compassion.

In 1970 he reluctantly announced a judicial inquiry under William Kaye QC, with very narrow terms of reference. The following January, Sir Arthur announced his resignation before the inquiry's findings were tabled.

The Kaye Inquiry found a corrupt system of payments to some in the squad. Ford, his boss Superintendent Jack Matthews, and former detective constable Martin Jacobson were jailed.

There was another side to Sir Arthur.

In 1963 my father, Fred, a policeman, was in Hong Kong extraditing a corrupt lawyer when he ran into Sir Arthur and Lady Ann (who was unsteady on her feet) on the steps of Government House just before Christmas.

'What are you doing here?' Sir Arthur asked. When Fred explained, Sir Arthur told him: 'Get home for Christmas to see your family.'

Fred baulked, predicting the government wouldn't pay for a second trip to get the suspect. Sir Arthur promised he would. And, unlike the bookies' promissory notes, he kept his word. My father came home and I was presented with a battery-operated Qantas Boeing 707 with flashing lights and operational stairs.

Caught with your pants down

Before Tom (No) Blamey became Australia's only homegrown field marshal, he was Victoria's Chief Commissioner of Police from 1925 to 1936, with a habit of misplacing both the truth and his trousers.

On 21 October 1925, three police raided Mabel Tracey's brothel in Bell Street, Fitzroy, to be greeted by a naked gentleman flashing (among other things) police identification, calmly declaring: 'That is all right boys. I am a plainclothes constable. Here is my badge.'

The badge was numbered 80 – Tom Blamey's. He claimed it had been stolen from his keyring and then dropped three days later at his Naval and Military Club letterbox. Despite his deputy saying he saw it on the chief's desk hours before the raid, No-Blamey survived.

Ten years later, when the head of the Criminal Investigation Bureau, Superintendent John Brophy, was shot in his car in the company of two lady friends, Blamey enthusiastically joined the cover-up. The first version was that he 'was accidentally shot in the right arm whilst handling his revolver'. Yet he was also shot in the cheek and chest (he survived because one shot deflected off the buckle of his braces).

When the accidental wounding story failed to fly, Blamey declared Brophy was shot on his way to meeting an informer as part of armed robbery investigations. Yet there was no manhunt.

The good mail was that Brophy was shot by a jealous husband while Blamey was in the back seat, sans trousers.

The 'green light' murder

When the man with the beard stood up and shot notorious armed robber Ray 'Chuck' Bennett on 12 November 1979, in front of police and inside the old Melbourne Magistrates Court, he knew exactly what he was doing and where he was going.

According to one insider, this was because the killer had been smuggled into the court complex a day before – hidden in the boot of a cleaner's car by two detectives for a dress rehearsal. The court was a maze – yet the killer ran directly to an internal car park hidden from the street to a corrugated fence where the tin had been peeled back for his escape.

The number one suspect was gangster Brian Kane, who wanted revenge on Bennett after he and two other men were acquitted of killing Brian's brother, Les.

As one detective of the time told me: 'We decided to stick with the Kanes . . . because they were more predictable, they had rules, they caught and killed their own . . . About two in the afternoon an informer told Angus [Detective Senior Sergeant Angus Ritchie, chief of the consorting squad] "it was an inside job from your office".'

The punch and the cover-up

When RJ Hawke, just-elected president of the Australian Council of Trade Unions, arrived as guest of honour and after-dinner speaker at the Victoria Police Criminal Investigation Branch's annual dinner, he fronted directly from a long lunch, spectacularly drunk.

Even so, the Police Association secretary Bill Crowley (who would rise to the rank of assistant commissioner) introduced Hawke as 'the future prime minister of Australia'. Bob continued to drink during the meal until it was his turn to speak. After all, the only drinking school harder than union delegates is hardened detectives.

He rose unsteadily and began with a joke flatter than his unfinished beer. 'CIB,' he started, 'stands for Criminally Insane Bastards.'

Some detectives staged a walkout during the speech but returned later, swapping their indignation for port and cheese. The other speaker, Chief Commissioner Noel Wilby, was given a standing ovation.

One of those present was a hard-as-nails Stolen Motor Car detective by the name of Rod Shedden, who approached Hawke to tell him he was out of order. 'He beat me with words,' says Rod, 'and we ended up shaking hands.'

As was the way of detectives from that generation, the night continued at the Police Club at the back of the Russell Street Police Headquarters.

'He was lording it over everybody saying: "I'm RJ Hawke, president-elect of the ACTU",' says Shedden. Witnesses say Hawke began flirting with one of the female bar staff, eventually putting her on his knee.

'I thought: "I'm sick and tired of this, bugger it",' recalls Rod.

He went over to remind Hawke he was a guest and should pull his head in. Hawke, never short of a word, said as the police union owned the club and he was the head of the ACTU, he was welcome at any time.

Shedden, a big man with fists the size of ham hocks, invited the much smaller Hawke outside for a more robust discussion. 'To his credit, he followed me out,' says Rod, now 82.

'He put his glasses in his top pocket and faced up and I went *bang*, knocking him arse over head. I was going to pick him up and give him a few rib ticklers to remind him to keep better manners but some of my mates grabbed me.'

By this point the future prime minister had lost all interest in the barmaid, the fight and the whole evening. 'I'd whacked him pretty hard in the head and he was unconscious.'

When Crowley descended on the scene, he went straight into cover-up mode, threw the still-dazed Hawke into a car and sped off, reversing into the wall of the Police Club in his haste.

On Monday, Shedden had to front his boss. 'Rod, what have you done? Half the force wants you sacked and the other half want you promoted.'

The twist is that a very laundered version of the story appeared in a small newspaper suggesting that following the speech there was a dispute at the Police Club and 'tempers became frayed'.

An outraged Hawke sued, alleging the article implied he was 'guilty of offensive behaviour in a public place and accordingly had broken the law'.

Shedden was told that under no circumstances could he give evidence, as it would be taken as an admission of assault. 'I was told if I opened my mouth, I'd be sacked and lose all my entitlements.'

The case was settled out of court.

In 1988 Rod Shedden retired as a detective sergeant, refusing promotion 'because all I wanted to do was to catch crooks'. And Bob Hawke, as Crowley (who became a life member of the association) had predicted all those years earlier, became prime minister.

I first learnt of the fracas more than 40 years ago and confirmed it with Rod over more than one quiet ale when no one was invited outside (except into the beer garden). But he was disinclined to go on the record.

I rang him soon after the 16 May 2019 death of Australia's third-longest serving and much-loved prime minister. Mellowed with age, Rod said yes, I could tell the story. 'The poor old bastard's gone now. Good luck to him.'

PART 2

CROOKS (AND THE NOT-SO-CROOKED)

What makes them tick? There is Judy Moran who lost two husbands and two sons to murder and then organised the killing of her brother-in-law but made the mistake of leaving the getaway car in her garage. A dead giveaway.

The dead crook whose ghastly wounds were blamed on hungry local turtles and the dog-loving hitman who was happy to kill a couple for cash but drew the line at shooting man's best friend.

The bodybuilder set to be deported who says he has been stitched up by one cop with a long memory. Despite spending nearly all his life in Australia, the courts have ratified a decision to kick him out because he was born in the UK.

A CRIME MATRIARCH OR MAYBE A MYTH

Underworld author-turned-killer-turned-inmate Judy Moran is two-thirds of the way through her minimum 21-year sentence for organising the 2009 murder of her brother-in-law, Desmond 'Tuppence' Moran, in a crime that would be laughable if it was not deadly.

Now 78 and with failing health, she is unlikely to ever see the other side of the prison walls. If she were to make her earliest parole date, it would be granted as she reached the age of 85.

A prison source not authorised to speak to baggy-arsed reporters told us in 2023: 'She's pretty frail these days, I reckon she's on her last lap.' But the source is no medical expert and Moran has proved many wrong before.

The source says Moran – a former TV chorus girl who craved the spotlight – is now unknown to younger inmates, who couldn't pick Judy Moran from Dame Judi Dench (although both have put on star performances in their long and colourful lives). While Moran is not queen of the convicts, she still knows how to get her views through to senior corrections officers – her complaints head straight up the chain of command.

Surfing the wave of her family's notoriety and her own personal tragedy, there was a time when Moran and drug boss Carl Williams' widow, Roberta Williams, were the go-to pair for commentary on the underworld.

Roberta has bounced around for years on the outer ring of social media relevance while Moran got sucked into believing she was an underworld player rather than just another victim.

Truth is, Moran has suffered terribly. She has lost two husbands – Les Cole (1981) and Lewis Moran (2004) – and two sons – Mark Moran (2000) and Jason Moran (2003) – to underworld murders.

Granted, Cole had long moved to Sydney when he was killed and Lewis hated her, but Judy Moran's anguish was real. For all the hundreds of glamour shots, there is one picture taken 20 years ago that tells the truth: she is slumped near a park, her face etched with grief. Her son, Jason, along with his friend, Pasquale Barbaro, had been murdered while sitting in a van at the Essendon North Auskick. Their bodies were still in the van when Judy Moran arrived. This was one of the rare times she let her mask slip. (In her book, she thanked those who did her hair and helped her choose outfits for her family's very public funerals.)

She had tried to build the contradictory image as a mother who refused to believe her sons had turned bad while simultaneously being someone who could pull underworld strings.

Perhaps she took offence because I didn't buy the Moran Matriarch brand. Many years ago, after several requests for a radio interview with an on-air team in Adelaide hopelessly out of their depth, I jumped on the phone only to find they had Moran waiting in some form of ill-considered (and quite unethical) 'ambush'.

When I later privately queried the producer, he pleaded inexperience, stupidity and naivety – and was right on all counts. When she was convicted of murder, he didn't request a follow-up interview. Funny that.

Moran wanted to argue that her son Jason was not the man who had killed underworld figure Alphonse Gangitano. Unfortunately for her, Gangitano and the radio team, the coroner had already concluded Jason Moran's alibi was false. He was present at the time of the shooting and 'implicated' in the murder.

But that was Judy – prepared to stare down the facts and bend the truth to her advantage, a tactic that failed spectacularly at her murder trial.

Judy Moran has made it clear she doesn't like me, writing in her book, *My Story*: 'Sometimes I feel I am at war with Silvester, that I am a soldier in the trenches with my bayonet fixed.'

On her book publicity tour, she was a nightmare, making more demands than Cleopatra. She required special assistance, including wheelchair access at airports. At the end of the trip, to the surprise of her handler, she got out of the chair and walked away.

I had the first version of the book pulped due to some lies I was not prepared to leave unchallenged. Judy's subsequent tantrum apparently made Hiroshima look like cracker night.

On a late-night visit to the famous Supper Inn restaurant, a group of young men spent their time glaring at me before storming out. (To be honest, the chopped chilli in the soy sauce was more dangerous.) When I rang Moran on a matter of no consequence a few days later, she volunteered: 'How was the food at the Supper Inn? Always tasty, isn't it?'

Moran, it seems, is a little like the Supper Inn's lemon chicken – a bit sweet and a little sour.

(An aside: at the Chinese restaurant my son, then a skinny 15-year-old, became quite protective, which I found quaint. A few years later, when he had filled out and was an accomplished boxer, I was relieved to have him with me when, not far from the same restaurant, two would-be crooks who had gobbled more steroids than wontons were looking for a confrontation.)

Moran did have a story to tell: one of violence, victimisation and tragedy.

Her father, Leo Brooks, was for years the doorman and one of the unofficial elders at the Carlton Football Club. Star interstate players often stayed with him. They soon found he was the sort of character who could find anything you needed from a fork to a forklift at vastly reduced prices. At times, his house was full of so much stolen property, it became known as Leo's Emporium. Moran was a keen student and became a first-class shoplifter.

Once, in later years, interviewed on TV in her home about the latest underworld rumblings, someone rang to tell me everything in the background of her neat house had been stolen to order.

Lewis Moran was involved in SP bookmaking, major thefts and, later, drug manufacturing with his sons. According to his mate Bertie Wrout, Lewis was a tight-arse who, following a feed at the Flower Drum, would insist on picking pockets on the way home.

He also beat Judy Moran before they separated, although he continued (begrudgingly) to support her caviar-and-champagne tastes. 'Beluga [$350 for 50 grams] and Cristal [$450 a bottle] are more my style,' she bragged in her book. (If it is a consolation, they sell tuna and orange cordial at the prison canteen at reasonable prices.)

Lewis Moran's legendary frugalness would cost him his life. When he decided to fight back against drug boss Carl Williams, who had ordered the murders of Mark and Jason Moran, Lewis put out a contract well under market rates and found no takers. (In fairness to Williams, he went to war with the Morans after Jason and Mark lured him to a park for a business meeting only to shoot him in the guts.)

The police, knowing Lewis Moran was on a list to be murdered, took the unusual step of asking the court to alter curfew bail conditions to make his routine less predictable.

Even so, he and Wrout went to the Brunswick Club Hotel every day between 5.30 pm and 8 pm to drink Carlton Draught. The added incentive was that one of the staff would slip them a few free ones.

You could set your watch on their arrival; the hit team certainly did. They burst in on 31 March 2004, killing Lewis Moran and wounding Wrout, who later mused they were shot for 'cheap beer'.

Judy was convinced Lewis had left a hidden fortune and that his brother, Des 'Tuppence' Moran, was holding out on her. Despite hating her, Des gave her a regular allowance, slinging her four grand a month. Eventually, he froze her, cutting her out of his will.

With media appearance money for the self-styled queen of the underworld drying up and book royalties reduced to a trickle, she decided to take matters into her own hands – or hired hands.

One slapstick attempt on Des Moran's life involved a mistaken identity, a balaclava that was too big and a scarecrow. The shot went through the windscreen of his Mercedes, lodging in the steering wheel. And the driver wasn't Des. Tuppence later complained to his car dealer that the Benz wasn't bulletproof, possibly thinking he was in Munich in the 1940s rather than Moonee Ponds in the 2000s.

Undeterred, Judy backed up for a second go. In May 2009, she borrowed $400,000 from Westpac, not volunteering on the paperwork she wanted the money to hire a hit team. Over the next couple of days, she bought two Chrysler convertibles and a Land Rover Discovery. Two of the cars were advanced payment for the hit.

Cynically, she picked the date of the murder to be 15 June 2009 – the ninth anniversary of her son Mark's killing. Her alibi was that she had been at the cemetery. She hoped Carl Williams would be blamed.

Des Moran was at his favourite Ascot Vale cafe when he saw the killers. All he could say was 'Oh shit' before he was shot dead.

Judy Moran arrived to perform as the grieving relative. One witness told police: 'Judy was crying and saying things like, "It should have been me, not Des. It's all about drugs and money."' She hugged a female acquaintance, who later remarked that while Moran was sobbing, there were no tears.

Detectives went to Moran's four-bedroom home, where one spotted the Fairlane getaway car in the garage.

Later, Moran, dressed more like a countess than a crook, jumped in the car wearing knitted white gloves and drove two kilometres to dump the Fairlane. As she walked home, an unmarked police car pulled up and a Purana investigator called from the window: 'Hi Judy, do you want a lift?'

It was a rhetorical question. It would turn out to be a one-way trip.

THE ONE THAT GOT AWAY FROM THE MOB

Australian gangsters, who tend to have the life expectancy of your average bumblebee, would do well to study the once feared Franzese US Mob family.

John 'Sonny' Franzese, said by US police to have killed or ordered 50 murders, died peacefully in 2020 aged 103. Which shows the Mediterranean diet, coupled with a lack of conscience, may be the secret to long life.

Franzese was born in 1917 but was not a prisoner to the old ways. In a conversation bugged by his son-turned-snitch, John Junior, he discussed his preferred method of body disposal. 'Dismember victim in kiddie pool. Cook body parts in microwave. Stuff parts in garbage disposal. Be patient.' This would indicate Franzese Senior was neither people nor environmentally friendly.

Understandably, John Junior disappeared into witness protection before he disappeared permanently.

His other son, Michael, became a made man and a mafia captain in the New York Colombo crime family.

The fact he is 72 and in Australia to tell his story is a testament to the Mediterranean diet and his unique survival skills. At one point, he was a dead man walking. Now he is a live one talking.

Michael's sliding-door moment came at 21. While studying medicine at university, he made an offer others couldn't refuse: to join the family's business after his father was sentenced to 50 years over a string of armed robberies. This meant Michael swapped the first law of medicine, Do No Harm, to the first rule of the Mafia, Do Harm If It Is Good For Business.

'I was visiting Dad in Leavenworth Penitentiary when I told him I was done with school and was going on the street. He said that if I was going to do it, then do it right,' Michael says. John nominated him to the Colombo family, where he was eventually in charge of 300 Mob guys.

The Mob business model may not be taught at Harvard, but it was effective nonetheless. Find a lucrative business, cut corners and then bully any competitors into retirement. The big-ticket item was bootlegging – not Al Capone's illicit booze but something even more lucrative: petrol.

Michael Franzese built an empire of 350 petrol stations, his own storage areas and a fleet of tankers. By using black market fuel and avoiding government taxes, he could undercut competitors. Those who were stubborn soon found their businesses firebombed. Most Mob violence 'was not personal, it was just business, although sometimes it could be personal'.

Franzese says at its peak, the business was generating $50 million a month with him making $2 million a week. He diversified into making movies, owning car lots and the construction business.

Hard to believe there was such a thing, but in 1986 he was listed by *Fortune* magazine as one of the 'Fifty Most Wealthy and Powerful Mafia Bosses'.

Headlines like that plus owning multiple luxury houses, a private jet and a helicopter was always going to bring police attention, and he was arrested over the gasoline scam. Looking back, Michael knew it couldn't last. 'Because of my father there was a target on my back from the start. He was arrested 18 times, indicted seven times and went to trial (and acquitted) five times.'

But times and his luck changed. The code of silence worked because insiders took an oath they knew, if broken, could cost their lives. But Michael says law enforcement started using anti-racketeering laws effectively, with threats of 100-year jail terms that turned insiders into informers.

'They began to fear the government more than the Mob. Law enforcement can use high-tech surveillance, but every big case is based on flipping people. Informants destroyed my life.' He says insiders facing life in prison are offered immunity, new identities and 'plenty of dollars' to turn on their Mob mates. The code of silence is dead.

During Melbourne's Underbelly War, the killings stopped when the Purana Taskforce flipped several key insiders, including one of drug boss Carl Williams' hitmen, his trusted lieutenant, plus Tony Mokbel's drug cook and one of his cabinet members.

And for 40 years, police have been pushing for US-style Racketeer Influenced and Corrupt Organisations (RICO) laws that can take isolated crimes committed years apart to establish a pattern of racketeering and can target apparently legitimate businesses that have been built on illegal funds.

When his business partner in the gasoline scam was prepared to testify, Franzese knew the gig was up. Faced with a possible life sentence, Franzese took a massive gamble – he would talk just enough to cut a deal, but not enough to end up dismembered in his dad's kiddie pool. He was on a tightrope, with crooks on one side and cops on the other.

He promised to give up Mob bosses but talked only about his crimes without implicating anyone else. 'I wasn't going to put people in jail.'

Then the prosecution played a ruthless card: they listed Franzese as a state witness in multiple prosecutions, telling him he was now a marked man and the only way to stay alive was to inform and jump into witness protection. It is an old cop trick, make it look like someone is talking so they have no choice but to talk.

Franzese kept sending messages from prison that he was not informing: 'But everyone does that.' It was when he didn't turn up to testify and was still in jail that his former colleagues saw he was true to his word, although some in his Mob family would never forgive him for walking away. He suspects if family boss Carmine Persico had not been jailed, he would be dead.

Even so, for many years he made sure his movements couldn't be predicted, moving several times, walking his dog at different times and locations and never going regularly to the same restaurants. Compare this with our crooks who have been gunned down after keeping more regular timetables than the railways.

Franzese was sentenced to 10 years, served five, paid $15 million in restitution and had $5 million in assets seized as proceeds of crime. He returned to jail for another three years (he says the government wanted to pay him back for not testifying) before finding God and realising he could make a lucrative and safe living talking and writing about crimes rather than committing them.

On his forearm he has tattooed Proverbs 16–7, which is: *When a man's ways please the Lord, he maketh even his enemies to be at peace with him.* In Franzese's former business, you need all the help you can get.

He is a fan dancer who knows exactly when to cover up. He has taken the skill of talking just enough to cut a deal onto the speaking circuit, providing an insight into the Mob without giving enough specifics to get himself thrown into prison or cooked in a microwave (how many minutes for a head, one wonders?).

He says that at his shows, he is always asked three questions: where did he hide the money, did he kill anyone, and what happened to missing teamster Jimmy Hoffa? 'You'll have to come to a show to find out.'

He says there is a fascination and at times a romantic image about the Mob, fed by countless books (he has written several) and

Hollywood movies. He says he tries to separate the realities from the myth.

Even gangsters fall for the Hollywood image. Drug dealer Rocco Arico was one of many to have framed pictures of *Scarface* in their homes, gangland murder victim Mario Condello could quote reams of *The Godfather* word-perfect, and 1950s standover man Freddie 'The Frog' Harrison was a regular at the Forum cinema to watch the latest Jimmy Cagney black-and-white gangster flick.

Melbourne and Sydney gangsters should take a break from watching reruns of *The Sopranos* and head off to one of Franzese's shows, where they could learn that for crooks a low profile is better protection than a bulletproof vest. In Sydney and Melbourne, hoods are shooting and bombing each other at an unhealthy rate that results in tit-for-tat retaliations, major police responses and multiple arrests.

'When guys are getting killed on the streets, it is usually a power struggle. If you want to be the boss, there isn't an election. You have to go to war,' he observes. 'But a war is bad for business. When it is in the public and in your face, law enforcement has to respond.'

While he has reformed, he warmly remembers the old days. 'I miss some of the guys and the good times. There were more good times than bad.'

But, he says, it ends badly for most. 'Just about every one of them ended up dead or in jail. Trust me, I am one of the few survivors.'

THE CREEP WHO CREPT IN, THEN CREPT OUT

Peter Oswald was a dashing navy officer, a police inspector, a respected psychologist, academic and – it has now come to light – a serial sexual predator.

For any number of reasons, on at least three occasions, Oswald has escaped justice. His latest and probably last close call was when two charges of indecent assault were dropped against the 74-year-old, leaving him to see out his final days in Thailand.

He was charged over allegedly assaulting a traumatised young policeman he was supposed to be counselling after a shooting. A submission by his lawyer detailing his chronic ill health and the challenges of returning from Asia during COVID has led the Office of Public Prosecutions to drop the charges, even though a magistrate had concluded the evidence was strong enough to proceed to trial.

In 1983, the injured cop limped into the psychologist's office on crutches, having survived a gun battle with an armed offender who later died. He left, shocked and traumatised, having been molested by then police psychologist Oswald.

'Simon' was in his early 20s and had been a policeman for two years.

Still shaken from the gunfight, he was encouraged to open up about his life by the seemingly concerned Oswald.

Soon in tears, Simon told of the loss of his mother when he was at the Police Academy and then confided that in his early teens, he had been molested by the notorious paedophile priest Michael Glennon.

'The psychologist talked to me about what the priest had done and asked for me to describe in graphic detail the acts I committed with him.

'I told him I felt ashamed to say and embarrassed, but he assured me it was OK and after some time he gained my confidence and I told him everything about what had happened.

'By this stage, I was very upset. During this time, the psychologist moved closer towards me and started to rub my leg gently . . . I was stunned and shocked. He looked at me in the eyes and continued to rub my leg and moved to my penis and then, for what seemed like an eternity, massaged and rubbed me. I felt sick.

'I felt like the small child from all those years ago in the church.'

Simon was ushered out to see Deputy Commissioner Eric Millar. 'I tried to tell the deputy commissioner what had happened, but I couldn't.'

When Millar asked how his meeting with Oswald had gone, he replied: 'Not good.'

'I had tears in my eyes,' Simon recalls. 'Then he [Millar] cut me off.'

In fairness, there is no way the senior officer could possibly have suspected what had just happened. But when Simon finally tried to complain, he was either ignored, or worse, treated as if he was the guilty party. He lost trust in senior officers and in 1998, after 17 years in the job, he resigned.

After giving evidence before the Royal Commission into Institutional Responses to Child Sexual Abuse, he felt strong enough to make a complaint to the police's Salus Taskforce, set up to investigate sexual misconduct by police.

He confided to friends inside and outside the force what had happened. This helped corroborate Simon's allegation to Salus investigators. One of those former colleagues, 'John', says: 'It changed him.'

John, who gave evidence at the committal hearing, says the decision to drop the charges was a 'real kick in the guts' for Simon.

By the time Salus began its investigation, Oswald had moved overseas, where he taught young men and women in Thailand on several subjects, including ethics. In September 2018, when he returned to Melbourne for an annual visit, he was arrested and charged by Salus detectives.

All those years ago, Oswald was recruited to usher in a new and enlightened era for policing. He was the first professional psychologist employed by Victoria Police. The plan was to give him a taste of street policing before promoting him to inspector, working on the theory that cops only want to confide in other cops. He was sent to the tough St Kilda station as part of his training.

Later, he would find any excuse to come back and hang around the young cops there. An experienced senior sergeant took him aside and said: 'Peter, what are you doing? You'll get a reputation.'

Then, on 12 May 1986, he was gone. There was no real farewell and no explanation. It was rumoured that because of allegations of sexual impropriety, he was given an ultimatum: resign or face a criminal investigation.

Around that time, a senior constable was charged with multiple indecent assault charges that began when the male victim was 12. The offender jumped bail. Months later, he was found in Queensland, extradited and convicted.

The original investigation found Oswald shared a house with the senior constable and the victim said Oswald was there when the assaults occurred. The investigation was stopped before Oswald was formally interviewed.

In the Salus investigation, police found that victim, now aged 50, living overseas. He said he had a new life and didn't want to be involved in any fresh prosecutions.

The senior constable – who was sentenced to 13 months – also refused to cooperate. Salus investigators could not interview senior police who might give insight into Oswald's resignation as they had all died or were infirm.

Those who can remember say Oswald was allowed to resign to avoid the criminal investigation and to avoid embarrassing the police department – a tactic known as 'beating the posse'.

A psychologist who studied with Oswald at the University of NSW remembers him as 'outgoing and charismatic': 'He was older than us when he turned up in our third year. He said he had been a trainee priest, and we knew him as "Peter the priest".

'He would run study groups at his house behind a church in Coogee.'

Once qualified, the psychologist found himself on the same military recruiting panel as Oswald. 'He said the only reason to join the navy was being able to bugger and be buggered. It was then I realised he was dodgy.'

A kid from Gippsland, 'Dave' joined the navy to learn a trade. At 16, he was accepted as an apprentice electrician only to find himself subjected to sexual assault, bashings and verbal bullying. In a bid to give him a new start, he was transferred from a ship based in Sydney to Melbourne, to help build *HMAS Cook*. As he was to drive back, a fellow seaman asked if Dave would give navy officer Lieutenant Peter Oswald a lift.

During that trip, in 1979, Dave found that Oswald was a trained psychologist and so confided that he had been sexually assaulted. Once at the base in Melbourne, Dave was again subject to brutal treatment – so much so that the commanding officer wanted to find him a safe place to stay. And what could be safer than to board with Oswald?

'It didn't take long. He plied me with alcohol and advanced on me,' says Dave. The assaults continued for three months.

Discharged from the navy as damaged, Dave was eventually diagnosed with PTSD. In 2004 he made a complaint to what was then called the Victorian Psychologists' Registration Board. 'They told me that his response to my complaint was that he was moving overseas for at least five years and that he wanted his registration to lapse. A hearing was held on the evening of 30 June 2004, and Oswald's barrister argued that we were friends and that he was not treating me.'

Oswald admitted to one drunken sexual encounter that he insisted was consensual. Oswald was a 33-year-old lieutenant, Dave a 20-year-old able seaman.

'The board stated that although they believed me, as they had no evidence of me being a patient, such as records of clinical visits, and that because it was over 20 years ago, they would not be ruling against Oswald.'

Dave no longer works and has 'considered suicide about a million times'.

'I have no friends and find it impossible to trust people. If someone does me a favour I think: "What do they want in return?"

'I can't hug my son and I can't hug my father.'

After examining a defence submission and Oswald's medical records, the Office of Public Prosecutions has filed a notice with the County Court to discontinue the case. A spokesperson for the OPP said: 'We can't comment on this matter at this time.'

Simon believes the original decision to allow Oswald to resign without being charged was a cover-up, and the latest decision to drop the charges is a cop-out: 'I am furious, and it has made me depressed, anxious and suicidal.'

Oswald could have been exposed and stopped when he was in the navy, the police and in private practice. Instead, those in authority chose to look the other way.

Instead, he was allowed to head to Thailand.

The allegations made by Dave and Simon have never been tested in court.

MR UNIVERSE v THE SUBURBAN COP

Former Mr Universe Gary Lewer is a polarising figure. To his many friends, he is an inspiration, a vegetarian, an anti-drugs campaigner and a fierce supporter of animal rights. To his detractors – including the police and then Home Affairs Minister Peter Dutton – he is an intimidator, a drug importer and the person behind a threat to 'nail your dogs to the door'.

What is beyond dispute is that, by accident or design, if you get on the wrong side of Lewer's massive bodybuilder's frame, bad things happen.

Lewer and his friends say he is the victim of harassment by police, who have fabricated a series of allegations against him because of a vicious vendetta. Police say many of the charges they have laid or would like to lay against Lewer haven't stuck because witnesses have been too frightened to give evidence.

That would normally constitute a stalemate. But as a four-year-old, Lewer arrived in Australia from Britain and, probably believing his parents had done it for him, he did not take up Australian citizenship. (This is somewhat ironic as he has won a record number of Mr Australia titles and represented Australia in 10 world titles, winning Mr World and Mr Universe.)

In 2017, after a series of police investigations, Lewer applied for and was granted a visa to stay in Australia. But when Dutton was sent a police intelligence dossier on the bodybuilder, it was the minister who did the heavy lifting. In 2020, he declared Lewer a person of bad character who should be deported to his country of birth in Australia's national interest.

Lewer, a man who could bench-press a woolly mammoth, did not meekly accept such a character assessment and appealed to the Federal Court. In the eyes of Federal Court judge Justice Bernard Murphy, who presided over the case, the muscled winner of world titles was, in fact, a loser.

Lewer's supporters say police are using the bodybuilder's ancient history against him and that the man, who should now be enjoying a peaceful retirement, has had a (nearly) spotless record for more than 25 years. According to an online petition, Lewer 'inspired thousands of people into fitness and good health. He now uses his following to bring awareness to the cruelty of animals'.

His Facebook page certainly promotes a healthy lifestyle and vegetarian diet, which means he has made many adjustments since he was convicted in 2004 of selling animal steroids to fellow bodybuilders.

The police dossier shows him as an alleged drug trafficker, arsonist, intimidator, organised crime figure and tax avoider. He has prior convictions for firearms, drug possession, breaking and entering, property and driving offences.

Lewer argued that Dutton's decision to deport him was unfair as it relied on a police report that was based on 'suspicion and innuendo'. The intelligence report in question finds Lewer to be involved in: 'Sophisticated criminal drug importation and manufacturing enterprises . . . [and he] possesses sound knowledge of police investigation methodology, is extremely disciplined in his criminal conduct to avoid detection and therefore is an extremely difficult suspect to investigate.'

Prosecutions failed, the report claimed, when 'witnesses have retracted their statements (in one case citing fear) and a Crown witness died'.

Although he had been under various forms of investigation for more than 35 years, Lewer was unlucky to come to the attention of a veteran local detective (who we will call 'The Pom') who made it his mission to expose the bodybuilder.

In 2013, he was charged over the importation of precursor chemicals from China that police allege could have been used to make ice valued at $500 million. The charges were later dropped.

It all began almost by accident when hazardous chemicals discovered in a rented property in Frankston were found to be the type used to make the drug ice. The Pom got hold of the case and would not let go.

The Pom was not working for a fancy organised crime taskforce. He went after Lewer while investigating all manner of local crime. 'I named the deportation investigation Operation Fairsky because Lewer and I are both £10 Pommies having travelled with our parents as young kids on the ship *Fairsky* which was a turbine steamship that went between Britain and Australia between 1958 to 1972.

'What different paths we chose when our families docked in Australia,' The Pom said. (Lewer denies arriving on the *Fairsky* and claims it is one of many fabrications.)

'Lewer was aware of this as when we were on speaking terms and he professed he liked me, which was short-lived, we spoke about being fellow countrymen, albeit that was when he asked me to look the other way.'

Lewer's supporters are calling foul, saying in their online petition: 'A police officer has grossly abused his powers by fabricating stories of "bad character" to convince the home affairs minister Peter Dutton to deport an Australian. The officer who has a long-standing vendetta against Gary is acting under the auspices of the Victoria Police. He has not produced any evidence to support any of the accusations he presented to the minister.'

The Minister had another view:

> I have also taken into account that the intelligence report states that intelligence holdings held by Victoria Police, the Australian Criminal Intelligence Commission and the Independent Broad-Based Anti-Corruption Commission indicate that Mr Lewer has been identified as a security threat against a serving police officer. I consider this conduct is serious, and poses a risk to both the police officer and the community, who relies on the police force to maintain order and protect the community from criminal activities.

Lewer told the media in 2024: 'If I read that document, I would deport me, too. But it is a fantasy.'

Lewer claims that after being examined by the Australian Criminal Intelligence Commission, he was cleared but the ACIC doesn't clear anyone. Testimony gathered under its coercive powers is inadmissible in criminal trials. And the ACIC only takes on cases of alleged organised crime figures of national significance. This does not mean he is an organised crime figure, but one thing is for sure, he ain't Snow White.

Lewer made an official complaint to police professional standards about The Pom. It was rejected. Lewer made an official complaint, complete with his own dossier, to the Independent Broad-based Anti Corruption Commission. It was rejected.

Police insist The Pom is a gun detective who refuses to blink, no matter how big the target. In 2014, the detective was made the Regional Investigator of The Year in the Mick Miller Awards for his work into Lewer and associates. Miller, the former chief commissioner, said he had studied the case and was proud of The Pom's determination and resilience.

The citation states:

> The investigation resulted in substantial seizures of chemicals, which at the time, were the biggest of their type. Interest in this

> investigation was recognised internationally through Chemical Associations and Drug Enforcement Agencies in America, Europe and China.
>
> The success of this investigation was a result of (The Pom's) tenacity and determination, as it embodied the definition of investigation 'as a search for the truth in the interests of justice and within the specifications of the law'.

He was also awarded the Australia Police Medal in the national honours list and the Medal for Merit for 'exemplary service to Victoria Police and the Victorian community'.

Recommendations for the APM and Merit Medal are reviewed by the police Honours and Awards Committee that involves a review of the nominee's whole career to see if there are any skeletons. The Pom's professional history was seen as outstanding.

So if he is a fabricator, he is a bloody good one.

After Justice Murphy declared Lewer should be deported, the bodybuilder contacted me to say The Pom was a nasty man who had a set against him and wanted to get even after the drug case collapsed.

'All allegations, suspicions, beliefs and conjecture referenced in the document emanated from investigations out of the Frankston Police Station [shit, fancy that].

'Note: Of the sixteen beliefs, suspicions and allegations contained in the document I was interviewed just twice, and charged ONCE only which was wholly withdrawn . . . all fourteen others are simply self-serving conjectures that neither [The Pom] nor anyone else EVER spoke to me about, NEVER.'

He seemed reasonable, articulate and persuasive. Except the courts don't believe him.

Justice Murphy found: 'It is uncontentious that Mr Lewer has been convicted of a range of offences including firearm, drug possession, violent break and enter, property and driving offences; and he does not pass the character test because of the terms of imprisonment imposed for the firearms convictions.'

He also pointed out that Lewer 'had been convicted of a range of serious offences, including convictions for violent offending in 1983 and drug related offending in 1992, 1993, 1995, 1997 and 2014'.

Lewer said that within days of our email conversations, a key witness in his case 'was tracked down by two undercover detectives to a property where he was working on that day only, and THREATENED . . . Amongst other things, they said: "Lewer going to the media is going to end badly"'.

Call me cynical but undercover police don't turn up and say they are undercover because, if they did, they would not be undercover.

The bodybuilder's court appeals against Dutton's decision were not based on claims of a vendetta, but that the Minister's decision was not reasonable and should not have been made on the basis of the material before him.

Justice Murphy found that Lewer and his legal team failed to show the material was flawed and therefore it was open to Dutton to make the deportation order.

Lewer says he made a living in the fitness industry including opening a series of gyms and that claims made in the intelligence document such as he 'has no known lawful means of income, has concealed assets and has amassed substantial hidden wealth from criminal drug and other activity; he has purchased two multimillion dollar properties, one of which he resides in, and the other of which his former spouse resides in; both homes are linked to fake companies' are false.

Surely if Lewer had produced financial, company and tax records showing an income stream consistent with his lifestyle, the credibility of the intelligence material would have been destroyed and Dutton's decision could have been seen as unreasonable. He didn't produce such records in his Federal Court actions.

Lewer's latest attempt to avoid detention is an appeal to the minister that he has become wheelchair-bound while in custody and that he may be of Indigenous descent.

The ice charges fell over when the Chinese government revoked a decision to allow two Chinese alleged co-offenders to give video evidence. No one knows why there was a change of heart.

The police intelligence report sent to Dutton (at the request of the Home Affairs Department) said Lewer 'has forged a powerful reputation in criminal circles as being a violent individual who has the proven behaviour and financial means to inflict harm on any person that provides to police information about his criminal activities'.

The report lists a series of alleged crimes in 2015 and 2016 linked to Lewer, including that he launched a wave of terror against a family building a retirement complex next to his former wife's Frankston home that would have affected their view.

First the excavator caught fire, causing $100,000 damage, and then a massive hole filled with water on the Lewer property caused a landslide that wrecked concrete work on the development next door. There were further fires on the construction site and two cars owned by the developers were firebombed. Their windows were smashed and police alleged the owner's daughter was followed by Lewer.

The girlfriend of a family member told police she received a phone call from a man she believed to be Lewer who threatened to blow up her house, burn her cars and 'nail her pet dogs to the front door' – an alleged threat that does not sit well with Lewer's stance on cruelty to animals.

In Lewer's court and media appeals, he failed to address the unfortunate events that befell the developer's family.

In his judgement, Justice Murphy referred to 'The Minister said that Mr Lewer and his son were subsequently convicted of criminal damage in relation to the deliberate flooding of the Smith construction site in May 2015 . . . causing damage of approximately $19,430 and major disruption to the progress of construction.'

Police also claim that in 2009, a gym owner who was intimidated into allowing Lewer to work out for free cancelled the arrangement when he found Lewer selling steroids in the car park and sleeping with his girlfriend. Then the gym burnt down.

Minister Dutton concluded: 'non-citizens such as Mr Lewer who commit such offences and engage in such conduct should not generally expect to be permitted to remain in Australia'.

Lewer's arguments that the intelligence dossier was flawed were rejected by Justice Murphy and then again by the Full Court on appeal.

Lewer has chosen not to ask for leave to appeal to the High Court as he would almost certainly lose. Instead, he is appealing directly to the new minister that he is too ill to be deported and needs time to explore whether he is of Indigenous heritage.

The former bodybuilder says he has been railroaded and that he is being kicked out due to a report filled with innuendo and suspicion but no evidence. He says that someone who has lived in Australia since Sir Robert Menzies was prime minister should not be bounced out by a kangaroo court.

But the Appeal Court said the case against him was compelling, with one finding:

> It was not irrational or legally unreasonable for the Minister to consider the content of the Victoria Police reports and to reason from the information contained therein that, despite the absence of conviction for the criminal conduct attributed to the appellant, nonetheless the sheer volume of criminal intelligence and the detail of the information pointed compellingly to the conclusion that Mr Lewer had engaged in serious criminal conduct and that in consequence his propensity to engage in that conduct was a risk to be appropriately assessed in informing the Minister's satisfaction that cancellation of the visa is in the national interest.

> The Minister was, in my view, entirely justified in joining all of the dots and in reasoning inferentially to that conclusion.

Lewer has been found to be a person of bad character and his attempts to rewrite history and blame one policeman for his predicament has failed.

But he is a victim. Intelligence is not evidence and Lewer has not been able to contest many of the allegations in a criminal court. He is being kicked out by sleight of hand, on the technicality that the former Mr Australia is not Australian.

Lewer came to this country when he was four. His criminal activities have been in this country and he has served jail time in this country. He may be a bad man, but he is *our* bad man.

He has lived here for more than 60 years, which means he is our problem. Yet the disabled 68-year-old can be put on a plane to become some other country's problem.

Those countries are filthy on us, particularly New Zealand, which has seen many of our crooks dumped back there because of an accident of birth. It is the diplomatic version of sneaking your rubbish into someone else's recyclable bin.

WHO'S WHO IN THE CRIMINAL ZOO

The private schoolboy was beginning to doubt the wisdom of choosing former standover man Mark 'Chopper' Read as his documentary subject for his senior-year assessment.

As he sat on the couch with Read about to film an interview, Chopper's dog, the fearsome-looking Kayser (named after his defence lawyer Boris Kayser) began to take an uncomfortable interest, placing his impressive snout close to the young man's lap.

'What's the matter?' Read asked. 'Haven't you ever sat with someone with no ears with a dog about two inches from your knackers?'

It was a rhetorical question, for while both Read and Kayser looked ferocious, their days of crime were behind them.

To show he didn't bear a grudge, Read once named a greyhound The Buggster after Tasmania's then director of public prosecutions Damian Bugg KC, who sent the self-confessed killer to jail on an indefinite sentence.

The greyhound was slow and unsuccessful, while the barrister was fast-tracked to become Commonwealth DPP and Chancellor of the University of Tasmania.

When finally released, Read moved to a Tasmanian farm with two terriers, Reggie and Ronnie, named after the notorious Kray brothers of London. Sadly, they had the same bloodthirsty streak as their namesakes and, after attacking a prize chicken, had to be put down.

Not that Read was a committed animal lover, once admitting to killing an enemy's small dog, barbecuing it with garlic salt and making the rival eat it with American mustard.

Crooks are often referred to as animals (dogs, jackals, hyenas, rats, maggots and stool pigeons), which is wildly unfair to the planet's non-human community. In fact, many colourful characters have an affinity for pets – often based on companionship but sometimes for practical purposes.

Prolific drug dealer and killer Dennis Allen kept attacking geese at his Richmond house, believing they were more territorial than guard dogs. As he dealt in cash, had more jewellery than Elizabeth Taylor and was a prodigious police informer, it was a wise investment – although he was to die in 1987 from a drug-related heart condition.

One of his relatives also had an interest in birds, but of the canary variety, until her favourite went missing during a police raid. She concluded a detective (who himself had a wildlife nickname) freed the feathered pet in an act of petulance. That is, until she opened the freezer to find the bird wedged between the fish fingers and the raspberry ripple.

Master armed robber and alleged gangland killer Russell Cox didn't stay on the run for 11 years after escaping from Long Bay's maximum-security Katingal by taking risks. He was a master of disguise with a number of aliases, including Mr Walker from *The Phantom* comics. Even his dog Devil (also from *The Phantom*) had a fake name, also answering to Butch. He and Devil ran early in the morning as Cox liked to be out of the house at sunrise, knowing police preferred to conduct raids at dawn.

One drug dealer laced his two Alsatian guard dogs' water bowls with amphetamines, leaving them with the physiques of greyhounds and the personalities of white pointer sharks.

Hitman and former poodle breeder James Frederick Bazley had more time for dogs than his victims. Bazley was paid $20,000 to murder drug couriers Isabel and Douglas Wilson, whose bodies were found buried in Rye in May 1979. The Wilsons were killed on the orders of the Mr Asia drug syndicate boss, Terrence John Clark, after corrupt police confirmed the couple were talking to Queensland detectives.

The hitman was instructed to kill the Wilsons' dog, Taj, and drop their car at Melbourne Airport to leave the impression they had fled overseas. He parked the car as per the plan, but refused to kill the dog, dropping it in Brunswick on the way to the airport.

Another gangster with a weakness for little dogs was Mario Condello, a qualified lawyer and a tooled-up mobster who once had ambitions to be a High Court judge. The big man liked to take his dog for an early-morning walk, using the same route past the Brighton cemetery. For a fellow connected with the so-called Carlton Crew and up to his armpits in the Melbourne gangland war, such predictability could be fatal.

In 2004, the Purana Taskforce found drug boss Carl Williams had put out a contract to kill Condello while on his morning walk. On 9 June, police made sure Condello was nowhere near Brighton as the two-man hit team assembled. In a sliding-doors moment, another large local with a small dog walked past the cemetery, leading the would-be killers to think they had found their man.

Confirmation came with a police bug picking up one saying: 'I'm going to have to walk up beside him and shoot him.' As there were 170 police hiding in the area, the gunmen were quickly arrested before they could move. Worried detectives were instantly relieved, as was one of the gunmen's bladders when he was handcuffed.

We will never know if the wrong man discovered how close he was to becoming a mistaken identity victim.

Condello was safe – for a time – but continued to be a creature of habit. Given bail on the condition he spent nights at home, he fell into a routine of returning around the same time. He was shot dead two years later when walking up his driveway.

The suspect in this case, the late Rodney Collins, disliked most people and preferred the company of a parrot he taught to cry 'not guilty' and 'I hate coppers'. Who says hitmen don't have a sense of humour?

It is not only the baddies who have affection for animals. Police dogs have a wonderful history of catching crooks and protecting their handlers, a lesson crooked Drug Squad Senior Detective David Miechel forgot when caught outside an East Oakleigh drug house he was in the process of robbing.

Found up a tree by a canine unit, he first tried to talk his way out, saying he was looking for the offender. When that failed, he punched the handler, which enraged police dog Silky, who proceeded to latch onto the suspect's thigh.

Miechel tried to punch the dog, which enraged the handler, who hit him with a police torch, fracturing his cheekbone and jaw. Miechel got a nasty scar and 12 years, while Silky got a plate of Meaty Bites.

For a time, the elite Purana Taskforce had its own office pet – a mature-age yabby found in a Castlemaine dam and kept in a 25-litre glass receptacle previously used to produce amphetamines. The container was seized from a lab owned by drug boss Tony Mokbel, and so the freshwater crustacean was named Tony.

Both yabby Tony and runaway Tony seemed to like boats. The drug boss escaped to Greece in a $340,000 ketch, while the yabby had a $2 toy one at the bottom of the tank.

Eventually, administrative staff bought a goldfish dubbed Zarah (after criminal defence lawyer Zarah Garde-Wilson who, incidentally, owned a snake called Chivas), but the yabby ate the fish, proving that Tony could not be trusted nor was fond of captivity.

This brings us to one of the great criminological and zoological mysteries of our time – the unexplained death of Australia's oldest armed robber: Aubrey Maurice Broughill.

When his body was found floating in a flooded Wodonga quarry in February 1999, the death was treated as suspicious. There was no reason for him to be there. He had no car, there was no record he arrived on public transport, and accommodation checks showed no bookings under his name. He was 73 years old, fit and a strong swimmer.

When the body was recovered, it showed he was wearing a striped shirt, his blue denim jeans were caught around his left foot, his belt was still fastened, he was not wearing underpants and was barefoot.

There was another reason to suggest this was no accident: Aubrey Maurice Broughill had no testicles.

One theory put to the coroner was the local population of eastern snake-necked turtles – which usually snack on insects, small fish, tadpoles and the occasional frog – attacked him after death. While the 25-centimetre turtle is known to carry on over carrion, no one can explain why it only went after one part of the anatomy. And when these turtles find a carcass, they use their front claws to shred the flesh into bite-size chunks.

Which seems at odds with the description of Broughill's injuries as 'a well-defined, incised-like edge measuring seven centimetres and extending to a more irregular ragged tear'.

This would suggest that unless the turtles were armed with scalpels and doing third-year medicine, they are not guilty.

Broughill had teamed up with some South Australian petty thieves and just weeks earlier was charged with 19 offences, including burglary and car theft. An Adelaide-based taskforce had connected this gang to the mysterious disappearance of four men over a seven-year period. Their bodies have not been found.

They were all drifters, just like Aubrey.

CAPABLE OF ALL THE IDIOCY IN THE WORLD

Wanted: hitman

Must be: capable of stealing a car and sprinting while carrying a firearm.
Must not be: allergic to wool balaclavas or gunshot residue.
Remuneration: negotiable.
Superannuation: not required.
Qualifications: IQ between a sea cucumber and a village idiot.
Career path: long stints in jail and probable death.

Wanted: gangster

Must be: attracted to headlines, steroids, gold jewellery and Instagram.
Must not be: allergic to tattoo ink, hot lead, dental surgery or Flower Drum fried rice.
Remuneration: millions in drug money to be laundered through property and spent at five-star restaurants.
Superannuation: not required.

Qualifications: multiple convictions for violence and a subscription to the true crime channel.
Career path: long stints in jail and probable death.

The latest in the long line of crooks given the gunshot redundancy package was Gavin 'Capable' Preston, shot several times in September 2023 while having a single-shot coffee over breakfast at an East Keilor cafe.

He had a date with death since his release from prison seven months earlier, after falling out with the sort of people who will do more than block you on Facebook. While his death is listed as a homicide, in many ways it was natural causes, as in it was natural that he would cause this.

Arrested more than 30 years ago, just out of his teens, he had no fear, detectives noted. The skinny 20-year-old assaulted a supermarket manager at the Northcote Plaza, with a witness saying the offender kicked the victim's head 'like it was a soccer ball'.

The arresting officer noted on Preston's file that he was likely to be mentored in prison and one day would kill. The prediction was sadly accurate.

Why he went off the rails is not known. At Sunshine Primary School, he was a well-liked kid who in grade six wanted to be a policeman.

The closest equivalent underworld murder was that of Nik Radev in April 2003. Radev, like Preston, was out of control and a threat to established crime syndicates – and, like Preston, he didn't see it coming.

Radev had just invested $50,000 cash in cosmetic dental surgery when he was ambushed in Coburg, meaning he was wearing new caps when he was capped.

Ever since reporters wrote crime stories on typewriters while smoking at the desk and sipping beer out of long-neck bottles (it was called work–life balance), crooks with overblown egos have been killing each other.

It is the height of stupidity and part of a cycle that usually takes about 20 years to complete. The reason it is dumb to shoot dum-dum bullets is it is bad for business, with shootings generating headlines and a massive police response. These crooks fail to realise the market for illicit drugs is so massive, everyone can get rich without getting shot, or that each increase in law enforcement powers – from phone taps to asset seizure, coercive hearings and anti-bikie and criminal association laws – was introduced in response to gangland wars.

Their role model should be Howard Marks, an Oxford University graduate who became the world's biggest cannabis supplier. He had his own freighter and connections in the UK, Mexico, Australia, the US, Hong Kong and Pakistan.

While other gangsters had nicknames such as Rent-a-kill, Muscles, Greedy and Machine Gun, Marks was known as Mr Nice, probably because he dealt with drug rip-offs the way Myer deals with shoplifting – writing it into the bottom line. He didn't shoot anyone; he just cut business ties.

(Marks once told me he spent a pleasant evening in Manila bar-hopping with Australian gangsters, a group of performing dwarfs and several local nuns, but that is another story.)

In Melbourne in 1963–64, we had the Market Murders, a struggle for control of Italian-based organised crime syndicate the Honoured Society. The war only stopped when Liborio Benvenuto was elected godfather. The peace lasted 20 years.

In May 1983, Benvenuto's four-wheel-drive was blown up at the wholesale market. In response, he said: 'I have no enemies, only friends at the market. I don't know why anybody would do this. I have never done anybody harm.'

There was another response. A year later, the tortured bodies of Rocco Medici and brother-in-law Giuseppe Furina were found weighed down in the Murrumbidgee River.

Benvenuto lived to a ripe old age before passing away of natural causes.

In October 1978, three men burst into notorious standover man Les Kane's Wantirna home and shot him dead. His body was never found. Ray 'Chuck' Bennett, Vinnie Mikkelsen and Laurie Prendergast were charged and acquitted. Thirteen months later, Chuck was in the Melbourne Magistrates Court facing armed robbery charges when he was shot dead by Les' brother, Brian, in an inside job.

Brian Kane was shot dead in the Quarry Hotel in Brunswick in 1982, with the suspects being prodigious hitman Rod Collins and escapee and armed robber Russell Cox. Neither was convicted.

The weedy and seedy Collins would die in prison serving a long murder sentence, while Cox became the rarest of beasts: a retired gunman.

Prendergast went missing in August 1985; his body never found. Four months earlier, Prendergast's good friend, hitman Christopher Dale 'Rent-a-kill' Flannery, went missing in Sydney. His body was never found.

Are we seeing a pattern here?

The Kanes married into the Moran crime family, with a young Jason Moran placing a death notice for 'Uncle Brian' (Kane) from 'Your little mate, Jason'.

Not that they learnt anything.

Mark and Jason Moran started a war with drug rival Carl Williams, shooting him in the belly. The Underbelly War resulted in more than a dozen murders. When the gun smoke cleared, Mark, Jason and Lewis Moran were dead, along with Carl Williams and his hitman of choice, Andrew Veniamin.

The underworld void was filled by Middle Eastern crime cartels and bikie gangs. And guess what? Twenty or so years later, they are doing the same dumb thing – shooting each other for fun and profit.

The staggering thing is how many ambitious young crooks are prepared to kill to order. And most of them aren't very good.

There have been dozens of fires at tobacco shops over a protection racket and a power struggle to control the illicit section of the industry.

The crooks who set the fires have usually set fire to themselves. Which means instead of carrying 9 mm automatics, they would be better off carrying tubes of Savlon.

Mongol bikies-turned-hitmen Aaron Ong and Josh Rider staked out a Croydon home for hours in November 2019 before following hardworking fruiterer Paul Virgona, leaving for work at 2 am. Either they, or the people who hired them, were too stupid to find the right house; they were following the wrong man.

They drew up alongside him on EastLink in a stolen Mercedes, shooting him seven times. They set fire to the Mercedes, escaping in a Volkswagen Amarok that would have been torched if police hadn't seen them.

Arrested because of clues in the car, they will serve more than 20 years in jail after refusing to say who hired them or identify the real target. The crooks who ordered the hit are laughing while Ong and Rider rot in prison.

Hitmen are sole traders without union representation and are often ripped off, as it is not the sort of job where you can lodge a complaint for wage theft. In fairness, they are more concerned with GSR (gunshot residue) than GST.

When Melbourne drug dealer Dennis Allen employed Roy 'Red Rat' Pollitt to carry out a hit, he paid him handsomely – with counterfeit notes. Carl Williams shortchanged his hitman the Runner not once but twice – not a great business strategy, as the paid killer ended up as a witness against Williams.

The hitman career path is roughly the same as that of a kamikaze pilot (minus the last glass of sake).

We have had a spate of abductions, bashings and stabbings of schoolkids where the alleged offenders are as young as 14. Somewhere in Melbourne, a cop is typing an intelligence report on one of these teenage offenders, saying he has no fear, will probably be mentored in prison and one day will kill. Just like Gavin 'Capable' Preston.

A MILLION REASONS TO REMEMBER A KILLER

The man on the end of the phone line was a serious gangster who had ordered a hit on an undercover cop, and he wanted a meeting. Who was I to argue?

The caller was Alan Williams, central to an underworld cartel connected to at least four murders, one failed hit, a suspicious death, corrupt cops in two states and a concerted effort to sabotage the criminal justice system. Williams wanted to tell his story, but he was also making a public plea to the underworld: don't kill me.

Williams became a target after he told police the notoriously bent NSW detective Roger Rogerson was the organiser of an attempted hit on his undercover colleague Mick Drury.

Williams' message to his former underworld associates was that while he had talked about Rogerson, he would remain silent regarding their affairs and was happy to disappear. Rather than be a dead man walking, he wanted to be a live one running.

He had good reason to be nervous. There had been one attempt on his life and his contact in the drug syndicate Drury infiltrated had been executed. That contact was Robert 'Jack' Richardson who,

39 years after his murder, is the subject of a promising cold case investigation that includes a million-dollar reward, fresh information and a tantalising DNA trace discovered on a bullet casing.

According to Senior Detective Leigh Prados, this case is far from cold. 'In a fresh homicide time can be the enemy, but in this sort of case time can be on our side.'

That's because the wall of silence cracks over time. Those who built that wall, and who killed to make sure there would be no leaks, are dead, infirm or in jail. 'The threat to people who know the truth has diminished,' says Prados.

At the time of the crime, the threat was very real – anyone seen as a weak link tended to end up dead. Now, the million-dollar reward could be handy superannuation for someone who has kept their mouth shut for four decades.

The murder of Richardson was one of the black cards dealt when NSW Drug Squad detectives wanted to find the source of heroin flooding into Kings Cross. To do this, undercover policeman Mick Drury infiltrated a syndicate at the lower end, hoping to climb to the top.

The first person to vouch for him was Sydney crook Frank Avery. As his reward for introducing the fox into the henhouse, Avery was found dead in a Sydney hotel with a heroin needle in his arm in July 1983. He was not known as a drug user.

The personable Drury soon won the confidence of middleweight Sydney drug supplier Richardson, a knockabout former Australian rules player with a minor criminal record. Tapping into a heroin supply had boosted him into the big time.

Richardson introduced Drury to the next link, Brian Hansen, a man of extreme interest to the NSW Drug Squad. The trouble was that Hansen's supplier, Alan Williams, ran out of Melbourne, which meant the job had to shift down south.

This was not a drama to the crooks but a big one for the cops. Victoria Police thought too many NSW detectives were corrupt, while the Sydney team thought Melbourne was out of its depth. Both had a point.

In late February 1982, when the NSW team arrived in Melbourne, there was a fair helping of tension and a large slice of distrust. Sydney kept crucial information to itself and Melbourne was slow to produce $110,000 in show money for the sting.

The job was saved because Drury and straight-talking Melbourne detective Johnny Weel trusted each other.

So it was arranged that on 4 March 1982, there would be a meeting at the Old Melbourne Hotel. Drury would show Hansen the money, he would contact Williams and they would be scooped up when Drury gave the sign.

Trouble was one of the surveillance team missed part of the briefing because he was buying sheets (on the instructions of his wife) at a sale at Myer. The bedroom bargain would prove very expensive.

Williams was reluctant to deal with Drury. He would later tell me: 'The deal was supposed to kick off at lunchtime, but for about nine hours, I smelt a rat. I didn't want to do the business. Brian, on the other hand, was insistent. He said he had counted the money and that everything was sweet.'

When Drury gave the signal, the arrest team streamed in far too fast, skidding past Williams' car by about 10 metres, giving the heroin dealer just enough room to plant the foot and escape.

That 10-metre gap cost lives. If Williams had been arrested in the car with the heroin, it was an open-and-shut case, but because he escaped, he became obsessed with sabotaging the prosecution.

Within a week, he had offered $30,000 to any cop who could swap the recovered heroin with harmless white powder at the forensic lab.

Williams went to a friend, hitman Christopher Dale Flannery, to use his Sydney police connections to bribe Drury. Williams said: 'I offered $30,000 at one stage, $50,000 at another stage, $100,000 and an open ticket in the end.' Flannery's connection was the notoriously corrupt cop, Roger Rogerson, who was so brazen that he summoned Drury to his police office to make the offer.

Richardson, Hansen and Williams were charged over the Old Melbourne sting. Without Drury, the case against Williams was weak. Even with Drury, the case was poor and Williams was ultimately acquitted.

According to Prados, the police who investigated Richardson thought he was 'a good bloke'.

Maybe too good. The man they called 'Melbourne Jack' indicated he was up for a chat with the right detective. The trouble was the wrong detectives also knew, which meant Williams' team was tipped off.

On 4 March 1984, two years to the day after the arrest and the day before the trial, Richardson went missing. He was last seen sitting outside a St Kilda ice cream shop with two men, 200 metres from Mickey's Disco, where Flannery had worked and was a silent investor.

Local detective Larry Proud recognised Richardson at the ice cream parlour and would have almost certainly identified Flannery if he was with Jack.

As Prados says: 'Richardson was seen with his hands in his pockets, looking relaxed.'

No one ever relaxed around Flannery.

Richardson was somehow lured to Strath Creek, 110 kilometres away, to be shot in the back of the head.

For Williams, there was still the outstanding problem of Drury. At a Sydney restaurant Williams, Rogerson and Flannery decided if money couldn't silence Drury, a bullet could. On 6 June 1984, Flannery, possibly with killer Laurence Joseph Prendergast, shot Drury in his Chatswood home.

Against all odds, Drury survived. By this stage, the threat was so high that Weel's children were being driven to school in a police car.

Flannery took a $50,000 deposit for the Drury hit but, according to Williams: 'Chris said not to worry about sending the other $50,000. The job hadn't been completed.'

Not everyone was so generous, as the next target was Williams.

On 18 September 1984, Dennis 'Mr Death' Allen and Roy 'Red Rat' Pollitt were waiting outside Williams' Lower Plenty house when a car pulled into the driveway.

They dragged the driver from the car, but it wasn't Williams. It was his brother-in-law, Lindsay Simpson. They shot him regardless.

Pollitt, who was convicted of the murder but claimed he was innocent, told me the killer wasn't wearing a balaclava. He knew he would be recognised and feared Williams would come after him. 'He was a poor bloke who was in the wrong place at the wrong time. I have been told that he [the gunman] ran down the drive and wasn't wearing a balaclava because it was at night. He looked in the car and thought: "Fuck, that ain't Williams." But he knew the guy would be able to identify him and tell Williams who would come after him.

'So it wasn't a case of mistaken identity; it was a matter of survival.'

Pollitt didn't bother to explain that while he was not the killer, he knew the details of the murder. Certainly, according to underworld sources, he was the killer and he was dudded by Allen, who paid him with counterfeit notes.

Next was Flannery, who even in Sydney was considered the loosest of loose cannons. He had killed up to 12 people and the unsolved Drury shooting was bringing heat.

On 8 May 1985, Flannery (at Rogerson's suggestion) agreed to informally meet NSW murder taskforce detectives in a bar.

The murder detectives were puzzled. Flannery was reluctant to talk, so why have the meeting? Chris was a psychopath but no idiot. He knew he was in danger and was moving regularly, staying in rented apartments and hotels under false names. The word is that Rogerson set up the meeting so he could follow Flannery to his new location.

The following day, Flannery went missing, never to be seen again.

Flannery had told his wife, Kath, he had a meeting set up with local Mob boss George Freeman, but when he tried to start his car the battery appeared to be flat. He returned to ask Kath to call a battery service, saying they would go to a movie when he returned.

The battery service started the car first time, suggesting the leads had been disconnected, then reconnected to make sure Flannery didn't take his car to Freeman's.

He was almost certainly picked up by Rogerson.

Kath went straight to the police saying she believed Flannery was already dead and was killed by Freeman. They went to George's home, knocked on the door and asked to come inside for a look. Freeman said without a warrant, they could go jump. They came back with the paperwork more than a week later – time enough for anyone to clean up a murder scene.

Four months later, Prendergast also joined the missing list.

Neither body has ever been found.

Prados says the Richardson case was reviewed in 2019 and deemed solvable. Fresh information suggests there are people who know the truth. He believes many of those love to flick through books like these.

'These people need to contemplate their position. They should find us before we find them,' Prados says.

Postscript

Here is a story I wrote about Pollitt more than ten years earlier.

*

In the underworld pecking order, paid hitmen are considered the lowest of the low. They lack the initiative to set up their own jobs and the morality to walk away from the business of killing strangers for money.

One of those was Roy 'Red Rat' Pollitt, a career criminal who was convicted of killing an innocent man in front of his wife and child.

Pollitt was on the run after escaping not once but twice from NSW jails when he was commissioned by Dennis 'Mr Death' Allen to kill drug dealer Alan Williams in the driveway of the victim's Lower Plenty home.

The plan was sabotaged when two Victorian detectives warned Williams of the ambush and advised him not to go home.

Williams' brother-in-law, Lindsay Simpson, was neither so lucky nor well-connected. When he drove into the driveway on the night of 18 September 1984, Pollitt was waiting.

Red Rat forced him from the car and made him kneel before shooting him in the head, despite the victim pleading: 'My name is Simpson.'

As a criminal, Pollitt was an abject failure. He was a teenage armed robber who became an institutionalised inmate and one of the most violent men in captivity. He did time with some of Australia's most notorious men, many who died courtesy of police bullets, underworld rivals or drug overdoses.

Pollitt did hard time in jails so brutal that two – Jika Jika in Melbourne and Katingal in Sydney – were later bulldozed on human rights grounds.

Yet Pollitt is an underworld survivor whose salvation has come in the strangest possible way.

Jailed at 18 in 1972, he would spend less than eight months on the outside (six of those as an escapee) over the next 36 years.

In 1977, he was one of seven inmates, including his great mate, the infamous Ray Denning, who carried out a mass escape from Maitland Prison, only to be arrested within hours.

Thrown into Katingal because of the escape ('It was a monster of a place that helped create monsters'), Pollitt started to paint as an alternative to stabbing fellow inmates.

He gave his first painting to Denning, who did what any good crook would do: immediately signed it with his own name before passing it off as his original to his aunt. (Denning died due to a suspected heroin hotshot after he became a police informer.)

Soon Pollitt realised he had a natural talent for painting, but this is not a feel-good story of immediate redemption, for the discovery didn't alter his self-destructive life. He remained a vicious crook, just one who could punch out an interesting picture inside maximum security. 'I was a bad case, a rotten egg – a bad spoke in the wheel. But who says you have to be a good person to paint?'

The first painting he sold, in 1978, fetched $70. According to art gallery director David Wemyss-Smith, who has long championed Pollitt's paintings, the first works were dark and disturbing, which is hardly surprising considering the painter.

This obvious talent was dominated by his world of revenge, violence and escape. For years, he says: 'It coexisted with my unfortunate and not-too-brilliant criminal career.'

While he was painting in Katingal, he pursued another hobby – planning an escape with six inmates, using a hacksaw blade smuggled into the prison by a female lawyer. Russell Cox was the last to join the unit in 1977, but when the rest of the inmates were in Maitland Prison for a court hearing, 'Cox the Fox' took his chance to slip away. 'Coxy didn't want to go last,' Pollitt claims.

Seven years later, it was the Red Rat's turn to run.

In 1984, he was three weeks from release in the NSW Mannus prison farm when a dispute over cannabis turned violent. As he lay in bed, a fellow inmate hit him on the head with an axe. 'I thought: "Bingo, someone got me on the scone." Then someone mysteriously stabbed him and I thought I better take off.'

And like Steve McQueen in *The Great Escape*, he took off on a stolen motorcycle minus a helmet. And, like McQueen's escapade, it ended badly when police ran him off the road and into a mud-filled culvert.

He was taken to Wagga police lock-up where an old mate tipped him off that staff failed to count the inmates to be transported away. He hid under the blankets until the van had gone, then wandered around wearing an old army greatcoat until he was noticed by the station sergeant.

Pollitt pretended to be a local vagrant locked up for being drunk and disorderly and was promptly released with the advice to head to the Salvos for breakfast.

Instead, he made the mistake of heading to Melbourne and into the care of 'that rotten Dennis Allen'. Friends took him to Allen's Richmond house. 'Dennis was sitting there in a bulletproof vest and two guns. They don't do that in Sydney.'

Allen offered him the contract to kill Alan Williams.

Pollitt may have left the criminal world, but the habit of never confessing dies hard. When we asked why he killed the wrong man, his answers were textbook gangster: 'I maintain to this day that I am totally innocent.'

He did, however, give details he felt would put the killer in a better light. I felt, rightly or wrongly, that Pollitt wanted to say the hitman was a little too professional to mistakenly murder someone. Bad on the CV, you see.

In the underworld, survival can be measured in centimetres. When he was finally arrested and returned to Sydney's Long Bay Jail, he was promptly stabbed by a fellow inmate. Police told his family he was going to die but, to the disappointment of many, he survived to run a prison marathon three months later.

Inside prison, he rediscovered painting. 'Something drove me to it,' he said. 'I couldn't express myself fluently, so I used paints. I didn't think I could make any money – it was just a calming influence.'

In 1990, he returned to Melbourne to serve a further 18 years for the Simpson murder and was denied paints for eight years until he saw old Jika guard, Shane Kelly, who had risen through the ranks to governor at Port Phillip Prison.

'He was a good man. I asked him if I could use my own money to buy some paints and turps and he said yes.'

He withdrew $400 – his prison savings – to buy art gear. That first painting sold for $1700 and the next for $2900.

As his bank balance swelled, one guard made a written complaint, but Kelly made it clear the maximum-security prisoner could continue. Soon, Pollitt says, he was put on the Port Phillip payroll to complete artwork for the jail.

'I started to realise this could be my ticket out of crime. I was never successful as a crook and I found I could make more money with paints than a gun.'

He was released on 18 January 2008, with $100,000 in the bank. A little over a year later, a client paid him a $20,000 advance for a commissioned work. Compare that to his biggest armed robbery haul of $23,000. One took weeks in an art studio to complete – the other years in a maximum-security prison. You do the maths.

'I had seen so many of my good friends die. It gets to you in the end. It was all so stupid. I have no desire to go back; they can keep it.'

Before the wooden-heads cry that Pollitt is profiting from his infamy, Wemyss-Smith, who is exhibiting his work at the Manyung Gallery in Glenferrie Road, Malvern, says most buyers are unaware of the artist's crime background. 'He is a perfectionist who keeps a low profile. We have collectors who are rallying around Pollitt's work.'

On matters of art, we freely acknowledge our interest waned when we downed the Derwent pencils back in primary school, so we turn for advice to our favourite art historian, Dr Penny Peckham, who says: 'Pollitt's Magritte-influenced work is very visually clever . . . while he may never be a big name, what he does is skilful.'

It should be noted that Dr Peckham has always been attracted to the slightly bizarre, which is why she dated your correspondent some years ago.

The only thing framed about Pollitt was his artwork. Roy's paintings didn't impress the authorities and he was ultimately deported to the UK, land of his birth.

BEAUTY AND THE BEAST OF CREMORNE

The tiny pocket of Cremorne, wedged between Richmond and the Yarra River, long ago graduated from industrial wasteland to valued inner-city living. At the hub is the renovated Cherry Tree Hotel, where locals wander in from the cold for a wood-fired pizza and a craft beer or on a mild day sit outside with dogs and prams, chatting with neighbours.

In the 1980s, while other working-class suburbs were becoming trendy, the psychotic serial-killing drug dealer Dennis Bruce Allen turned a small slice of Cremorne into a gangland ghetto. How many he killed is anyone's guess (detectives say 11, while Allen bragged his total was 13), yet police kept him on the street by allowing him to successfully apply for bail even though they knew he was a one-man crime wave.

Allen made between $70,000 and $100,000 a week from drugs and was on bail for 60 different offences with sureties of $225,000, then the price of five inner-suburban homes.

He invested heavily in properties in the Cremorne pocket of Chestnut, Stephenson and Cubitt Streets, using them for an illegal brothel, to house relatives, traffic drugs, kill enemies and dismember victims.

Now we can reveal he used them for another purpose. For more than two years, he kept a young model prisoner, turning her into a drug-addled sex slave and an accessory to murder.

Jenny was the good girl with a sense of fun and a self-confessed rebellious side. She was expelled from Ave Maria College at 15 when a teacher on a bus 'saw me chasing a boy and smoking in my school uniform'.

That summer, holidaying at her grandparents' home, she was urged by friends to enter the Miss Rye competition and did it as a dare. She won, aged 16.

Jenny became a Miss Victoria and Miss Australia contestant at the age of 17, was picked up by a South Melbourne agency and contracted as a Myer lingerie model. 'Everything took off from there. It was my dream job – I always wanted to be a model – and then it turned into a nightmare,' she says.

The turning point was moving into a South Yarra unit with a friend. 'She was the sister of my first boyfriend. He told me to keep away from her because she was bad news. I didn't understand; I had lived a very sheltered life.'

The friend was dealing heroin out of the unit and persuaded Jenny to smoke drugs to beat her nerves before a TV shoot. 'It totally changed me. I was not in control and a total mess.'

Eventually the flatmate persuaded her to go to the Cherry Tree to meet her supplier, the very pub that was Dennis Allen's local. 'He didn't like Dennis and when Dennis turned up with Jason Ryan [Allen's young nephew], he left.'

Even though Allen was the drug dealer from central casting, wearing overalls, at least a dozen gold chains (usually provided by junkies in exchange for drugs) and covered in tattoos, the girls stayed and partied.

The next day, at Allen's Chestnut Street home, Jenny's mate left. 'Then he stood in front of me and said: "You aren't going anywhere." He raped me that night.'

She says she became his sex slave, imprisoned by fear and a never-ending supply of drugs, once being kept awake for 21 days on a diet of amphetamines and takeaway food. When she tried to escape, he beat her, shackled her with chains, kicked, stabbed and tried to drown her. 'He fired a shot right between my legs inside the house. He used to hit me up with speed all the time. He said if he killed me, no one would ever find the body.'

Allen's then lawyer, Andrew Fraser, recalls: 'She was so young and innocent. I think she suffered from Stockholm syndrome and couldn't leave. Dennis got her on the gear [drugs] and kept her on the gear. He wrecked her life, no doubt. I watched her disintegrate before my eyes.'

As Allen took massive doses of speed, he would stay awake for weeks at a time – sometimes deciding to renovate one of his properties at 2 am, using a sledgehammer to smash out a wall. A builder around the corner would be called in to finish the job.

In the time when the world had largely shrunk to a few streets in Cremorne, Jenny witnessed three murders and had to clean up after one – Wayne Stanhope, who was shot dead inside Allen's home in August 1984.

> He was just out of jail and Dennis invited him for lunch. Jason [Ryan] and I got some KFC. He [Wayne] wanted some speed and Dennis tried to kill him with an OD [overdose].
>
> They went to the Cherry Tree for a few drinks. When they came back he put Wayne's favourite music on. I was sitting on the floor. Wayne went to the record player and Dennis pulled out a gun and went bang, bang. Wayne said: 'Dennis what are you doing?'
>
> He emptied it into his head. He got another gun from Jason – bang bang, and emptied that into his head although he was already dead.
>
> He then told me to pass him a knife, then he slit his throat.

> He rang his brothers to help and they dragged him onto the tiles. Dennis said: 'Don't you bleed on my carpet.'
>
> They dragged him outside, there were trains going past. We had to clean up, there was blood everywhere. He told us to burn our clothes in the incinerator. He told me: 'You open your mouth and you're off.'
>
> I thought I was going to have a heart attack. Jason was vomiting. He was a nice kid; he didn't have a chance there.

In 8 November 1985, Jenny was in a bedroom playing with Allen's two young children when she heard shots. Allen had ambushed Hells Angels associate Anton Kenny in the next room. 'Dennis told me to take the kids to his brother's place [Victor George Peirce].

'Victor pretended he was not that bad but he was a nasty, vicious person, he would rip your eye out if you crossed him.'

She was ordered to buy lime and concrete. Peirce and Allen used a chainsaw to cut the legs off the victim and the remains were dumped in a 44-gallon barrel which was filled with concrete and rolled into the Yarra.

Occasionally they would leave Cremorne and stay at a motel, but that was only when tipped off by a corrupt detective that they were about to be raided. When Allen wanted Jenny to get a gun licence, the same detective drove her to the city office to apply.

'I used to hide Dennis' gun in my pants,' she recalls. 'I was terrified it would go off.'

The centre of Allen's social life was the Cherry Tree, despite repeated attempts to ban him. One night at an inner-suburban pub when a cover band was playing, the lead singer ignored the drug dealer's request to play a Bob Marley tune – until Allen followed him into the toilet and stuck a gun to his throat. The singer returned and performed reggae complete with a West Indian accent.

Once, when his captive told the crazed drug dealer she was leaving, he seemed to react calmly. 'He stood there and let me pack my stuff.

He let me get to the car and then went bang, bang, shooting out the windscreen and tyres. He bought me another car.

'There were these tiny, gorgeous puppies from his dogs, Julie and Fatso. He shot every one of them – he was getting worse and worse. He would take shots at the tower clock and the neighbour's cat.'

There is no doubt the information Allen provided to stay out of jail led to many arrests. There is also no doubt that it was a scandal that a man who provided heroin for 100 people a day through an inner-city massage parlour and banked $7000 a week was given the green light by police. His insurance policy was to pay off friendly cops with cash and information.

Eventually Jenny fell pregnant and had a son by Allen. He began to let her visit her mother with the boy; one night, she just didn't come back.

By this time, Allen was losing his power, his faculties and his health. A police taskforce was investigating him over 11 cases – a fatal shooting, three suspicious drug overdoses, two missing persons and five confirmed homicides.

In March 1987, Allen was charged with the Stanhope murder, but he was already terminally ill, his chronic heart disease brought on by prodigious illicit drug use.

On 13 April he died, aged 35. 'Thirteen was his favourite number, it was the devil's number and he was the devil. He said he killed 13 and I reckon he hung on to die on the 13th,' says Jenny.

She made statements to police and moved to Queensland, later living with a policeman she met at a nightclub. 'I spent five years looking over my shoulder. My life was in complete chaos. He took the life I wanted and turned me into something else.'

RIVALRY IN A DEADLY TALE OF TWO CITIES

Like New York and Chicago, Australia's largest cities – Sydney and Melbourne – have always engaged in a little healthy rivalry.

Sydney may be older, but Melbourne was the home of the first federal parliament. Sydney has the Gay & Lesbian Mardi Gras, but we have the Moomba Parade. They have the Sydney to Hobart Yacht Race, but we have the Yarra Birdman Rally. They have the Opera House, but we have Captain Cook's Cottage. They have rock oysters while we have (inedible) penguins. Sure, they have Hyde Park, but it is not a patch on Gumbuya Park.

Sydney has thrown money at horse racing to try to usurp the Melbourne Cup, had a nibble at the grand prix, then abducted and brainwashed Buddy Franklin, who was perfectly happy playing footy with his Hawthorn mates until they offered him more money than Donald Trump's legal bills.

In crime, there has been a clear divide between Sydney, traditionally built on the vice and drugs trade, propped up by corruption – hence the name Sin City – while in Melbourne, it was protection rackets, Painters and Dockers and military-style armed robbery gangs.

Standover man-turned-author Mark Brandon Read once declared the Sydney underworld was filled with hoons and pimps: 'Sydney may have all the razzle-dazzle, but most of the deadly serious work gets done in Melbourne.'

Today, Melbourne and Sydney have one thing in common: both are in the midst of deadly underworld wars. Since 2020, there have been 23 gangland murders in Sydney, largely related to fighting over a missing cocaine shipment, warring gangland families, bikie power struggles and possibly bad table manners. In Melbourne, gangsters are proving smoking is bad for your health with 30 arson attacks connected to the illicit tobacco market.

In Sydney, they have turned the natural order of things upside down. It used to be you decided to kill an enemy, put out a contract, followed the target then stole cars for the job. NSW detectives have found there is a new and improved version of a transport share service for crooks – an underworld Uber system.

In a sign Sydney police are getting in front of the game, they have seized more than 20 stolen cars parked in selected locations to be used as getaway vehicles for violent crimes, including gangland murders. In the cars, police found petrol-filled jerrycans to be used to torch the vehicles, gloves, balaclavas and false numberplates. Police say the cars are auctioned on an encrypted site.

For many years, Sydney crims made the trip to Melbourne about as well as a crate of oranges infected with fruit fly. One of the first to try to muscle in was Percy Charles Neville, who stood 194 centimetres tall and weighed 130 kilograms. When he tried to stand over businesses that were already being stood over, the big man was on borrowed time. In April 1951, local hood Normie Bradshaw shot him dead in Flinders Lane. Bradshaw was acquitted of the murder, but while criminal law didn't get him, the law of gravity did. Ten years later, he was one of four people killed when their light plane fell out of the sky into the bay off Mornington, with rumours the carburettor pump had been doctored.

Stan 'The Man' Smith was another Sydney crook who wanted to expand into Melbourne. When he arrived at Tullamarine airport, waiting police miraculously found a matchbox full of hashish in his top pocket, usually only used to display a decorative handkerchief. Smith is said to have cried out 'I'm being fitted up', no doubt a reference to his tailor-made suit.

When he returned home (after serving one year), he vowed to never return to Melbourne because 'the cops run red-hot down there'. While Melbourne had trams, many cops in both capitals were happy to railroad the right crook.

Police from the two states for years had a mutual distrust. NSW cops thought the Vics were incompetent cowboys, while the Vics thought Sydney detectives were slippery crooks. At one joint operation, the NSW boss broke the ice by saying: 'We'll promise not to steal anything if you promise not to shoot anyone.'

Many years ago, notoriously corrupt NSW detective Freddie Krahe turned up at Russell Street Police Headquarters uninvited to see a Melbourne detective: my father, Fred. He asked Silvester to take a walk and, outside the nearby museum, said he wanted a Sydney crook facing charges in Victoria to walk on bail and, to facilitate his freedom, he would appreciate it if his prior convictions were lost. 'There's a drink (bribe) in it for you,' Krahe added.

When Silvester said he didn't work like that, Krahe said: 'Please yourself' and walked off without even going inside the museum to see the stuffed Phar Lap.

Later in court, the defendant's lawyer addressed my father in the witness box: 'You will agree my client has no previous convictions.'

On the contrary, Silvester said, and read into evidence three pages of crimes. The crook was refused bail and Krahe presumably pocketed the bribe money, claiming the Vic cop flipped on the deal, meaning everyone was a winner except the crook.

One of the biggest crimes in Australian history was the 1977 mafia-ordered murder of Griffith anti-drugs campaigner Donald Mackay.

While the murder was in NSW, the plotting occurred in Victoria, which opened the possibility that a group of Melbourne detectives under Carl Mengler in Operation Trio could lay conspiracy to murder charges.

Enter the head of the NSW Mackay murder team, Detective Inspector Joe Parrington, an honest if profoundly arrogant investigator. When he arrived in Melbourne to be briefed by detectives he stopped them with: 'I don't talk to the monkeys, I talk to the organ grinder', before demanding to meet Mengler. Joe, it would seem, was the one carrying on like a peanut.

Despite the fact Parrington hid evidence he planned to use in a later murder prosecution, Trio charged and convicted the gunman, James Bazley, with the conspiracy.

To be fair, Melbourne crooks who tried to expand into Sydney also had a habit of failing. Judy Moran's first husband, Les Cole, was shot dead in Kyle Bay in 1982.

Prolific Victorian hitman Christopher Dale 'Rent-a-kill' Flannery moved to Sydney after he was acquitted of a Melbourne murder. He set up shop as a deadly gun for hire, initially charging $50,000 for a murder and $10,000 for a bashing. In 1984, he charged double his usual rate to kill NSW undercover cop Mick Drury to stop him testifying in a Melbourne case. He took a $50,000 deposit but didn't claim the rest when Drury survived the shooting.

When NSW police tried to stop him trying to shoot half the gangsters in town, he told one senior officer: 'You're not a protected species, you're not a koala.' Big mistake.

In May 1985, he left to see crime boss George Freeman and was never seen again. Unsurprisingly, Freeman could not help police with their inquiries.

One Melbourne crime figure who went to Sydney and returned without incident was expert safe breaker Graham Kinniburgh. When he was charged with serious offences, Melbourne detectives went to Sydney to give evidence. Kinniburgh was acquitted and, coincidentally, they all returned on the same flight – the cops in economy seats and Kinniburgh in business.

These days, the old ways have died. The drug trade and cybercrime no longer recognise international, let alone state boundaries. Bikie groups have national runs, cocaine imported into Sydney ends up in Melbourne nostrils, and Middle Eastern crime groups have loyalties to cartels, not postcodes.

Police work has changed from the days when Joe Parrington was happy to sabotage another police force's investigation. Senior cops know cooperation rather than competition is the only strategy that can work.

WHY EGO SHOULD BE A DIRTY WORD

Multi-millionaires and gangsters have a lot in common. They are risk-takers, can never have enough money, are often addicted to wedding cake and all are welcomed without reservations at five-star restaurants, even when not wearing socks.

Multis gain access to political heavyweights through large donations. In NSW in the 1960s, 70s and 80s so did gangsters. And both classes like to hide their donations and hate paying tax.

Gangsters, like multi-millionaires, grow their wealth through multiple investment strategies and outsourcing, plus they provide job opportunities.

For example, your modern crime boss imports cocaine, manufactures speed locally and supplies illicit cigarettes for local tobacco shops (the type that get burnt down).

They also provide employment opportunities for arsonists, hitmen, bent accountants, criminal barristers, dogged detectives and luxury car sales people.

But there should be a difference. Multis are usually happy to be photographed at charity fundraising events for A-listers, while gangsters should be happy to hide in the shadows.

Take Sydney crime boss Abe 'Mr Sin' Saffron, who spent a fortune donating to charities and another fortune suing anyone who called him Mr Sin. He wanted to be remembered as a benefactor rather than a crook.

The reality is that he was a killer, blackmailer, arsonist, hoon, pimp and dirty rat.

Now we have a class of gangster that is no longer happy with a fortune – they want fame as well. They are on social media, showing off their luxury beach resort accommodation, their bikini-clad companions, new tatts and high-powered motorbikes.

There are professions where being visible is valuable. The stop-go person at road and building construction sites needs a large stop-go sign and a reflective vest. For if you can't see a stop-go person, how can they make you stop, or indeed, go?

The lead in musicals such as *Oklahoma* can't hide behind the cardboard chuck-wagon. They have to be centre stage while belting out 'The Surrey with the Fringe on Top'.

And who wants to see the *Rolling Stones* if Mick Jagger is singing 'Midnight Rambler' from a rocking chair with a shawl over his knees?

There are occupations where being invisible is invaluable.

An undercover police officer doesn't wear a uniform, and surveillance cops don't have blue lights on top of their sneaky cars. And you don't paint a stealth bomber bright orange.

There are certain creatures that should avoid the spotlight. They include rabbits, escaping prisoners and the greater sooty owl.

A grey nurse shark doesn't dress as a grey nurse. It is grey on top so if you look down it blends in with the darker sea and its underside is light so if you look up it blends in with the sunlit water.

Snow leopards are white to blend in with – you guessed it – the snow. Tigers hide in the jungle while lions blend in with the plains. The king of beasts doesn't need to wear gold jewellery to show it is the king of beasts. Eating antelope tends to prove the point.

The first natural enemy of the gangster is ego. For them, it is a dirty word. If they just got on with their business, quietly making money by filling a demand for illicit products, such as cocaine and cheap tobacco, they would be off to a gourmet restaurant for a bellyful of salt and pepper shrimp.

Instead, they fall for the Hollywood mobster image and go all Al Capone on us (as a role model Al was a stinker, going to jail for tax evasion, then going mad and dying of syphilis).

Not happy with a giant slice of the pie they want the whole pie – and the bakery as well. Take Melbourne's tobacco war. Two syndicates were making millions a month, then decided to go to war to create a monopoly. Each week we'd hear of another smoke shop going up in smoke. Crime wars get people dead, get authorities cross, and get others arrested.

Take the big four banks. Sure they might nibble on each other's tail every now and again for show, but they are happy to co-exist with all four making a fortune. When was the last time you heard of a NAB hit-team doing a drive by on a Westpac branch?

Back to the laws of the jungle for a refresher. If two lions each have an antelope, they eat their antelope and then go to sleep under a tree. They don't fight each other, so one has two antelopes plus life-threatening bite marks.

The second enemy of the gangster is publicity. Gangsters who end up on the front page end up in the court list or obituary pages.

Liborio Benvenuto was for decades the Godfather of the Honoured Society. He avoided publicity, drove a nondescript four-wheel drive, wore a check overcoat and a brimmed felt hat and died peacefully of old age.

Alphonse Gangitano courted publicity, wore an expensive cashmere overcoat and designer sunglasses, had the nickname of 'the Black Prince of Lygon Street' and was shot dead in the laundry of his suburban house wearing only his underpants.

Drug dealer Carl Williams called himself 'the Premier' because he claimed to run the state. He ended up dead in Barwon Prison with his head caved in.

Joseph 'Squizzy' Taylor was the best-known criminal of his day. He and rival crook John 'Snowy' Cutmore shot each other dead in a Carlton gunfight in 1927. Taylor was 39.

Sometimes even multi-millionaires don't know when it is time to be a little discreet. Such as when the CEOs of Ford, GM and Chrysler flew their private jets to Washington to ask for a $25 billion government handout after the 2008 stock market crash.

When a French queen was advised that starving peasants didn't have funds for bread, her suggestion that they eat cake as an alternative was probably ill-considered.

There are those who fly under the radar when facing criminal charges and those who dance in front of it.

Majid Alibadi is hardly a household name, but he is certainly no shrinking violet. Alibadi, 25, is facing more than 20 charges, largely relating to alleged firebombings and car thefts. Like any other matter before the courts, Alibadi is entitled to the presumption of innocence, but the usual strategy between the day you are charged and the day you appear before a jury of 12 is to try to keep a low profile. Our Majid seems to have other ideas.

Granted bail in February, he was picked up outside the Melbourne Assessment Prison in a Rolls-Royce accompanied by associates in a Lamborghini. The prison is across the road from the Victoria Police Centre, and the best bet is that the show of wealth was aimed at the detectives looking out the window who'd arrested Alibadi.

Police applied for his bail to be revoked and in court alleged Alibadi was a key executive in Kaz Hamad's syndicate.

Hamad was not in a geographic position to refute the claims as he has been deported from Australia and is allegedly running a network from Iraq.

Police alleged the syndicate sent Alibadi more than $270,000 for his legal expenses. It is unlikely such a donation would be tax-deductible.

The court was told Alibadi purchased the personalised number plate 'MEOC', allegedly an abbreviation of the police claim that he was a 'Middle Eastern Organised Crime' figure.

Colourful characters have often had fun with their number plates. Drug boss Tony Mokbel had the plates RUDARE – a phonetic question to surveillance police he believed were following him – and gangster Dennis 'Greedy' Smith had initialised plates on his Rolls-Royce, the same Roller he used to deal drugs from the driver's window.

At Alibadi's bail hearing, Senior Detective Matthew Lindsay told the court the accused enjoyed first-class travel, luxury holidays and five-star dining. 'I believe Nobu is a favourite,' Lindsay told the court. 'When he was in custody and offered a meal, he asked if Nobu was available.'

(We recommend the Lobster Shiitake Salad ($88), the Peruvian Rib Eye ($165), a Tiramisu Martini ($28), a bottle of the Devil Sake ($280) and the hard-to-find Penfolds 76 Shiraz/Cab for $1900.)

The good news for Alibadi is that he was granted bail. The bad news is for medical reasons he will have to give Nobu a miss for the moment.

He has been released from prison to attend a live-in rehabilitation facility that charges $60,000 for 90 days – that's around $650 a day. The centre, the court was told, would treat Alibadi's addiction to methamphetamine, cannabis and alcohol.

He will wear an electronic bracelet while on bail. It will be a change from the usual multiple gold chains favoured by many.

New unexplained wealth laws introduced by Attorney-General Jaclyn Symes mean suspected crime figures will have to prove their flash cars and gated mansions have come from legitimate sources, which may be difficult when, for many of them, their last legitimate job was working part-time in a pizza joint when they were a teenager.

'If you've got it, flaunt it' may be the correct philosophy for a bare-bellied burlesque dancer, but may turn out to be a poor strategy for those who want to survive in society's underbelly.

WHY WE NEED INDEPENDENT COPS

In Winston Churchill's first speech as prime minister, he told UK Parliament: 'I have nothing to offer but blood, toil, tears and sweat.'

A modern spin doctor would have the PM lose the cigar, put on a hi-vis vest to make the following announcement at a Spitfire factory built in a marginal seat: 'We will establish a steering committee to develop policies to lift productivity in an environmentally responsible manner while achieving our short- and long-term goals in a time frame agreed upon by the appropriate stakeholders.'

Our leaders today are trained not to answer questions but to recite platitudes like performing parrots. I suspect if Churchill heard modern politicians refer to infrastructure and unavoidable shortfalls, he would throw up (or at least double swallow his Pol Roger).

Politics is our version of a black hole, sucking in and destroying initiative and independence. Heads of government departments used to be picked on ability, not on political persuasion. Their advice was to be fearlessly independent while the ultimate decisions were to be made by the elected ministers.

Judges were selected on experience and wisdom and given tenure until compulsory retirement so they couldn't be influenced by governments. And senior police were appointed to retirement age to enforce the law, not act as an extension of the government.

Compare that to the US where police chiefs, two-bit sheriffs and judges all the way to the Supreme Court are political appointees, which means a president can influence the justice system years after they have left office because their judges remain in place.

In Australia, we have moved slowly towards the flawed and at times corrupt American system. If a senior bureaucrat gives unpalatable advice, the government appoints external consultants until they are told what they want to hear. Party flacks and hacks have the ministers' ears while the career professionals sit in the waiting rooms watching daytime television.

Federal Attorney-General Mark Dreyfus is swimming against the tide by scrapping the Administrative Appeals Tribunal which he says too often has become a greenhouse for political turnips.

This notion of independence is not some outdated convention. It stands, as we shall see, as the watertight door to protect us from seeping corruption. Individual cops have a duty to enforce the law that can't be usurped by politicians or even senior officers. The control creep here is that senior police are now put on contract, which means they can be terminated without appeal at the end of a set time.

Many decisions are made by politicians with elections in mind. Police were given a new 24-hour station in a coastal town that happened to be a swing seat. The trouble is they didn't want it because when the town reverted to a sleepy village after the tourist season, it was ridiculous to keep it open to arrest the odd angry walrus.

To understand the importance of police independence, let's play Good Cop/Bad Cop.

The Bad Cop: the bent-as-a-banana Queensland commissioner Terry Lewis.

Between 1970–76, the Queensland police commissioner was Ray Whitrod, a thoroughly decent and scrupulously honest career cop. As well as being straight, Whitrod was smart – smart enough to know his freshly promoted inspector Terry Lewis was a political limbo dancer and a crook to boot. As Whitrod couldn't sack Lewis, he chose to send Slick Terry 750 kilometres away from Brisbane to Charleville. He thought, not unreasonably, that the slippery inspector couldn't work against him from the backblocks. But Queensland back then was anything but reasonable.

The cunning, if unintelligible, peanut farmer-turned-premier Joh Bjelke-Petersen secretly flew to Charleville twice to meet Lewis. The fix was in. First, he moved the police minister, who was Whitrod's ally, and then he waited.

When Whitrod put in his recommendations for the next assistant commissioner, cabinet, at the urging of the premier and now without the support of the police minister, ignored them and appointed Lewis, jumping more than 100 more qualified senior police. Whitrod, his independence crushed, resigned on principle.

Rather than realising the error of his ways, Joh appointed Lewis commissioner.

Whitrod was fiercely independent and an outsider while Lewis had been mentored by the corrupt (and slightly mad) former commissioner Frank Bischof.

What could be better than to replace the annoyingly honest Whitrod with a local puppet? The unspoken deal was that if the commissioner did what he was told and was prepared to be a political tool, the government would turn a blind eye to corruption. The premier and the commissioner were, in effect, holding each other's testicles with an understanding neither would squeeze.

About 10 years later, the system imploded, leading to the Fitzgerald Inquiry into corruption. Lewis ended up in jail.

Evidence included that when his bribe package was on the light side, he remained courteous saying: 'little fish are sweet'.

Tinned sardines, from the prison canteen, are not.

The Good Cop: Victoria's Chief Commissioner Sinclair Imrie (Mick) Miller.

The careers of Miller and Lewis were similar – on paper. Both were awarded Churchill fellowships (Miller in 1967 and Lewis in 1968), they were appointed police chiefs in the 1970s, were smooth movers, were long-shots to be appointed chief, would rule for a decade and were young – both were 48. And that is the end of the similarities.

Miller was honest, spoke his mind and stared down any political interference. When Miller was appointed assistant commissioner in 1971 the then chief, Reg Jackson, told him: 'You weren't my choice.'

A year later, when another assistant commissioner refused an out-of-hours call for an emergency, the police operator rang Miller, who returned to duty. The emergency was a group of schoolkids and their teacher had been abducted from their one-class school at Faraday.

He worked closely with education minister Lindsay Thompson until the hostages were saved and kidnapper Edwin John 'Ted' Eastwood was arrested. In February 1977, Eastwood committed the same crime at the Wooreen State School. Again, Miller and Thompson teamed up.

A few months later, with Jackson due to retire, he lobbied heavily for his deputy. Victoria had been through two police scandals that resulted in judicial inquiries, and premier Sir Rupert Hamer wanted someone fresh. Thompson recommended Miller, who became chief commissioner in June 1977.

There lies the difference. Hamer wanted someone honest and who could run the force without needing political direction. Bjelke-Petersen wanted someone dishonest and as malleable as political putty.

Today, all senior cops know the only way to tackle organised crime is to pool information and resources. When Miller urged the same strategy 40 years ago through the Australian Bureau of Criminal Intelligence, he was deliberately sidelined by cops more interested in lining their pockets or keeping power.

Lewis served 10 years as Joh's tame cop. He was ordered to stand down in September 1987. Joh crashed and burned a few months later.

Miller served Labor and Conservative governments. It is fair to say his politics leant to the right, yet well after both had retired, Miller would regularly lunch with his ex-police minister, Race Matthews, who was well to the left.

Despite not being politically aligned, they both understood the need for police to be at arm's length from the political process and to enforce the laws of the government of the day.

When Sir Edward Lyons, a close buddy of Joh and a political ally of the National Party, was caught driving with a blood alcohol level twice the limit – you guessed it. The charges disappeared.

When a police minister mentioned to Miller his government driver had been booked for speeding, Miller asked for details. Within days, the minister was puzzled when the chief commissioner handed him the booking officer's details. Asked why, the politician was told firmly he should ring the country cop to congratulate him on his exemplary work. The minister made the call, and never again tried to pull a string.

KERR'S SLEDGE WAS NO CRIMINAL ACT

There is little doubt Matildas captain Sam Kerr made a goose of herself when she argued the toss with a London cop after throwing up in a cab during a post-match celebration of her hat-trick against Liverpool.

But when did being a goose become a criminal offence?

Kerr is alleged to have called the cop who was dealing with her, PC Lovell, a 'stupid white bastard' after Kerr refused to pay a surcharge to have the cab cleaned. It was a spectacular own goal.

She appears to have made a hat-trick of mistakes – she threw up, failed to pay the required fee and then got lippy with the law.

The incident occurred on 30 January 2023. Nearly a year later, she was charged by post for allegedly using racially aggravated words that caused alarm and distress.

PC Lovell was no doubt only doing his job. However, as a rule of thumb, a career in policing requires not becoming alarmed and distressed at robust verbal interactions. For those not so inclined, occupations such as librarian, museum curator or emperor penguin carer await.

Sam Kerr is 167 centimetres, of slight build and has no criminal history. The only person who should be frightened of Kerr, OAM, is a goalkeeper. She was a feisty, full footballer – a striker who didn't strike, not a bikie with a knuckle duster.

The taxi driver took Kerr to the Twickenham Police Station in busy London Road next to the excellent, family-run Greek Cook and Grill restaurant in the hope of settling the dispute. She would have been better off investing in a souvlaki than a slanging match (two skewers, homemade chips, dip and salad for £15.70. Bargain).

PC Lovell was not alone. Inside the 24-hour station were fellow police officers, batons, handcuffs and, in all probability, a pie warmer.

Twickenham recorded 15,352 crimes in 2023. Kerr's three-word sledge is now alleged to be another. The station is down the road from the international Twickenham Stadium, meaning the local police would often deal with over-refreshed rugby supporters.

Not so long ago, someone in Kerr's condition may have been put in a cell for four hours to reflect on life and then released without charge. Are we better off with court dates to deal with a brain fade? It smacks of shenanigans that had some of our police (who could swear like pirates on the rum punch) charge people with offensive language and give sworn evidence they nearly fainted when hearing the f-bomb uttered in public.

In New York, the great columnist Jimmy Breslin exposed such fake outrage when a policewoman of Puerto Rican descent named Cibella Borges was sacked for posing for racy pictures (as a teenager, before she joined the police), later published in a periodical named *Beaver*. The magazine was purchased by a police officer (no doubt attracted to the wildlife title) who, having identified a colleague, handed it to multiple male police officers, all of whom chose to stare long and hard at the photos before turning their heads in horror.

The complaints led to a hearing and termination.

Breslin wrote:

> The cop took the magazine to his sergeant. The sergeant was aghast. The sergeant gave the magazine to the lieutenant. The lieutenant was shocked. When Cibella was told about the magazine she went downstairs and found the lieutenant showing the magazine to a whole group of cops.
>
> The police department should have been proud of the pictures as they prove that at least one member of the force is in marvellous physical condition: most officers are in such deplorable physical shape that if called upon to pose for pictures they would first put on overcoats.

Breslin's caustic wit embarrassed senior cops. Borges was eventually reinstated, reaching the rank of detective sergeant before retiring.

Here in Victoria, the chief secretary, Sir Arthur Rylah, banned the book *Lady Chatterley's Lover* in the 1960s, arguing you couldn't possibly allow teenage girls to read such filth. Rylah, who on occasions would refresh himself with a morning whisky, kept copies of *Playboy* in his desk drawer to admire models often just out of their teens.

To suggest that Kerr's alleged sledge is racially charged is just plain silly. Vilification is used against people who have been the victims of traditional oppression. Yet case law in England suggests otherwise. A black man was convicted after telling two parking officers in Sheffield to get back 'with your white uncles and aunties'.

Kerr has been charged with an offence serious enough to draw a maximum of two years jail. It is part of a drift where we make laws for bad behaviour by declaring it criminal behaviour. It is the cholesterol of the system, clogging the arteries of justice.

Kerr's jury trial is set for February 2025, two years after the event. It is listed to last four days over an alleged three-word slur. Jury trials are usually reserved for the most serious offences, not for slurring soccer players. It is proof the British system of justice – here and there – has gone bonkers.

The Victims of Crime Commissioner Fiona McCormack has produced a detailed report that shows the majority of victims are dissatisfied with the system and would not enter it again. 'Victims are asking for a criminal justice system that delivers justice for them,' she found.

If the criminal justice system was a business, it would have shut its doors years ago because its core customer group – the victims – hate it.

Committal hearings are redundant and only force victims to tell their stories yet again, cross-examinations that should take hours can take days, and the ridiculous delays mean offenders are often bailed to commit further crimes.

And still we produce more laws to deal with bad behaviour when the system is failing to efficiently deal with serious crime.

At the football, for no apparent reason, a supporter turned and yelled at me: 'What are you looking at, Skeleton Head?' Rather than being alarmed and distressed, what passed for my friends (quite rightly) fell about laughing.

Words reflect the user, not the recipient. If someone yells a bigoted slur at the footy, the majority see that person for what they are: a pathetic racist. Those who don't are pathetic racists themselves.

We have progressed. Too slowly, for sure, but we are moving. And it is community-driven, not forced by legislation. We ban the Nazi salute and give a tiny group of powerless right-wing fanatics what they crave: attention. In Europe, there is a history of evil, ultra-right-wing political movements and such modern reincarnations need monitoring.

The number of hard-core fascists in Victoria would be flat out having the numbers to make a footy team. Public vision of them 'training' by hitting heavy boxing bags shows they would struggle to take on two angry nuns equipped with wooden spoons. They would fade into obscurity if not for their greatest allies – the far left. When the failed fascists roll out to yell clichés, the far left roll out to yell at them. And the confrontation, not the Nazis, becomes newsworthy.

Recently we went to the police front lines and saw members of the Public Order Response Team deal with abuse that would make a dockworker blush. Yet none of the PORT officers appeared alarmed or distressed. None required counselling or therapy such as finger-painting or listening to whale songs in a darkened room while inhaling Amazon rainforest incense.

Isn't it time we concentrated on the main event and stopped worrying about silly sideshows?

No one thinks Sam Kerr is a criminal. So why (unless her lawyer's move to have the case chucked out as an abuse of process succeeds) is she to stand trial in a criminal court?

NINE LIVES RUN OUT FOR THE CAT-BURGLAR

Ian Hardy wasn't the first policeman to tackle the man in black they had been chasing for years, but he was the one who settled the issue beyond reasonable doubt.

Despite being outnumbered, the suspect on the ground was desperate to free himself. Across the road was a park where the pre-dawn darkness would provide the master escape artist the chance to disappear. Given a few metres break, his pursuers would have no chance – after all, he had beaten them before by running, hiding in plain sight and once swimming into Port Phillip Bay.

Hardy, a crack shot, drew his pistol but instead of pulling the trigger used the butt to crack the man in the mask over the head. It was at that moment that Australia's most prolific cat-burglar, John Harvey Rider, knew it was all over.

How many jobs he had pulled will never be known but over more than seven years, he robbed hundreds, and perhaps thousands, of homes – usually with the occupants tucked up in bed. His logic was simple: he was after cash and jewels and if the owners were out, so were their wallets, rings and necklaces.

He scaled multistorey buildings, disabled alarms, climbed drainpipes, leapt from balcony to balcony and stayed for hours inside homes, sometimes serving himself a snack from the fridge (smoked salmon on rye was a favourite).

He left no clues and no sign of forced entry so that often his victims didn't know they had been robbed until they looked for their jewellery.

On the day he was caught, he was wearing skin-tight black pants, a black skivvy and a matching black mask. Under his skivvy was his specialist utility belt containing knives, a screwdriver, spanner, scissors, clothes pegs and cotton attached to fish hooks (used to lower louvre windows to the ground without making a noise).

Hardy, now in his 80s, asked the man his name. 'John,' was the response. 'Just John.'

'Well, John. You've led us a merry dance,' Hardy said.

'Would you believe this was my first time?' Rider asked more in hope.

'Don't treat me as an idiot and I won't treat you like one,' replied Hardy and Rider, then 33, responded with 'Fair enough.'

Hardy and his crew had been called to a residential block in Elwood. It was 4.30 am on 19 March 1973, and the Elsternwick senior detective had been working nightshift for six months trying to find the burglar dubbed 'The Cat'.

They set up a cordon and waited. Hardy heard a series of dogs bark as Rider scaled backyard fences. Eventually one of the police grabbed his legs as he tried to climb another but even though three cops were holding him, Rider would not give up – until he was cracked on the head.

Despite the robust nature of their initial greeting, the Cat and the Cop (assisted by the adept Senior Detective Ian 'Bluey' Fountain) developed a bond and soon were chatting freely. 'I asked him how many he had done. He said: "Successful ones? Just over 800." I asked what is a successful one? Rider said: "One where I got more than

$5000 in cash and jewellery." I said: "How many unsuccessful?" He said more than 1000.'

When Rider told Hardy if he had made the park, no police would have caught him, his captor said: 'You wouldn't have got there. I would have shot you.'

The official police estimate was 4000 burglaries and his haul between $500,000 and $1.5 million, with the jewels sold overseas and the gold melted down.

For the first few years, he lived in Sydney masquerading as the owner of an interstate taxi truck company. His roster was three weeks in Melbourne, robbing as many as four homes a night, six days a week, and the next two in Sydney, living the life of a Porsche-driving playboy.

The private schoolboy-turned prowler says he took to running and strength conditioning while a student at Geelong Grammar's bushland Timbertop campus, was able to run more than eight kilometres a night between jobs and developed a rock-climber's grip that enabled him to enter high-rise homes that seemed impenetrable.

Years later, after he served his jail term, I saw his climbing ability first-hand. He became an associate of *The Age's* charismatic, sports car-driving crime reporter Steve Ballard. Rider was a visitor at late, long and liquored-up police rounds dinners and on one such early morning, we watched from the courtyard as he effortlessly scampered up a drainpipe to the second floor of BJ's restaurant in Collingwood, where he stood and drank a stubby.

It was a long way up, for when we threw a couch from the window around 5 am, it did not survive. However, *The Age* cadet who was stuffed in the oven did. (It was not turned on. Even back then an attempt to cook a junior reporter would have been considered bullying.)

When Rider and Hardy finally started the formal interview process, his statement was taken on a manual typewriter without a tape back-up. A few years later a royal commission headed by Barry Beach QC (now Supreme Court judge) found police sometimes took confessions where the suspect would speak freely then, for reasons never explained, refuse to sign the statements. Such statements could be fair or fabricated, depending on the ethics of the cop driving the typewriter. This tactic was referred to by the cynical (or the well-informed) as 'the verbal'.

When Hardy told Rider he wanted to interview him over hundreds of robberies, the Cat said: 'I'm not going to sign my life away. I will sign up for 15 robberies if you let the rest go.'

True to his word, over the next few days Rider confessed to the 15 and signed each page of the confessions.

A senior officer told Hardy to interview Rider over the hundreds of unsolved burglaries.

'I told him he wasn't going to talk, and I was told it didn't matter if he didn't sign.

'I said: "No, I'm not verballing him."'

Unsurprisingly, other police were assigned the job and managed another 20 confessions, all unsigned.

Rider would chat to Hardy off the record, telling him how he sat on a roof and watched the police below scurry around looking for him, how he slid under a mattress leaning on a wall as police ran up and down the driveway metres from him and how he swam 500 metres out into the cold Port Phillip Bay and then a kilometre down the beach to escape.

'He never told me a lie – he just didn't tell all the truth,' Hardy says.

Over seven years he hit homes in Toorak, Caulfield, St Kilda, Elwood, Gardenvale, East Kew and Brighton, learning breathing patterns to check his victims were in deep sleep, sometimes hiding under their beds if they stirred.

He often found his victims over-reported their jewellery loss and under-reported the cash because the jewels were insured while the money had not been declared. Not all thieves wear balaclavas.

An expert scuba diver, Rider hid the gems and gold in an underwater cave before it was sent to his fence.

'We found a gold cigarette lighter at his house. It was the only thing we found that was stolen and the only thing we were ever likely to find,' says Hardy.

In December 1974, he pleaded guilty to 15 counts of burglary from eight signed and seven unsigned statements, with Rider saying: 'I regarded the whole operation as a game of chess between myself and the police [and] felt a terrific sense of achievement.'

He was sentenced to 10 years with a minimum of seven. He served four years and nine months.

Hardy thought once Rider went to Pentridge that would be the last he would hear from him. 'But while he was in jail, he got a message to me asking that I go and see him. He told me a rapist I'd locked up who was about to be released planned to kill me.' Sure enough, the offender began a campaign of harassment that included an arson attack on Hardy's house. Eventually the crook lost his obsession and moved interstate.

Another time Hardy was instructed to drive to Pentridge on a secret assignment. 'For some reason he [Rider] was given permission to go to a party.'

Another time Rider invited Hardy and his wife, Lorraine, to Pentridge as his guest to watch him in the play *The Caine Mutiny*. 'Don't tell them you are a copper' was the Cat's wise advice.

'We sat in a hall full of crims – it was a great play,' Hardy says.

On his release, Rider said he was finished with crime but, like a leopard that can't change its spots, the Cat still had a taste for cream. He went back to his old ways and was convicted of breaking into 58 Sydney homes in 1983.

He was sentenced to 17 years with a minimum of seven. On release he moved to Queensland and appears to have retired. Hardy still carries a respect for his adversary. 'He was an amazing man, he really was.'

PART 3

CRIMES & CONSEQUENCES

There are cases that make people change the way they live. The disappearance of Eloise Worledge, 8, from her Melbourne bayside home in 1976 was one of them. Doors were locked and windows bolted when parents felt their children were no longer safe in the family home.

The police worked every angle but the case remains unsolved. Now we know there were paedophile teachers working at her school – a fact hidden from the police looking for Eloise's killer.

Would it have made a difference? We will never know.

Then there are the freezer files: cases where smart forensic scientists froze exhibits from crime scenes and waited for DNA technology to catch up. Rapists and killers who thought they were free are learning justice can move very slowly.

FREEZER FILES HELP CATCH A RAPIST

There is a small group of people – long retired – who are still solving crimes. They are not detectives or profilers or tea-leaf readers but forensic experts with the unique capacity to see into the future.

From the early 1980s, they would take material from crime scenes and place samples in their giant freezer at Macleod, even though at that time they were next to useless. The back-to-the-future plan was to keep the evidence on ice and wait for technology to catch up.

They are known as the Freezer Files, containing thousands of samples waiting to be matched. When DNA technology had been trialled, tested and accepted in court as compelling evidence, the thawed samples could create hot answers in cold cases.

At first it was a simple scientific procedure: enter the DNA profile from the sample in the national database and see if it matched a convicted offender. This helped to solve more than 100 cold cases, such as the Shepparton rapist identified 20 years later after his DNA was taken when arrested for burglary in Queensland.

They also uploaded more than 500 DNA profiles from the samples and found some matches with other unsolved sex crimes, indicating the offenders were serial attackers.

But there is a hitch. Today, when a suspect is convicted of a sex crime, the DNA sample is entered into the database. But before 2000, samples were not routinely collected from offenders. Police have collated a list of 300 names, just from 1985 to 1993, of convicted rapists who have not been scientifically tested against unsolved crimes.

Once these freezer cases were tested, many crimes were solved, but there were more than 100 that remained unmatched, meaning the offenders' genetic profiles were not on the national system.

These cases were listed for review by eight detectives in the Sex Crimes Cold Case Unit. Among them was Senior Detective Phil Drews, who was given a file called Operation Megaliths.

The good news was that samples from the case had been tested in 2012 and a DNA profile of the offender established. In 2017, the case was reactivated and the following year, it was given to Drews.

The bad news was when he opened the original file, it was dangerously thin. It contained the victim's statement, some forensic reports and little else. The original investigators' master file had been destroyed. 'There were no known suspects,' says Drews.

The victim was a Ballarat woman, 38, whose husband had died four years earlier, leaving her to care for their five daughters, aged six to 15.

After watching a movie with her kids on a Friday night, she went to bed to be woken around 5 am on 22 July 1990 with someone's hand over her mouth. There were two men in her house, both wearing balaclavas and woollen gloves. The terrified victim asked: 'Who are you?' and one answered: 'I'm a secret admirer.' He then threatened the children: 'If you don't do as you are told, I'll kill them.'

During the attack, when the men heard a noise, one calmly went to investigate. Clearly they knew she was the only adult in the house and no one would be returning that early morning.

They continued the attack, with one warning: 'Don't tell anyone, or I'll kill the kids.' To add weight to the threat, one said: 'I know you have a 16-year-old girl.' (She was 15.)

Terrified, the victim rang her mother, saying she didn't want to report the crime. When the 15-year-old ran to a neighbour to get help, the neighbour took it upon herself to ring the police.

The local detectives conducted the investigation by the book. They checked with neighbours to see if they had seen anything suspicious and looked at all the woman's friends and associates. This was not a case where police had a suspicion but lacked evidence; they had no suspects at all.

Drews had no suspects, no existing crime scene, a 28-year-old case and a DNA sample that didn't match any known offender. The tools of modern police would be no help. There was no CCTV, no mobile phone records or credit cards to track.

Drews had to rely on hunches, half-leads and a paper trail. 'It was a bit like entering a time machine.'

What he did have was a comprehensive statement taken by Ballarat detective Paul Jolly, who knew his trade. Drews studied it not so much to review what had happened, but for what it said about the two men in the masks. 'Crime scene behaviour can be telling,' Drews says.

One man said he was a secret admirer. He mentioned the age of one of the daughters but got it slightly wrong, indicating he knew the family but wasn't close. They wore balaclavas but didn't bother to disguise their voices. Was it someone the victim could recognise by sight but had not heard speak? Someone close geographically but not socially? Perhaps a delivery driver, service provider, shop assistant or everyman who lived nearby?

Not a bad theory, but theories don't crack cases. Drews went to the Ballarat Police Station and pulled three years of arrests books, going through them line by line, looking for anyone with a potential link.

There were six, including a man charged with the minor offence of handling a couple of bottles of stolen rum. A closer look showed he had prior arrests for family violence and had been the subject of intervention orders. His name was Brett Braddock, 26, the father of two young children. And he lived up the road.

There was nothing to suggest he and the victim had ever met, although he could see into her property from his home. Naturally police at the time had knocked on his door and asked if he had seen anything suspicious. Braddock, not unreasonably, said he had been asleep.

The case faded, Braddock's marriage failed, he moved 260 kilometres away, remarried and had three more children, all daughters.

On 25 January 2019, there was a knock at his door. It was the local policeman from the one-cop station with a letter from town. The letter was from Phil Drews, explaining details of the case and why he was requesting Braddock provide a DNA sample.

There were no tricks, just an honest explanation of why the DNA could assist the cold case investigation. Braddock, who was standing next to his wife, didn't hesitate to cooperate.

The fact that Braddock didn't hesitate led Drews to believe he was innocent. Until the test came back, saying the odds were that he was 100 billion more times likely to be the offender than anyone else.

'He freely provided the sample, saying he had nothing to hide,' says Drews. 'I think because his wife was standing there, he may have felt he had no choice.'

It was then that Drews contacted the victim to tell her they had found a suspect.

After the assault, she felt she couldn't live in the house and had to move to emergency accommodation. She would never sleep in a double bed again. Because she had five children to raise, she had tried to block out her memories until Drews knocked on the door.

'She was apprehensive, and I told her we were doing this for her, and we would only do what she felt was best for her.'

She decided she wanted justice. Faced with a determined victim, a relentless investigator and an overwhelming DNA result, Braddock had no choice but to plead guilty. He claimed he was addicted to alcohol and marijuana at the time and had no memory of the attack. No one believes him.

County Court Judge Patricia Riddell sentenced him to 12 years, two months with a non-parole period of nine years.

Riddell praised the original work of Senior Detective Paul Jolly and that of Drews and the Cold Case Unit: 'They did not rest or abandon this case despite its age. They did not give up. They renewed their search to identify and apprehend the offender in 2018, some 28 years after these events.'

Braddock appealed, looking for the sort of leniency he didn't give his victim. The Supreme Court knocked him back.

But this case is far from closed. There were two offenders, and Braddock has refused to name the other man. 'This is not a case of two drunks stumbling into a house. It was planned, they were wearing gloves and balaclavas,' says Drews.

Braddock was an introvert with a small circle of friends. He was known at the local go-kart club and was unemployed.

Drews knows that in such premeditated crimes the two offenders would be close – close enough to trust each other to remain silent. Which means police believe the other rapist was at that time one of Braddock's small circle.

Detective Sergeant Mark Farrugia from the Cold Case Unit says: 'We are not stopping. We are determined to bring the second offender to justice.'

HOW JADE BROKE THE CYCLE

Jade Allen has no right to be here. She should be dead – just another kid born into hell who didn't have a chance. Born addicted to drugs due to her mother's heroin abuse, she was only days old and still critically ill when abducted from hospital by her father, a notorious drug trafficker and multiple murderer.

'I was very sick when Dad came and just stole me from the special care ward. No one had the guts to try and stop him,' she says.

Her dad was the notorious Dennis Bruce 'Mr Death' Allen. Kath Pettingill, Allen's mother, recalls in the book, *The Matriarch*, that he took the baby from the Royal Women's Hospital: 'He brought Jade home to me and said: "You've got a granddaughter" . . . He brought her about 10 o'clock at night, pissed.'

She says Jade's mother, Sissy, discharged herself from hospital. 'She (said) she wanted to see the baby. She didn't want to see the baby. She wanted the smack underneath the mattress in the bassinet.'

It was a portent of what was to come.

Before she could walk, Jade saw drug abuse; before she could talk, she witnessed mindless violence; before she was old enough to go to school, she was an orphan – her mother killing herself in 1986 while in prison, leaving a note to her two daughters that she was sorry but just wanted the pain to stop, and her father dying of heart disease brought on by massive drug abuse in 1987.

Jade was too young to comprehend. 'I never felt scared. I felt safe and loved. I remember the violence, but it wasn't scary because that's all I knew.'

The chaotic violence around Allen was off the map. Bodies in the backyard, family members ordered to clean blood stains, hostages beaten with bats and brooms and a man shot dead while changing a record. His body was never found.

Allen was a police informer on bail for more than 60 offences, a contract killer and a man who would go days without sleep living on massive doses of speed. Sissy was part wife, part accomplice and part prisoner. She was beaten, once left overnight chained to a washing machine, bashed with a gun butt by Allen, stabbed and dumped in the boot of her car.

Allen's sister-in-law, Wendy Peirce, told me: 'Dennis opened the boot. Sissy was in there with her throat cut. It wasn't ear to ear but she lay there, just gurgling. It was awful. I was helpless. He just slammed the boot shut and I spun out. He told someone to drive her somewhere and just leave her in a Dumpmaster. I got her dropped off at a railway station so someone would find her and take her to hospital. That saved her life.'

Jade's memories, understandably, are sketchy. She remembers parties, gold lights, her father sharpening giant knives on a stone, fish tanks filled not with colourful species, but piranhas and small sharks. There is a picture of him apparently giving her a cigarette when she was one.

Her babysitter was cousin Jason Ryan. 'I looked up to Jason. He would give me chips with sauce.'

Years later, Jason Ryan would become a key police witness against members of the family charged with the October 1988 ambush murders of Constables Steven Tynan and Damian Eyre in Walsh Street, South Yarra. There is a picture of her sitting on the knee of her uncle, Trevor Pettingill, one of the four men acquitted of the police murders.

She says she was supposed to be raised by Dennis' half-brother Victor Peirce. Victor, a career armed robber and gunman, was also acquitted. In May 2003, he was shot dead in Bay Street, Port Melbourne.

Jade says her father, wealthy from drug dealing, made out a will to look after his two daughters. His mother, Kath Pettingill, was executor. 'We were supposed to have had a Catholic education. There was nothing. She has had nothing to do with us.' She says even now she would like Pettingill to hand over any items from her father.

She went to seven primary schools, spent most of her time crying in toilets and was told a series of false stories about her parents' death, including that they died in a car crash. She said that it was only when she read Kath Pettingill's book that she learnt the truth. 'I was 12 or 13. It had a massive impact on me.'

Sissy's mother, Heather Hill, took on the task of raising the two girls. Heather had six daughters. Three died, two from overdoses and one from suicide.

'I resented my mother (for taking her own life). As a mother, I don't understand how she could leave her kids,' says Jade.

But she says she loves her father, even though he was a killer. She remembers being left at the bottom of steps in Housing Commission flats to play by herself while family members took drugs inside.

'Nan was a recovering alcoholic. She tried her best and always tried to keep us away from that (Allen) family.'

We meet in a trendy cafe in Carlton. She is nervous, laughs readily then is moved to tears as she talks of her darkest times. She is a fighter, but the battles have taken a toll.

Eventually she moved to Queensland to live with Sissy's sister, Kellie Carter-Bell. But Kellie was caught in a toxic, violent relationship.

The father of her children hunted her down and attacked her, plunging a knife into her heart. Amazingly, she survived. (After more than two decades of violence, Kellie escaped, survived and is now a powerful advocate against family violence.)

'She moved to me in Year 7. Jade had seen so much,' says Kellie.

Jade went on the run, making a small amount of cash from babysitting. 'I now know I was groomed.' When she was 15, the 24-year-old father of the children she looked after started to drop around at home during the day when his de facto wife was at work. 'He drove me around in a nice car, bought me clothes and gave me speed,' she says. By the time she was 17, she was pregnant.

The father beat her. 'My son learnt to crawl over to me when he was bashing me on the floor.' They would go to a country property where he would shoot at targets. 'I was so scared he was going to shoot me and bury me there. They would never have found the body.' Soon it began the usual spiral – lost years, drug addiction, bad friends and a twilight existence.

The prospect of a second child made her face reality. She escaped her violent partner, hid in a women's refuge and eventually returned to Melbourne.

Jade Allen hates seeing her father portrayed as a monster – even though he was. She detests her grandmother, Kath, feeling she failed to provide any help when it was needed.

She could have gone down the same path as many of that clan – drugs, self-destruction and premature death. But somehow, she didn't. Three of her four children live with her. They have a three-bedroom public housing flat that is the family oasis.

'It is our little castle,' she says. 'I want to protect my children.'

Kellie Carter-Bell says: 'She is an amazing woman. Her strength is amazing. She has struggled, then thrived, struggled and thrived again. She has fought her demons and won.'

She is proud of her home. 'I have OCD, so I am always cleaning. If I stop, I think and thinking is not always a good thing.'

Eventually she turned her obsession into her business. She is a one-person professional cleaning company, often preparing AirBnBs for the next visitors.

Jade the survivor has done the near impossible. She broke the cycle.

A SURVIVOR'S LESSON ON RESILIENCE

The rookie teacher at the tiny country school was startled during morning recess when some of the kids ran into the single weatherboard classroom, yelling: 'There's a man outside with a gun.'

His initial reaction for someone so inexperienced was remarkably calm, believing his nine primary school students were more at risk from overactive imaginations than an active shooter. He thought the gunman was probably 'some harmless hunter out shooting rabbits'.

Then he saw him – the man in the balaclava – pointing the handgun straight at the teacher's chest, saying: 'Don't try anything fucking smart or I'll shoot you.'

Rob Hunter had been the sole teacher at the Gippsland town of Wooreen for just nine days at his first posting after three years at teachers' college. He was 20 years old. He'd slipped into his new role, having been welcomed into the Wooreen dairy township with a local barbecue a few days earlier.

The children – six girls and three boys from six families – ranged from seven to 11 years old and grade two to six. They were, according to Hunter: 'a dream – co-operative and well-behaved, from families who loved them dearly . . . All different in their own ways, all full of potential. They were all so keen to please, eager to impress, willing to work and hungry to learn'.

The man with the revolver and wearing a Collingwood beanie as a balaclava was Geelong Prison escapee Edwin John 'Ted' Eastwood, 26, who five years earlier pulled the same crime 270 kilometres away, kidnapping a teacher and six students from Faraday.

Hoping it was a simple robbery, Hunter volunteered: 'I can write a cheque. How much would you like?'

The gunman responded: 'No, mate, that's not the sort of money I want.'

He remembers Eastwood as nervous, distracted and sweating profusely when he initially grabbed them.

When a grade-five girl asked: 'What's your name?' the gunman eventually responded 'Ted', not even attempting to provide an alias. Eastwood always craved the spotlight – even if it was held by armed police.

His planning was so poor that he had tried the kidnapping at another country school earlier before randomly choosing Hunter's class. His ransom note had the name of his original target, Allambee, crossed out and replaced with Wooreen.

Trying to remain outwardly calm for the sake of the children, Hunter managed to unplug the electric clock to leave a clue to the time of the abduction. It stopped at 11.10 am.

Eventually, Eastwood produced a ten-metre dog chain to bolt the kids together. As he made Hunter lie on the floor to chain his wrists, one of the grade-six girls asked: 'Ted, what are you going to do with us? Where are you going to take us? How long are we going to be away for? When will we get back?'

'He answered: "You'll only be away until I get what I want. Don't worry, just do what I say and I won't hurt you. But if you do anything silly, I'll shoot the teacher",' Hunter recalls.

Under unimaginable stress, Hunter was angered by the most trivial matters. Eastwood had a sign prepared to give him breathing space. On a torn piece of cardboard, he had printed: *HAVE GONE ON A NATURE STUDY TRIP, WILL BE BACK IN ONE HOUR!*

'This annoyed me,' Hunter recalls. 'He had written a notice, making out that it was me who had written it. It made me angry. How dare he? Despite the crazy circumstances, I was also irritated by the way it was written. His use of capital letters was wrong.

'Any primary teacher worth his weight uses every opportunity to model and teach the use of correct upper, and lower-case letters. I would not have written that note in capital letters.'

What did the kidnapper want? His ransom demand was as stupid as his initial plan.

In a note to education minister and Deputy Premier Lindsay Thompson, he demanded the release of 17 of the state's most dangerous criminals, an arsenal of weapons, $7 million in US currency, 100 kilos of cocaine, 100 kilos of heroin and a late-model car with a full tank of petrol (with $US7 million, he couldn't buy his own juice?).

Eastwood gagged and blindfolded Hunter before taking his chain gang to his stolen Dodge truck. The kids were put in the back while Hunter was forced onto the front passenger-side floor. 'He yelled at the children, all crammed in the back cabin: "You kids keep down. When we're passing any cars, keep your heads right down or bullets will be flying."

'"You mongrel! They're my students you're yelling at," Hunter recalls thinking. "How dare you threaten them like that?"'

Eastwood's plan was doomed from the start. Not only was he a bad kidnapper, he was a bad driver, hurtling along gravel roads and throwing the chained children around the floor of the truck, leaving them frightened and one bleeding.

'The gunman called out to the children: "Keep your heads down or watch out! If I see you waving to anyone, I'll shoot someone."'

Then he ran into a truck.

Eastwood jumped from his disabled vehicle and took the two men in the logging truck hostage: 'Don't try anything fucking smart or I'll blow your heads off.'

He had 12 hostages, but another truck rolled around the corner and he grabbed the two men on board, bringing the number to 14. When a Kombi van pulled up with two women on board, he added them to the list – 16.

He jammed them all in the van and eventually drove to his camp site for the night, where they shared tinned ham and stolen chocolate. That night, Eastwood bragged about the Faraday kidnapping and declared that this time if confronted by police 'he would shoot it out with them; he wouldn't be going down alone, he would shoot some of them, too'.

When news of the kidnapping broke on the radio, Eastwood was delighted. 'It was like he was sitting back getting ready to enjoy the unfolding of the story, with the essential ingredient of the media giving him publicity.'

In the darkness, truck driver Robin Smith slipped his chains and crept out of the camp site. 'I'm sure that if Eastwood had woken up at that moment, he would have shot Robin,' writes Hunter. Smith then jogged more than 10 kilometres to a farmhouse to raise the alarm.

English was not the farmers' first language and it took Robin some time to convince them he was an escaped hostage.

By 6.45 am, Eastwood, the prison escapee, realised he had let one of his prisoners escape. He bundled his remaining 15 hostages into the underpowered van and took off. Almost immediately, police were on his tail.

'Eastwood, holding his revolver in hand, put his hand and arm out the window while he was driving and took some shots at the police cars chasing us. I couldn't believe what I was seeing,' Hunter writes.

Police fired at the tyres, but one bullet ricocheted through the cabin. Eventually, Eastwood was shot in the leg and arrested.

On Monday, 7 November 1977 – 38 weeks after Eastwood walked into the Wooreen Primary School – he pleaded guilty to 16 counts of kidnapping, three of theft of vehicles, three of using a firearm to avoid arrest, one of escape, one of burglary and one of theft. He was sentenced to 21 years, with a minimum of 18, and was released from jail in 1993.

Hunter refused to be defined by the kidnapping and continued to teach around Victoria, retiring after 44 years in education. The key, he says, was to let go of his anger towards the kidnapper and reject his desire for revenge.

He now delivers those lessons in school lectures, entitled Health After Hurt, to teach kids about mental resilience.

THE TRUTH BEHIND VICTIM-BLAMING

On the rare occasions I am allowed to leave the office and engage with humans, I am often asked: 'When are you going to retire?'

The question, while confronting, is quite reasonable, considering I look about 100 years old and in urgent need of a walking frame.

Despite this impression, the answer is I have no plans to move into a nursing home any time soon as the only thing left working in the present state of decrepitude is the teeth, which means my food does not, as yet, require processing in a blender.

I actually enjoy what I do – expressing random thoughts in this column in return for a small stipend that helps pay for life's necessities, such as cabernet merlot, blue cheese and chocolate-covered almonds.

The alternative would leave me the most boring man at the pub, mumbling incoherently through a mouthful of salt-and-vinegar crisps, telling those who aren't interested how I think the world should work.

We are often defined by what we do, not who we are. Worse still, there is a secret system of affording people a value based on their occupation. This is particularly true in the world of crime, where we make a snap judgement on the victim using this unspoken order of rank.

A young man who may have a future as an AFL player is considered more valuable and newsworthy than a young man who is very good at chess. A young woman has more to lose if she is pretty than one who is not. That is, of course, only if she is a 'good' girl and not a 'naughty' one.

When Michaela Dunn, 24, was stabbed to death in a Sydney CBD apartment in August 2019, she was quickly identified as a sex worker. Her profession did not define her, for she was a young woman loved by her family, respected by her friends, filled with optimism and entitled to live a full and happy life.

There is a reason for the judgement and it is not necessarily a moral one. If we can 'blame' the victim, it makes us all feel a little safer. If the person has engaged in behaviour that we would not, then we feel less at risk. If a skydiver dies, it is sad. But if a swimmer is taken by a shark at a popular beach, it is terrifying; it could have been us.

There is no greater example of this than Kaera Douglas, the repeated victim of domestic violence escalating to being shot in cold blood on a city street.

On the conventional metre of sympathy, she should be off the scale. She was young, smart, pretty, white and a former private school student from the posh suburb of Toorak.

Except for one thing; she was a stripper and her partner a bikie. There is no doubt she made bad choices but that doesn't make her a bad person. She is the victim, not the offender.

When she appeared in court over a minor police charge – a package worth less than $100 was delivered to her home and she kept it, hardly the Great Bookie Robbery – she was still identified as a 'former stripper'.

'I've worked so hard to get my name out of the mud and then this happens. It is so disappointing,' she says.

For more than a decade, she has battled physical and mental scars, plus a slice of guilt that two strangers who tried to save her were shot, with one losing his life.

A natural extrovert at her Catholic private school, she was the self-confessed class clown who harboured an unusual ambition. 'I always wanted to be a stripper. I was attracted to the beauty and glamour. I just wanted to look like that.'

After Year 12, she and a friend went to work at Camp USA holiday sites, but she had another secret plan on the trip – to become an exotic dancer in Manhattan.

Armed with a fake ID (she was under-age), she started in a back-street venue before moving to bigger, Mafia-dominated clubs.

'I loved the money and attention', finishing each shift with at least $1500 in cash. Perhaps that's where she developed a weakness for bad men. Returning to Melbourne in 2002, she was soon associating with the city's gangsters, including the notorious Jason Moran.

'I got involved with the Moran crew. I wanted to be in with them – there were drugs, fast cars and money. And they liked to spend it. It was fun.'

Sometimes she would be invited to the Moran crew's business lunches, usually held at a Japanese restaurant in Moonee Ponds, but if there were secrets shared, she didn't hear. 'I was so self-involved, I didn't see what was going on.'

It was when she moved to Sydney that she met Christopher Wayne Hudson. If you were to have a relationship with a bikie, Hudson should have been the last choice. He had defected from The Finks to the Hells Angels, which sparked a bikie war. He was always dangerous and constantly in danger. He hurt some people while others wanted to kill him. He was erratic, armed and a heavy drug user.

Not that Douglas had the maturity to see the danger. She saw him as romantic, handsome and devoted to her. 'We were head-over-heels together. It was magic,' she says.

That is, until Mother's Day 2007. She still doesn't know what triggered him to kick the hotel door off its hinges and punch her in the face. 'I just kept apologising. I was thinking I must have done something wrong.'

Later, he made her eat a meal in the dark so he didn't have to look at her battered face.

Over the next two months, she was beaten, choked and tortured by the increasingly unhinged Hudson.

'He told me he had already found the place he was going to bury me. I knew he would eventually kill me. He loved bashing women. He was sick for it.

'He made me stand up, then choked me to see what shade of purple I would turn. He broke my ribs and left welts all over me.'

The outgoing, confident young woman was soon broken. She felt if she told her family, they would be in danger, and she was too scared to run because 'I knew he would find me.'

It was early on Monday, 18 June 2007, just as city workers were arriving at their jobs, that Hudson finally imploded. First, he beat and kicked a woman in a strip club before dragging her into King Street. Then he saw Douglas, who had just arrived on Hudson's orders to drive him home.

'He grabbed me and said: "Today is the day you are going to die." I tried to make a run for it, then he shot me in the stomach.'

Two men – solicitor and father-of-three Brendan Keilar, 43, and Paul de Waard, a 25-year-old Dutch backpacker – tried to step in.

The word hero has been devalued over the years but the actions of these two men were truly heroic. Hudson was a huge man, inflated by a diet of steroids, who was beating a woman. Whether or not they knew he had a gun, they both knew they were risking serious physical injury.

De Waard was shot in the chest and stomach; Keilar was shot and died near the corner of William Street and Flinders Lane.

Witnesses told police the gunman hesitated then pointed the gun under his own chin as if considering suicide. Self-preservation overrode the impulse and he dumped the gun, a .40-calibre Llama Mini Max, before escaping.

He surrendered to police two days later with a self-inflicted wrist wound, and was later sentenced to life with a minimum of 35 years.

After emergency surgery, de Waard survived but only just. Douglas was in intensive care for two weeks and hospitalised for a month, losing a kidney in the process.

When she woke, she had to deal with the trauma but also the guilt that two good men had made great sacrifices for her. They were seen as victims, but she was treated as part of the problem.

'I was 24 years old and I felt I was never given the privilege of being a victim. I had to get on with it. I felt as guilty as he was. Why did I stay? What was it all about?'

She had nightmares for years and was diagnosed with PTSD. She wrote to Hudson in prison: 'I wanted to know why. He couldn't tell me – I have no answers.

'It took me years to understand it had nothing to do with me and everything to do with him. I wasn't special, I was just the girl at the end of the chain when he snapped.

'It took me three years to decide that I needed to embrace life to honour his [Brendan Keilar's] sacrifice.

'I want to be someone worth saving.'

When I wrote a story suggesting the Hells Angels may expel Hudson, he wrote me a chatty letter from prison saying he was still a member. The note was on HAMC letterhead. It was light-hearted and quite entertaining, but lacked one element – remorse.

THE REPTILE AND HIS CROCODILE TEARS

Justice Elizabeth Hollingworth didn't need to make a legal ruling or deliver a solemn lecture to shut down the sham unfolding before her in the Supreme Court.

At the back of the court is Sven Lindemann, the man pleading guilty to murdering his partner Monique Lezsak in a frenzied knife attack.

As prosecutor Kristie Churchill reads a chronicle of events, Lindemann begins to sob. When this did not make him the centre of attention, he ramps it up to apparently inconsolable wailing. Finally, Justice Hollingworth steps in and steps up.

'Just a moment. Would the accused sit up?'

She looks at the cold-blooded reptile, saying sternly, 'Stop the crocodile tears. You haven't shown any real remorse, don't do loud sobbing in the back of the court distracting us please.

'I'm not persuaded by that, that you're remotely remorseful. I've seen the evidence, just stop interrupting us please.

'Sorry, Ms Churchill, he was just getting louder and louder and it's unacceptable . . . It's not remotely persuasive. It's a bit late for him to pretend he's remorseful.'

It is fair to say there is nothing that can be said about Lindemann that could reduce his guilt – condemned as he is by his actions and words.

Sometimes defence barristers have to try and defend the indefensible and this was the lot of Lucinda Thies.

After the dreadful details of the crime are read Thies takes the well-travelled path of suggesting her client is remorseful and acted out of character. It is clear the no-nonsense Hollingworth thinks this is complete nonsense.

The judge stops the barrister to describe the pathetic performance of her client as the barrister couldn't see, as Lindemann was behind while she was at the Bar table facing the judge.

'He put his head in his hands, he was shaking. It was the most dramatic – given the material I've seen about his complete lack of remorse for her (the victim), to be doing that; turning it on, apparently for my benefit.

'I do not accept he has genuine regret for what he did to Ms Lezsak . . . The moment I told him to pull himself together, he sat upright, he was miraculously able to control his emotions and I maintain my description of crocodile tears.'

Any suggestion of remorse is sunk by his own words in a prison phone call to his parents where he continues to blame his victim.

'It was as though she poured petrol on to the fire . . . That woman wrecked all of that for me. She wrecked everything for me. It was a blackout. She ripped my heart out of my chest and she took everything from me.'

Little wonder Justice Hollingworth is unimpressed. You get the feeling when the judge does sentence him his tears may be very real.

Kaera Douglas, the partner of Jye Carter, the father of Monique Lezsak's twin children, was apprehensive the first time they met. But any concerns immediately melted away.

'I met her in December 2022. She welcomed me with open arms. She was the most beautiful person both inside and out that I have ever met. She was amazing. I thought we would become great friends for life but we didn't get the chance.'

Douglas is a family violence survivor, repeatedly beaten and choked by her boyfriend, bikie Christopher Wayne Hudson, who took her dignity, her independence and very nearly her life.

On the morning of Monday, 18 June 2007, just as city workers were arriving at their jobs, Hudson began to beat Douglas in the street.

Solicitor Brendan Keilar, 43, and Paul de Waard, a 25-year-old Dutch backpacker, tried to step in. Keilar was shot and died near the corner of William Street and Flinders Lane. De Waard and Douglas (who lost a kidney) were both shot and survived.

Douglas is speaking to us because she believes Lindemann should be jailed for life. (One feels Hollingworth would agree with her but she may be constricted by the need to provide a sentence discount due to the killer's guilty plea.)

'He is a cold-blooded killer who has shown absolutely no remorse. He doesn't deserve to walk among us. We have to change the culture of a minority of men responsible for an epidemic. This has to stop.'

Lezsak's mother-in-law, Annette Carter, remained close with the family and regularly visited to see the twins.

The first time she met Lindemann she found him 'weird'.

'He was all over me and in my face. He wanted all the attention and I was there to visit the twins. It was all about him, he was a real show pony.'

At dinner he moved next to her to say she reminded him of his own mother before bursting into tears.

She feels he wanted to dominate the time to keep her away from her grandchildren. 'I thought of Monique as my own daughter. She was a beautiful person. I still can't comprehend that she is gone.'

Lindemann's self-serving suggestion that he snapped and blacked out is self-deluded, pathetic and contrary to the facts. His actions make him a monster, his excuses make him a coward.

Here are the facts. Lezsak, 39, a caring mother to her twins, Lily and Leo (not their real names) was devoted to fitness, winning several elite bodybuilding competitions.

Lindemann, then 51, was also a bodybuilder (he later tries to blame the use of steroids for his murderous outburst).

They became a couple but Lezsak remains concerned with Lindemann's cold relationship with the twins. It is as if their presence interferes with the attention the 'show pony' craves.

On a trip to Queensland Lezsak meets a man and they begin to exchange texts.

In early May 2023 Lezsak tries to end her relationship with Lindemann. In the next two weeks he veers from abusing her to self-pity to seeking couple's counselling.

Lezsak has transferred her savings to Lindemann for a deposit to buy a family home. They remain living with her parents in their Endeavour Hills home.

He finds the identity of the other man sending him threatening texts.

On the night of 29 May, she leaves the family home twice to get away from him and later sleeps in her daughter's room. Lindemann enters the room for another blazing row. Lily wakes crying.

Lindemann contacts his work to say he will not be coming in. Around 6.15 am on 30 May he enters the kitchen as Monique's father, Zoltan, is preparing for work. He tells Zoltan his daughter is crazy and he will grab his possessions and leave.

Lily and Leo are on the futon in the living room talking to their grandmother when they hear screams from the master bedroom. It is 7.32 am.

Lily, 10, runs in to see her mother being stabbed so violently the knife breaks.

Lindemann punches and strangles the wounded woman while dragging her from the ensuite to the kitchen to grab another weapon from the knife block.

Lily yells: 'Leave my mother alone.' He screams at Monique: 'You have ruined my life.'

Unbelievably the little girl manages to kick and disarm the bodybuilder, snatching the knife and throwing it on the kitchen floor. He grabs another, again breaking it in the frenzied attack.

A second time Lily grabs the weapon but he gets another. He uses six knives to stab her 17 times.

Lily continues to fight although she is injured five times and will need stitches in three wounds.

Injured and seeing her mother being killed before her, she uses voice recognition to call emergency services on 911. The call is automatically transferred to Triple Zero. Lezsak's mother Maggie Peril hears Lily pleading: 'Stay with me Mum, stay with me.'

Lily tells the Triple Zero operator her mother is dead and the killer is in the house.

The operator transfers the call to a police sergeant. She tells the police officer she has tried CPR but Lezsak is dead. Both the mother and the daughter are covered in blood. Lily says to the sergeant: 'My heart's shattered in pieces, my mum, I loved her so much.'

She is pleading with her mother not to leave her.

It is now 7.36 am and as the mortally wounded woman and her injured and heartbroken child lay on the dining room floor Lindemann retreats to the bedroom where he jumps online and transfers $71,000 of their mutual funds to another account, apparently trying to hide it from his victim's family.

This is hardly the actions of someone, through grief, anger or drugs, who has lost control.

He then stabs himself.

Police arrive and rescue Lily who screams at them to save her brother who remains in the house. The police cover his eyes so he doesn't see his mother's body.

They find Lindemann injured from his self-inflicted wounds. He says: 'Let me go. She ruined my life.' Police start first aid until ambulance officers arrive. In the ambulance he repeats: 'She ruined my life.'

Douglas says Lindemann 'is a butcher. I hope (Lily) receives a bravery award. She fought so hard to try and save her mother'.

Lezsak's former partner Jye Carter says: 'I want Monique to be remembered. We both loved the kids so much. He shouldn't be able to do a plea deal. I want the world to know what he has done. Life with no release is the only answer.'

A judge can't sentence someone on gut feel. They have to look at similar cases and sentence within those fence posts. Otherwise, we would have hard judges and soft judges with justice dispensed on a flip of the coin.

What Justice Hollingworth felt about the case will never be known and doesn't really matter. She had to give Lindemann a discount, not because he showed remorse but because he saved the witnesses, particularly Lily, from the trauma of testifying.

The Supreme Court judge said Lindemann only felt sorry for himself and his family – not his victim and her two children he should have protected.

He was sentenced to 31 years with a minimum of 25. Justice Hollingworth said that without Lindemann's guilty plea she would have given him 37 years with a minimum of 31. If he lives long enough, he gets a second chance.

There will be no second chance for Monique.

A FEW SECONDS REVERBERATE FOR YEARS

The ex-cop with a reputation sits quietly at a picnic table at a little stop at a little country town on a perfect autumn afternoon. Even though these days he tends to hunch and keep his head down, he is still physically imposing.

A few metres away is a wire rack where locals leave plants and herbs for anyone to grab. It is that sort of community. Next door is the old-style general store he ran with his mother. It has been in the family since 1946. It is boarded up now. They closed the main street bridge for repairs and the through traffic stopped. Then COVID hit.

'We were selling 300 pies a week, buying $1000 worth of stuff from the bakery. Then there was the virus.' His voice trails off. It often does.

As we talk, his pet cats climb on the table and nestle into the big man with the salt-and-pepper hair and moustache. They are often his only companions. 'I prefer my own company,' he says.

Cliff Lockwood was just 19 when he left the peace of a tiny town to join the police force. 'I know it sounds funny, but I just wanted to do good. Nineteen was way too young. You don't know anything.'

After graduating, he was sent to Flemington, an area with a steady stream of angry, violent crooks. Lockwood soon developed a reputation as an old-school cop happy to take them on. 'I was taught you should never be frightened of them. You join the police force to stand between the bad and members of the public.'

His then sergeant, John Stubbs, remembers: 'He was a first-class crook catcher, full of enthusiasm. He wasn't much at paperwork. He would lock one up and want to go out and catch another.'

He stuck in that area and eventually became a detective. 'I wish I hadn't. I would have liked to have stayed in uniform. Driving the (divisional) van is an exciting job because you are stopping crime. We pulled a car over in St Kilda and found a girl who had been abducted. We probably saved her life. It is better than being in a suit and coming around the next day when it is too late.'

One of the most successful armed robbery gangs of the time was the Flemington Crew, led by Victor Peirce, Jedd Houghton, Graeme Jensen and Peter David McEvoy. Before each job, the gang had a thief steal two Holdens, one to be used for the armed robbery and the second hidden a few kilometres away as the clean getaway car. Their car thief's name was Gary Abdallah.

On 11 October 1988, Jensen was shot dead by armed robbery squad detectives during an attempted arrest. Just before dawn the next day, Constables Stephen Tynan and Damian Eyre were ambushed and murdered in Walsh Street, South Yarra.

The Flemington Crew were the suspects. (Peirce, McEvoy and two others were charged and acquitted.) The police were lured to Walsh Street to check an abandoned Holden, probably stolen by Abdallah.

Lockwood was tasked to arrest Abdallah for a violent crime that had nothing to do with Walsh Street. In March 1989, a young man was deliberately struck by a car then reversed over in King Street. The driver was Gary Abdallah.

'It was pretty serious,' Lockwood says. 'He wasn't just clipped. There were tyre marks on his body. He was lucky to survive.'

Lockwood says he knew Abdallah but not well. 'I may have charged him, I can't remember. I knew the name and had previous dealings with him. He was an active car thief.

'I have been asked, did I like or dislike him. I never judged any of them, it just didn't matter.'

On Sunday, 9 April 1989, Lockwood and his partner, Senior Detective Dermot Avon, arrested Abdallah and took him to his Drummond Street two-level flat to search for evidence and an accomplice. According to both police, Abdallah grabbed what they believed was a loaded handgun and threatened them.

Lockwood fired his full six shots at Abdallah, then grabbed Avon's gun, who had drawn his weapon but not fired, to discharge a seventh – and fatal – round. The gun found next to the dying suspect was a fake.

Lockwood later told Homicide: 'I saw that he was holding what I believed to be a .357 Magnum revolver . . . I think he was holding it in his right hand and was using his left hand to support it . . . He was bringing the revolver up to the firing position when I first saw it . . .

'I screamed at him: "Drop the gun, drop the fuckin' gun" a couple of times. He screamed: "I'm not doin' nothin", or similar. I just kept screaming at him to drop the fucking gun. I started shooting at him and he kept raising the gun at me. I must have shot six because I took Dermot's gun and shot one from his, I think. The last shot he dropped to the ground. We rolled him over and pushed the gun away. Avon was giving him mouth-to-mouth.'

A neighbour said: 'All the time I heard the bangs the male voice was continually yelling out . . . "Put the fucking thing down".'

So why would a man pull an imitation firearm when all police post-Walsh Street were a touch jumpy?

Abdallah knew he was a Walsh Street suspect and had been told police were planning to murder him. Months earlier, his friend and fellow Walsh Street suspect Jedd Houghton was shot dead by police when they tried to arrest him near Bendigo. Perhaps Abdallah pulled the gun because he thought he, too, was about to be shot. The truth is only he knows.

Lockwood and Avon (who did not fire a shot) were charged with murder. The prosecutors did not allege it was premeditated and the replica was planted. They said while the first six shots could be construed as self-defence, the threat was gone by the time Lockwood grabbed his partner's gun and fired the final bullet. Both men were acquitted.

Lockwood believes there was never enough evidence and they were charged to satisfy media outrage. 'I don't feel any guilt. He brought this upon himself with a stupid action.'

Coroner Hal Hallenstein found that 'Abdallah has contributed to a sequence of events leading to him being fatally shot by picking up and pointing at Lockwood an imitation revolver reasonably believed to be real.'

The rumours persisted that Abdallah was unarmed and the gun was planted. But why? Abdallah, the car thief, had already been interviewed over Walsh Street and was terrified. The taskforce had released him and knew he would be re-arrested for running over the policeman's son in King Street.

The plan was for the taskforce to move in and use the fresh charges as leverage to try and turn him into a prosecution witness against the main Walsh Street offenders. His death was a blow to the taskforce.

The prospect of being sentenced to a large slice of his life in prison changed Lockwood. 'It was time to get out and live my life. I wanted to travel and have as much fun as I could.'

He worked as a locksmith in Melbourne before he and his then wife headed to Darwin, hoping to join the Northern Territory police. She was accepted while he was rejected.

'I rang them before I left to see if there was a problem with my background and they said it wasn't. In hindsight, it was a waste of time. They had no intention of allowing me in.'

Lockwood worked in Darwin, Bali and East Timor in travel, car rental and as a taxi driver. But his reputation followed him. Often, he says, local police would tell others he was the ex-cop acquitted of murder. 'The common thing I get is people saying he bloody well deserved it. That's not what I want to hear.'

Life spiralled out of control for Lockwood. He began taking drugs and in 2009 was arrested for trafficking pseudoephedrine.

He doesn't claim innocence but says he was set up. He says he was taking drugs with a woman in a hotel who persuaded him to deliver the tablets to 'Andy', an undercover police officer.

'I went on a bender with her then she gave me a bag of Sudafed tablets to deliver. It was a stupid thing to do. A momentary lapse in the fog.'

He pleaded guilty and was sentenced to 17 months, serving eight. The once lock 'em up cop found a new perspective by becoming an inmate with local offenders and people smugglers. Prison, he says, was good for him.

'If you take the embarrassment out of it, if I had my time over again, I wouldn't change it. It was a very enlightening time.' He says many inmates need treatment, not punishment. 'There has to be a better way.'

'I used to be a red-necked hater. Now I think most people in jail have made bad decisions. There are very few really bad people.'

Back in Victoria, Lockwood has been diagnosed with PTSD. There is broken sleep, anxiety, depression and lethargy. 'You can't put it aside and stop thinking about it. There is nothing you can do about it. Some police on the ground think I have gone to the dark side. They treat me with suspicion and that bloody hurts. The dark side – imagine that.

'I am still loyal to the cause. I always have been.'

When I caught up with him in 2021, Cliff Lockwood had reached rock bottom and was trying to climb back.

When former colleagues found out about his plight, they reached out, held working days to restore his home and to reconnect with him.

In February 2024, he died alone in his mother's shop that had become his home.

Jon Hargest / Newspix

Helen and John Magill. There was no justice for their murdered daughter Jane Thurgood-Dove.

AAP Image / Supplied by Victoria Police

Kaera Douglas

Above: Kaera Douglas was shot by her boyfriend and then judged by strangers.

Left: Ju 'Kelly' Zhang. Police wouldn't rest until they found her body.

Victoria Police

Walsh Street victims Damian Eyre and Stephen Tynan.

Victoria Police

Murderer Sven Lindemann and his victim Monique Lezsak.

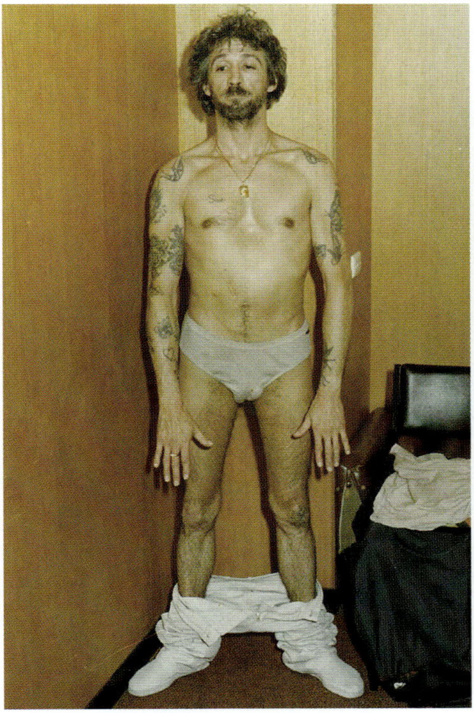

Hitman Rod Collins.

Bodybuilder Gary Lewer: happier days.

Trevor Pinder / Newspix

Judy Moran arrives at the Supreme Court in Melbourne.

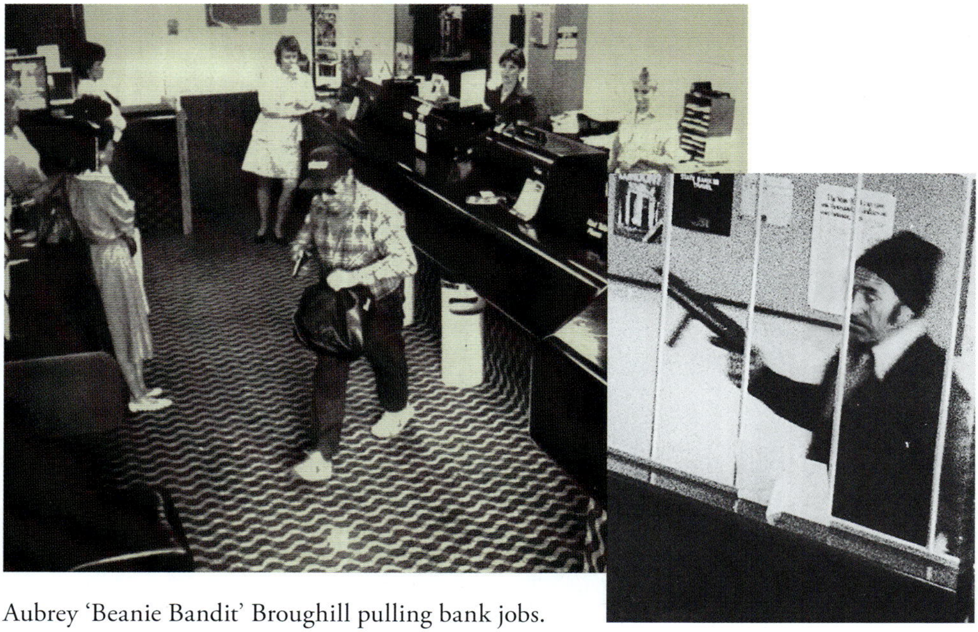

Victoria Police

Victoria Police

Aubrey 'Beanie Bandit' Broughill pulling bank jobs.

Victoria Police

Victoria Police

Hells Angels raids at Greenslopes.

Hells Angels hitman
James 'Jim Jim' Brandes.

Victoria Police

SOG ram robbers at Melbourne Airport.

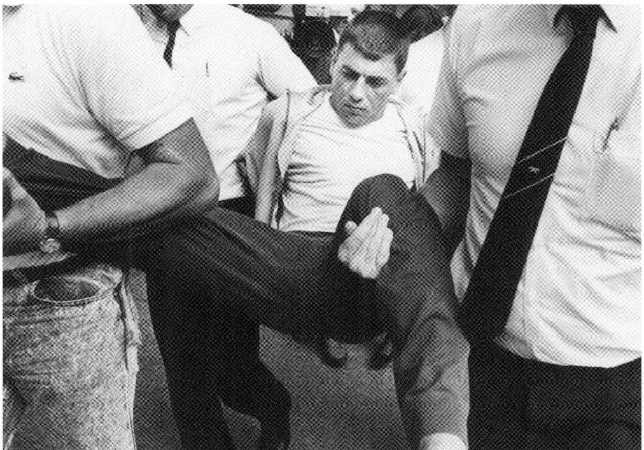

News Ltd / Newspix

Victor Peirce, one of four men
charged with the Walsh Street
murders, dragged to court.

The Age

Notorious criminal Dennis Allen points a gun at his mother, Kath Pettingill, during a party in Richmond.

The Age

Russell 'Mad Dog' Cox (centre) is arrested by police following his escape from prison.

The Age

Ex-policeman Cliff Lockwood.

Kerley Family

Left: Michelle Kerley's police graduation photo. She turned crooks into informers but at what price?

Below: *Underbelly* actor Caroline Craig (left) with Michelle Kerley. Craig's dramatic character was based on Michelle.

Kerley Family

Jimi Kelly

Positive vibes: AFP cop Jimi Kelly with wife Emma.

Paul Maher

Victoria Police detective Paul Maher with Sir Don Bradman.

AFP

Georgia the AFP hi-tech dog.

'CYBER COP' STAKES OUT DARK FRONTIER

The O'Loughlin clan is the greatest tribe in the Victoria Police, with 18 of the family joining the force. For years, it looked like Darren was going to be the odd one out.

Bootmaker Albert O'Loughlin and his wife, Sylvie, had eight children, with all five boys – Barry, Neil, Robert, Geoff and Doug – joining the force. Barry, an Armed Robbery detective sergeant, died in a car accident in 1972. Robert, Geoff and Doug became superintendents and Neil retired as deputy commissioner.

Robert and his wife, Shirley – also a police officer – believed their son, Darren, would take another route (unlike his brother and sister). His marks at school were not promising; like many, when a subject didn't interest him, he shut down.

At the age of 15 he turned up for work at Frankston's Hades Hot Bread Kitchen, with his shifts starting at either midnight or 2 am. Welcome to the workforce.

Darren didn't know it, but he was about to receive unique police training when his father won an eight-month scholarship to study hostage negotiation and counterterrorism. In 1978 the family went with Robert to Singapore, Hong Kong, Thailand, Greece, Italy, West Germany, Holland, Britain, Ireland, Canada, Fiji and the United States. Young Darren was taken on police ride-alongs and scuba-dived with police diving teams. (He absorbed the intricacies of physics needed for diving, proving he could absorb what mattered to him.)

Back in Melbourne, he started an apprenticeship as a fitter and turner before deciding a stint of hard study would beat a life of hard factory work. With the help of his girlfriend, he spent two years studying to pass the police entrance exam. 'Spelling was my big weakness,' he says.

In late 1983, he arrived at the Police Academy that had become a second home to the O'Loughlins.

Soon he was working in the melting pot of St Kilda, learning to develop a rapport with victims and criminals. During a stint working with the National Crime Authority, he was seconded to work on the 1988 Walsh Street murders. Less than six weeks later, O'Loughlin identified one of the suspects, Jedd Houghton, inside a Bendigo pub. A few days later, the heavily armed Houghton was shot dead in a Bendigo caravan park by the Special Operations Group. The head of the SOG at the time was one of Darren's uncles.

Darren transferred to his home patch of Frankston as a detective and had a lucky escape when he managed to roll a police car on the Nepean Highway. In hospital, he stood up to head to the toilet when a nurse ordered him to stop moving, informing him he had a broken neck. For seven weeks he lay in a bed with his head tilted back so far, they mounted a television upside down for him to watch. Eventually, a piece of his hip was used to realign his spine.

Working as a detective in Frankston was both 'good and bad', he says. The good was that as a local boy, he knew where to find the crooks. The bad was that as a local boy, he knew some of the crooks.

One was a mechanic he charged with handling stolen car parts. Despite being guilty, the mechanic felt it was a breach of some unwritten code to be arrested by a fellow local lad and vowed revenge. 'He wanted to take me out,' Darren recalls.

One night Darren saw he was being followed and – thinking they were traffic cops looking to pinch a local detective – he gunned the car to lose them. Turned out it was the manic mechanic, who was later charged with firearm-related offences.

One shift Darren was hoping for a quiet one so he could leave the office on time and head home for his son's second birthday. That is until he got the call that a protective services officer had stolen a gun from the office and was threatening to kill his girlfriend.

Darren and fellow detective Peter Sterling strapped on their bulletproof vests and drove off to Beach Street, Frankston.

'We heard this guy was jumping neighbourhood fences and trying to escape. We got out of the car and I went up the driveway of the house.'

When he spotted the offender, O'Loughlin pulled his gun and told the man to put his hands in the air. For a moment it looked like he was thinking of complying, before slipping his hands behind his back and producing the stolen gun.

The offender put the gun to his own head. Darren kept his pointed at the clearly disturbed man's chest. When another policeman opened the side gate, the offender trained his revolver on the second cop. Although he would have been justified in taking a shot, O'Loughlin yelled at the man to regain his attention.

For five hours the two sat facing each other, both with guns cocked and fingers on the trigger. After hours of talk, they agreed to remove their trigger fingers. It was a tiny but important victory.

Darren told the man it was his son's birthday, and it wouldn't 'be very pleasant if [the offender] blew his head off or hurt me'.

Finally, the police managed to get him a phone connected to a negotiator. The advice was more practical than psychological. 'Whatever you do, don't lean right.' An SOG sniper was in position with a clear shot, unless O'Loughlin moved. He didn't. The thought of a bullet in the back of the head does wonders for one's posture.

Finally, a police dog distracted the man, allowing an SOG officer to jump the fence and crack him over the head with a shotgun.

Darren knew the way Frankston changed when, in just seven weeks in 1993, a serial killer murdered three women: Debbie Fream, Elizabeth Stevens and Natalie Russell.

The city was in lockdown, shopkeepers escorted women to their cars and police knew the killings would continue until the offender was caught.

O'Loughlin was conducting some door-to-door checks when some of his colleagues in an unmarked car screamed to a halt and told him to get in. They were to support Homicide who were heading off to check out another suspect – Paul Charles Denyer.

Within a few minutes of meeting Denyer, lead investigator Rod Wilson had a gut feeling he was the one. 'He was just a little too co-operative.'

It should have been the end for Darren, but he was told to hop in the Homicide unit to escort Denyer back to the station. At this point, he was just to be a body in the room.

O'Loughlin, a practising Christian, stood silently praying for the truth to be found.

Denyer looked at him and said: 'That man is trying to get into my head.'

He said the expression on Denyer's face was darkly distorted. 'I saw the evil those girls must have seen.'

It turned out O'Loughlin and Denyer had been seen by the same minister, who had sensed the evil in the serial stalker, kicking him out of the church and describing him as a wolf in sheep's clothing.

When Wilson finally trapped Denyer during questioning, it was during a break the killer saw Darren's crucifix and said: 'I see you are wearing a cross under your shirt. Are you a Christian?'

Senior Detective O'Loughlin said he was, and Denyer said: 'OK, I killed them, all three of them.' O'Loughlin then became part of the interviewing team as Denyer enthusiastically confessed.

At the end, a senior officer remembers seeing him sitting in the office, blankly looking out of the window. 'He looked pretty shattered.'

Back in the mid-1990s, Darren started to show an interest in home computers just as police were taking their first baby steps into the world of e-crime. He was recruited to the Computer Crime Squad, set up in a tiny area inside the Crime Department's St Kilda Road building.

Long before the Dark Web, there were chat rooms, and soon O'Loughlin and the team identified a paedophile ring who thought they were communicating in secret. One was a self-declared wizard who bragged he could provide children. The squad established a false identity to infiltrate the group. 'We were able to place an order for minors to be delivered,' says Darren.

The drop-off point was nominated as the Shrine of Remembrance, for two reasons: it was an open area where 'the wizard' would be unable to hide and 'we were pretty lazy, and it was across the road from the office'.

Then there was a sliding-door moment. O'Loughlin sat the sergeant's exam, receiving an impressive 85 per cent pass, but as there was a glut of candidates that year, the promotion bar was set at 86.

Miffed by the arbitrary decision, he resigned, moving into the world of cybersecurity, first for accounting firm Ernst & Young. Soon he was studying ethical hacking in New York, returning as a qualified trainer in the dark arts. He was ahead of his time.

In 2021, the Crime Department boosted the Cyber Crime Division in response to the largest growth area in organised crime.

'We are thinking of running Hackathons,' says Commander Mick Frewen. The aim is to hire the best hackers to defend systems against local and international cyber-extortionists.

Police have asked for nearly 50 legislative amendments to help them deal with a new class of crime.

When Darren was employed by one of the big four banks, one of the general managers challenged the security team to try and crack his password. Within hours, they sent a message with it. As the general manager was writing a note of congratulations, O'Loughlin took over his computer to write that his team was inside the system watching what he did. 'We were perched on his shoulder while he worked.'

Now the chief information security officer for the digital giant NTT, Darren protects the company and clients from the ever-present threat of cyberattacks, an area of crime he says is 'enormously underestimated'.

'There are two reasons for the attacks; to make ransom demands or to steal intellectual property. It is state-funded espionage.'

THE MYSTERY BEHIND A LOST GIRL

Rarely can we pinpoint a time when our world changed, but on 12 January 1976, when a little girl was stolen from her Melbourne home, it altered for the worse.

Eloise Worledge, 8, was taken from a bedroom in her family's Beaumaris home and was never seen again. From that day on, parents locked the back door and kids were no longer encouraged to roam on their bikes until dinner time.

We look back and think it was the time when we lost our innocence. Turns out, we weren't looking in the right places. Just two streets away from Eloise's four-bedroom family home was her school, Beaumaris Primary. Her parents could not know they were sending her to a place that kept dark secrets for decades.

During the 1960s and 70s, four paedophile teachers – Gary Arthur Mitchell, Grahame Harold Steele, David Ernest Keith MacGregor and Darrell Ray – molested between 50 and 100 students, a fact unknown to the Eloise Worledge investigators.

Police looked at 10 suspect categories: sex offenders in Melbourne's south-east, sex offenders within Australia involved in child abductions or who broke into houses, known local prowlers, local service providers, babysitters, tradesmen, door-to-door salesmen, government agencies with contact with the Worledges, and staff and parents at Beaumaris Primary School.

Senior staff were told of allegations against two of the teachers, but the concerns were not passed on to police. If they had, the investigation would have taken an entirely different course.

That no teacher was ever a suspect is backed up in the 2001 police review of the Worledge case: '[The original detectives] were unsuccessful in uncovering any evidence or creating new leads that could assist the investigation.'

If police had known her school was riddled with child molesters, they would have been on the shortlist of suspects.

In 1976, Eloise was about to enter Year 3. MacGregor was a Year 3 sports and guitar teacher, placing him in contact with a wide range of students. He left the school at the end of 1976 – the year Eloise disappeared. This, of course, does not mean he was involved in any way, only that important information was concealed from police.

What happened at Beaumaris Primary is now central to an inquiry, headed by Kathleen Foley SC, and while it is not a criminal probe, perhaps some of the witnesses might know if Eloise was in any way connected with the teachers.

A local resident told us a friend of Eloise's had said the missing girl confided to her there was a teacher 'who was creeping her out'.

Brian was a student at the school at the time, and a friend of Eloise:

> David MacGregor, my grade three teacher. I remember him being quite a good teacher but that he was a disciplinarian. I was usually a pretty good kid who, to this day, is a bit of a rule follower, but I remember one day getting in trouble and being whacked on the bottom by him with a timber metre ruler that he kept near his desk.

I also remember him being quite open to the kids in class that he was a nudist – a very strange and inappropriate thing to say to a group of eight- and nine-year-olds.

I was also a good friend of Eloise Worledge. I was eight at the time when Eloise went missing, and it still is a very upsetting part of my childhood.

My sister and I used to grab onto the frame of our beds at night and make sure that our bedroom windows were shut even on hot summer nights because we were so frightened that we would be abducted like we thought Eloise had been. I remember having play dates at her house and dancing to songs in her side yard. She was a happy, trusting, kind and gregarious kid.

The school administration building burnt down around 1996, I think, so I imagine there's not too many old records. I always thought that fire was odd at the time and have wondered if it was arson to destroy records and potential evidence, or a fire started by a victim in anger.

Given what happened with the teachers who have been named, I wonder if there is a connection to Eloise's disappearance. Was she abused by one of these child abusers, did she see something at school or somewhere else, did something happen to her brother, Blake, and did she stand up for him? That's all speculation and, unfortunately, we can't ask Blake because he died around 1997 in a tragic road accident.

So what do we know of the case?

Eloise was the eldest of three with a sister, Anna, and a brother, Blake, to Patsy and Lindsay Worledge. Bright and creative, she was becoming more outgoing through Brownies.

Behind closed doors, her family was falling apart. Patsy was outgoing and popular while Lindsay was razor sharp with a tongue to match. 'He was often described as thinking of himself as intellectually superior,' a 2001 police review concluded.

Four months before the abduction, Patsy had asked for a separation. Lindsay agreed to leave by his wife's 33rd birthday on 10 January – two days before Eloise disappeared. He reneged on the deal, adding to the tension. The parents had told the children their father was preparing to move out.

On Monday, 12 January, Lindsay had a speaking engagement, went to lunch, returned briefly to work and, as it was a summer break, headed to the pub, where he shared a carafe of wine and a jug of beer with colleagues.

He went home and played Monopoly with the children then returned to drinking, polishing off a couple of scotches, a bottle of wine with dinner and then sat drinking port until he fell asleep in front of the television.

When Patsy came home from her jazz ballet class, the flywire door was unlocked. A police report found 'the front door was unlocked and wide open. It was not an overly hot night'.

Patsy told detectives that the passage light was left on for the children, then switched off by the last parent to bed. On this night, police found that 'Lindsay Worledge did not turn off the passageway light.' At 4.45 am, Patsy left her bedroom to go to the bathroom and noticed the passage light was off, leading police to believe Eloise was grabbed in the early hours.

At 2 am, Daphne Owen-Smith from 66 Scott Street (150 metres from the Worledges) heard the cry of a child and the sound of a car door slamming. Another neighbour heard a car door slam around the same time.

Eloise's window was open, the flywire cut and rolled up from the inside. It was a wind-out window, opening 38 centimetres, which meant it would be difficult for an adult to clamber out from the inside.

Police dismissed the theory that an opportunistic child molester walked into a strange house, grabbed Eloise, spent time setting the scene as if the victim were grabbed through the open window, then walked past sleeping parents to escape. Police concluded: 'On balance, based on all the information on-hand, it appeared more likely that the person or persons responsible for Eloise Worledge's disappearance had effected their entry and exit through a point other than her bedroom window.'

Original investigator, Detective Senior Sergeant Jan Lierse, told me: 'I believe she was taken out the front door, which had been left unlocked.'

Detectives believed it was someone the child knew. Soon the main suspect was Lindsay Worledge, with the theory he wanted to punish Patsy for ending their marriage. While Patsy grieved publicly, Lindsay appeared cold and aloof. But if we learnt anything from the disastrous case of baby Azaria Chamberlain (taken by a dingo in 1980) – where her mother, the sometimes expressionless Lindy, was blamed and wrongly convicted of murder – people mourn in different ways.

Within days, Lindsay Worledge was interviewed as a suspect. More than 20 years later, he agreed to a lie-detector test that proved inconclusive.

More than 25 years after Eloise disappeared, a police review found: 'At the conclusion of investigations into Lindsay Worledge, no evidence in regard to his involvement has been uncovered.'

Lindsay died in 2017 and Patsy in 2022, neither knowing the truth.

There are many things we don't know. But what we do know is that if the authorities at the school had passed on concerns about the behaviour of some of the teachers at Eloise's school, the investigators would have asked: was the little girl ever in their classes? Had any of the teachers been to the Worledge home? Could a trusting kid have been lured into the night by an authority figure such as a teacher?

They would have checked if Patsy Worledge and David MacGregor met when they were studying together at teachers' college and whether there had been any ongoing social interactions that would have put the child molester in contact with the Worledge family out of school hours.

Back then, it would have been a hot tip. Now, there is nothing left but a cold trail.

HE WAS A SMART CRIM, BUT NOT AS SMART AS THE COPS STALKING HIM

When the handcuffed international drug courier landed at the police lock-up just before lunch, he quietly mentioned he was a vegetarian and politely requested two poached eggs with a 'little bit of salt and pepper'.

The response was swift and to the point; he received a clip to the back of the head and was told he could 'have a pie like everybody else'. Welcome to Australia, son, and have a nice day.

It was January 1982 and a simpler world.

For decades, the major crooks in town were armed robbers and dock workers well known to police. They committed crimes with their mates, married suburban sweethearts and drank in the same pubs as their fathers. But by the late 1970s, drugs began to change the criminal landscape and a new breed, lured by unimagined wealth, began to set up syndicates with international connections.

Traditional police methods of talking to informers and looking for signs of affluence among established crooks no longer worked. Detectives took years to catch up, resisting change and refusing to look beyond the usual suspects in their own backyard. Petty bickering meant policing agencies rarely worked together and half-smart crooks easily picked holes in the law enforcement fabric.

Chief Commissioner Mick Miller knew these old tactics were obsolete and set up the Bureau of Criminal Intelligence to tackle modern crimes with modern methods. The BCI soon discovered a new syndicate whose key figures were straight out of a pulp thriller. They included the Chiang Mai vegetarian; a counter-surveillance expert with virtually limitless access to near-pure heroin; the champion pole-vaulter hopelessly in love with his South American girlfriend; the beautiful daughter of a society family; and the rogue former private schoolboy codenamed 'M'.

The BCI chief knew such a syndicate was beyond the resources of one police force and proposed a unique alliance of state and federal agencies. 'I can recommend only one course of action and that is to set up a national strike force, whose charter would be to gather evidence relating to this suspected organisation. The law of conspiracy may be the most convenient. The officer in charge of the strike force should be given discretionary powers to dispatch his personnel anywhere in the world.'

As a result, a taskforce of Victorian detectives, Australian Federal Police and customs agents was established. It would be known as Operation Aries and become the template for investigating sophisticated drug syndicates.

This confidential briefing paper remained just that for more than 20 years until it was unearthed by your correspondent while sorting through the desk drawer of a man who had died just weeks earlier. His name was Fred Silvester and he was then the head of BCI. And he was your correspondent's father.

The main target, M, was David McMillan, an English-born chancer with an eye for pretty women and easy money. He came to police notice after he imported an obscenely expensive American roadster and police inquiries found he had nine identities, a series of safe houses in Melbourne, Bangkok, London, Hong Kong and Brussels, and made

11 overseas trips in one year. He appeared to be succeeding in business without really trying.

Police found he had a list of 43 women from Melbourne, Sydney and London he used as couriers, 38 birth certificates and 27 passports under false names.

Some of the women didn't know they were being used as mules. Others did. The syndicate would buy cheap china souvenirs, place them on top inside the luggage and smash them. The women were instructed that, if their bags were selected for a search at airports, to cry when the luggage was opened seeing the broken 'precious' artefacts.

What made McMillan a near overnight success was his addiction to risks and his sharp mind. And it was this combination that always brought him crashing down, first leading to his expulsion from Caulfield Grammar, when he tried to manufacture LSD in the school lab, and then to long and repeated prison sentences.

McMillan (who was living with the beautiful Clelia Vigano, a member of the famous Vigano restaurant family) was smart and knew it. That was his problem. Even when he found he was the target of a massive police operation, the gambler couldn't walk away.

'If I'd listened to any of my lawyers, I might not have kept going. The stress, expense and danger of operating under the eye and electronic ears of Operation Aries were too great. But instead of changing my ways, I just pretended to,' he wrote in his book *McVillain: The Man Who Got Away*.

(Disclaimer: Your correspondent was so impressed with the initial manuscript, he invested in its publication. This can be justified on only two grounds: public interest and private greed.)

Speaking from his London home, McMillan reflected that it was part arrogance and part curiosity that led him into an obsessive game of cat-and-mouse with Aries.

He knew he was hot when he heard surveillance units on his police scanner talking about following a car as it backed out of the drive just as he was doing the same thing. His suspicions were confirmed when a travel agent told him police were asking questions about a list of clients, including many of McMillan's carefully crafted aliases.

'I just thought, to hell with it, let's see where this goes.' The answer would be a long prison sentence.

McMillan says at 21, he was broke and virtually homeless. Three years later, he often would have around $1.5 million in cash. But a series of spectacularly bad business ventures and a series of failed criminal ones smashed his nest egg.

He was persuaded to invest in cannabis production, where you need people prepared to do the grunt work and a property to sustain the crop. His partners failed on both counts. 'The spartan life was not for them. It would appear they felt their first job was to go to their tailors.' Then there was the property. 'The only thing you could grow there was mould in the bathroom.'

Meanwhile, Aries, led by Detective Superintendent Jimmy Williams, was closing in.

According to Victorian detective Neale Fursdon, who worked on the syndicate's Thai connection, Supahaus Chowdury, the taskforce entered the arrest phase expecting to catch the main players in the act. Chowdury was an anti-surveillance expert and police followed him across the country as he took planes and public transport from Perth to Sydney, then to Canberra before taking a bus to Melbourne.

Even though McMillan knew he should stop, greed destroyed all sense and on 5 December 1981, he met Chowdury, who was carrying two cutlery boxes containing heroin.

For police, the deal went like clockwork. A surveillance member watched the exchange in a lane at the Mercy Hospital and called in the arrest team. But he was in a black spot and his radio message went unanswered. The suspects escaped.

McMillan would later brag he picked the location because he

knew it was a dead spot. Police say it was dumb luck rather than smart planning.

In January 1982, Aries arrested McMillan, Clelia Vigano, former champion pole-vaulter Michael Sullivan, his girlfriend Mary Escolar Castillo, Chowdury and several others.

Sullivan asked for a pole to train in jail. The request was refused.

A month later, Vigano and Castillo died in a deliberately lit fire at Fairlea Women's Prison.

Then there was the mandatory elaborate escape plot. The plan was to land a helicopter inside Pentridge, grab McMillan, Sullivan and Chowdury, then use a Kings Cross make-up artist to disguise them before flying to the Philippines, while keeping an ocean-going yacht as a second escape option.

An ocean-going yacht used to ferret away drug suspects? Surely not. Yet it proved to be true and a former British soldier was convicted over the conspiracy.

(An aside: the police took rooms in the hotel next to the soldier and, while keeping him under surveillance, managed to steal a large number of mini spirit bottles from the room service trolleys.)

The prosecution became Victoria's first super-trial. It sat for 100 days, the Crown called 175 witnesses and the transcript ran for 8000 pages. The jury deliberated for a record eight days and became so chummy they went on a picnic together.

According to McMillan, a jury member had applied to be a policewoman and the trial was adjourned while she sat an entrance exam. 'I am sure she was not biased,' he observes with such irony you could hear the rust.

McMillan, Sullivan and Chowdury beat all but one charge, but were convicted of conspiracy and sentenced to 15 years each.

McMillan went in aged 26 and was released when he was 37. Chowdury became a jail pastry cook and then returned to Thailand. Sullivan never recovered from the death of his girlfriend. 'His love of life was gone,' McMillan says.

A few years after he was freed, Sullivan died from leukaemia.

When McMillan was released, he found himself under police surveillance but soon slipped back into his old ways. However, the world had changed, even if he hadn't.

In late 1993, he was arrested in Thailand carrying drugs and faced execution or a sentence of 99 years. Three years later, he became the first person to escape from the notorious Bangkok Hilton – Klong Prem Prison. A further stint in a Pakistan jail showed that while McMillan was clever, he remained a slow learner.

Now in his 50s, he has decided that writing about crime is much easier than committing it.

Ain't that the truth.

THE MENTAL TOLL OF THE ROAD TOLL

Peter Bellion has saved the lives of hundreds he has never met and observed the death of thousands he couldn't help. Perhaps that is why he fought the signs the job he loved was eating him alive.

For more than 20 years, he was a crash scene investigator and reconstruction expert for the Major Collision Investigation Group, which means he has seen more violent death than just about anyone in Australia.

He retired at 51, battling chronic PTSD, having made the mistake of sacrificing his mental health for what he saw as his professional duty.

Every year he investigated about 100 fatal crashes, reconstructing what went wrong. It was a science but not an academic exercise in speed, force, impact, mechanical failure and driver error.

He saw their broken bodies, heard their relatives' cries, filled his lungs with the smell of death and was cross-examined by lawyers who slept soundly in their homes while Bellion was sifting through the carnage.

Yet his first fatality was almost gentle in comparison. As a young constable, Bellion went to a Cheltenham accident where a Ford ute had slammed into a smaller sedan driven by an elderly man. 'He had a grazed head and I talked to him thinking he wasn't too bad. I was shocked to find he died in hospital.'

It was the first of more than 2000 cases where he saw first-hand the frailty of human life.

It was during his civil engineering studies at Caulfield Institute of Technology that he found there was a chronic lack of speed data in fatal collisions. It became a career passion to use education and enforcement to lower speeds and he was one of the driving forces in the effective Transport Accident Commission (TAC) 'Wipe Off 5' campaign.

When he joined road policing, the annual toll was about 700. When he finished it was about 250. Yes he made a difference, but at what cost?

Like all recruits, Bellion received a grounding in general policing and was three weeks out of the academy when a house burglar pulled a shotgun on him.

He managed to arrest the offender without shots being fired. Not much later, a bikie tried to pull a knife, only to be stopped when the young cop proved to be quicker, handcuffing his wrist before he freed the blade.

By 1988 he moved to Traffic Operations, then to a career combining his policing and engineering skills as an accident investigator. And there lies the problem. Too good to lose and too valuable to move, he spent decades staring at horrors the rest of us would instinctively turn from. He should have stopped but Bellion ignored the signs that his immersion in tragedy was seeping into his bones.

He talks with a steady voice and red eyes. It is an effort but, as always, he doesn't take the easy road, hoping his story will help other emergency service workers put up their hands.

'It is a prick of a condition,' he says.

When Bellion first suffered PTSD, the tragedy is he was not protected from himself. He returned to the same work environment until his condition became chronic, which will now have to be managed for the rest of his life.

His former boss, retired Inspector Bernie Rankin, says: 'Peter is an absolute champion and an acknowledged world expert. He has paid a terrible cost for his dedication and there is no doubt we should have done better by him.'

So how much is too much?

In March 2007 he went into the Burnley Tunnel after a pile-up and subsequent fireball melted cars and left three dead. It was the eighth birthday of one of his daughters.

After 16 hours immersed in this cocoon of death, he took a call at work. It was from a relative of one of the victims looking for a sliver of hope. Although DNA would be needed for official identification, Peter already knew there was none.

Within three months he was at the Kerang rail disaster, where a truck hit a train, killing 11 people. When he returned home, he glanced at the television to see two of the victims, young girls in their school uniforms, just like his primary school-aged daughters. 'I just broke down and had to walk out.'

Then taking his son to school, he followed the usual routine of stopping for coffee (hot for him, iced for his son).

'I looked down and there on the front page of *The Age* was a picture of one of the boys (from Kerang). He was a young footballer, just like my son.'

All of a sudden, he found himself confronted by uncontrollable shakes. He later discovered his body was releasing massive doses of adrenaline in response to his stress. It was then he rang his senior sergeant to say: 'I'm not right, I need a bit of space.'

One of his releases was his love of golf, but he knew he was in trouble when, while walking the 13th fairway, he burst into tears. Even then he went home, showered and went to work, where he suffered 'a bit of a meltdown'.

He took months off only to return to a series of tough court hearings. Always fit, he found exercise helped to combat his stress until he went overboard. On holidays, if he woke up with the sweats at

2 am, he would 'smash out hundreds of push-ups' and, before a shift, he might ride 40 kilometres on his bike at 3 am.

To give him some relief, then Traffic Assistant Commissioner Ken Lay brought him to work on some long-term projects. But policing has changed. Once there were safe harbour positions where stressed police could work away from the trauma of operational duties but these jobs are now done by civilians.

Now police are either put on sick leave or sent on the road. Bellion applied for senior sergeant general duties positions but eventually returned to what he knew.

His first job back was a quadruple fatal in Hallam. 'Welcome back' was all he could think.

The symptoms returned and became progressively worse, such as a stubborn rash, night sweats, panic attacks, racing pulse, flashbacks, anger and suicidal thoughts. Then it truly unravelled not at a crash scene but a 2014 court case.

The driver was ice-affected, the case should have been straightforward and the barrister's only tactic was to attack the expert witness. It was Friday and the lawyer said he would have just a few questions for Monday.

'It had been deliberately dragged out and I think he just wanted me to sweat for the weekend. I thought: "Really, do we have to do this?"'

'The judge asked if it was OK with me, and I said: "Nup."' He then began to sob and the court was adjourned.

He spent the weekend expecting to return to court on the Monday to give evidence. 'I woke up and rang the boss and said: "I'm stuffed, I can't do this anymore."'

'It was as if a dam wall had broken and all the incidents flooded back day and night.'

When he closed his eyes, about to lift weights in his backyard, the crash scenes and the bodies returned in his version of 'the top hundred hits'.

'It was just flash, flash, flash.'

Bellion has retired after nearly 30 years of service, with 26 years investigating car crashes.

PTSD sufferers are taught to recognise and avoid stress triggers, which will always be a battle for Bellion. The family home has been gutted and rebuilt so there are few reminders of the calls he took to head out on the road.

But the triggers are everywhere. The sound of a police helicopter can bring on violent shaking, for it would hover overhead while he sifted through death scenes.

He has investigated deadly crashes on most of Melbourne's main roads and Victorian highways, which means when he travels anywhere, there are deadly reminders. If the shakes hit, he will pull over, which means a 30-minute trip may take 90 minutes.

While PTSD has damaged his memory and concentration, he can recite the location, make, model, colour and speed of vehicles involved in his investigations.

Some sufferers battle alone but Peter's wife, Michelle, three children, friends and former colleagues are there for him.

Another of his great supporters was his father, Mervin, who died at home on 7 December 2014. At the end he was there for his father as his father had been for him. 'I helped put him in the body bag and zipped it up. I thought that is the last time I will ever be doing that.'

And he has found an unexpected ally – a young black lab he is training as a guide dog.

Although not an assistance dog, Laurenz has learnt to pick up the signs of stress. 'If we are out walking, he can sense my breathing changes and he will nudge against my legs as if to say that was then and this is now,' Bellion says.

THREE SECRETS OF POLICE SNEAKINESS

I'm not sure I agree with the Oxford dons who define the word sneaky as 'behaving in a secret and sometimes dishonest or unpleasant way'. Some of the best cops I know are sneaky with a capital S.

This doesn't mean they are bent, or bash artists. It means they are smart enough to use tactics that aren't taught in the Police Academy to catch crooks.

We were reminded of this when reading an excellent article by Ed Caesar in *The New Yorker* (yes, we read more than *Bacon Busters* magazine and old Hawthorn footy records) on the history of police eavesdropping on criminals.

Caesar tells us that way back in 1895, a New York cop who once worked for a phone company suggested putting in an extra circuit, known as a wiretap. For 20 years, police secretly listened to whomever they pleased.

When it was exposed and there was outrage, Commissioner Arthur Woods said: 'You can't always do detective work in a high hat and kid gloves.'

Perhaps the extreme version of this is the Sean Connery cop

character, Jim Malone, in *The Untouchables*. 'You wanna know how to get Capone? They pull a knife, you pull a gun. He sends one of yours to the hospital, you send one of his to the morgue.'

While the world has changed since the days of Al Capone, in the police world there remain the Three Ss of Sneakiness: Surveillance (electronic and physical), Snitches (informers) and Spies (undercover cops).

Surveillance

Back in the 1950s, when senior constable and later chief commissioner Mick Miller wanted illegal gambling venues observed, his squad came up with several original tactics. They once dressed as abattoir workers carrying bins of offal next to an SP headquarters in western Melbourne. On another occasion, one stood alone in a suit carrying flowers near a Spring Street target, pretending to be waiting for a date. When the girl didn't show, he sadly placed the flowers in the bin but was able to report on the movements in and out of the building for a later raid.

When Deputy Prime Minister Jim Cairns was a Victorian policeman (the first with a tertiary degree), he was assigned to follow people the chief commissioner didn't like, including reporters. In November 1936, he was in a shootout with murderer and armed bandit Bill Cody. Gentleman Jim, an avowed pacifist, got his man without putting a bullet in him.

A few years ago, as part of a super-secret Australian Federal Police operation, they followed a would-be hitman on the way to a job, ready to grab him before he pulled the trigger. The crook had an anonymous-looking older sedan for the job – too old, as it turned out, as it broke down not once but twice on the way, meaning he missed his moment.

In the early 1980s, there was a series of small explosions at the homes of crooks recently acquitted in courts, with some witnesses identifying a yellow Ford Cortina in the vicinity. In a strange coincidence, the surveillance branch was using a similar vehicle, which means, of course, some mad bomber must have had an identical car (cough, cough).

When the tales of corruption in NSW were getting to mammoth proportions, Victoria Police slipped over the border to confirm a few things. The information on-hand was that crime boss Abe 'Mr Sin' Saffron was paying $750 per club to local police and $5000 a week to senior police. This was only a slice of the protection racket, with Deputy Commissioner Bill Allen in charge of the purse. Allen was as rotten as (vegans, look away) a chop.

The mail was that once a week, Allen would leave headquarters and head to Parliament House to divvy up the takings. Sure enough, as Victoria Police watched, Bill left right on time and headed up Macquarie Street to feed the crooks.

While physical surveillance remains a key component of investigations, the electronic version is all the rage now.

Think of the massive An0m sting that allowed the Australian Federal Police and international partners to download 27 million messages from crooks who thought they were using a safe app.

There was a time when police illegally bugged telephones. NSW cops were the best, running a truckload on crooks that discovered corrupt relationships with politicians, lawyers and judges. They were eventually published as *The Age* Tapes. Federal police had their own tapes and, after a hastily organised barbecue in Sydney, sent the tapes and transcripts to the bottom of the harbour, leaving the secrets to sleep with the fishes.

Victoria had a smaller unit, known to a handful as the Broom Closet. The information from the tapes was laundered to appear as if it came from informers. The Closet was shut once senior police learnt of its existence.

Many years later, police would drop stories in the media to excite phone chatter from crooks. When we wrote a story relating to a particular drug dealer, a police officer rang to say the suspect must be a Naked City fan.

That Saturday morning, a homeless person tried to sell the dealer's phone to a St Kilda pawn shop. Apparently, on reading the column, the target had thrown it in a bush.

One crook only ever talked while walking his dog, so police bugged the pet's collar. The subsequent tape contained grunts and the odd bark.

Snitches

Crooks are sometimes made offers too good to refuse to become secret informers. Brian Latch, known as Mr X, was an informer in the 1960s. When a respected journalist ghosted his book, Latch dobbed him into the tax department for working an extra (unclaimed) shift at a newspaper.

A hitman who worked for now deceased drug dealer Carl Williams was turned because Williams had short-changed him and expected the killer to plead guilty. When Williams was asked to look after the hitman's elderly mother, he sent her a paltry $1500. The hitman made statements to police and forced Williams to plead guilty to multiple murders. In 2010, Williams' own plans to snitch hit a hitch when he was murdered with the stem of an exercise bike seat in Barwon Prison.

When well-known NSW armed robber Raymond John Denning was arrested at the Doncaster Shoppingtown about to pull a job, he decided to change sides and become an informer. At one hearing, an unimpressed ex-colleague threw a large bone on the ground, saying: 'There's your lunch, you dog.'

He died of a drug overdose six weeks after his prison release that was almost certainly a hotshot.

One of the most successful snitches was a professional musician who was a trusted insider in Tony Mokbel's drug empire. He not only provided information to police but bugged phones of the syndicate leaders, eventually sucking the guts out of the ring's computer, providing police with rock-hard evidence of drug transactions.

Rumour has it he received a $1 million reward and was relocated with a new identity and now, in all probability, is playing the saxophone on a cruise ship.

Spies

To be an undercover cop, you have to be prepared to be hated. Crooks see it as the ultimate betrayal: you befriend them before turning them in.

Probably Victoria's first undercover cop was Nick Cecil, who would strum his guitar in pubs in the 1950s. But while he sang, he would identify the local SP bookmakers and then place bets with marked notes used later to prove the case.

In Mildura, the squad had one of their detectives, a handy centre half forward, sign up with a local side. After a month of near best-on-ground performances, the cops arrived to lock up the SPs on the information he provided. The cop may have been the best but not necessarily the fairest.

Young Queensland Police recruit Keith Banks was plucked with little training to go undercover gathering evidence on drug traffickers. 'Being undercover is like being an informer: you get close to people to betray them. I met some bloody good blokes who happened to be drug dealers.'

I asked him if it was traumatic. He responded: 'You could get on the gas, smoke weed and there was no supervision. You had guns and a shitload of cash. What's not to like?'

COMMON GROUND

Brett Stevens was wearing shorts as he sat on his couch watching the tennis on TV when his wife ripped into him, accusing him of losing his humanity.

Sitting on his lap was his police-issue pistol. In the gutter outside was a dead bandit.

The teenage gunman and his partner had tried to rob a Bondi hotel porter dropping off the takings in a bank safe, but the security guard fired back, hitting the 18-year-old in the heart.

Stevens says the wounded bandit yelled 'I've been hit' and collapsed. The off-duty policeman grabbed his own gun, strapped on body armour and ran outside to the teenager, who died where he fell.

'There were women crying, and I was thinking: "What are they upset about?" That's how bad I had become.'

It is only now, years later, that the former Sydney cop sees how the sharp end of policing blunted his compassion, leaving him with little sympathy for those on the wrong side of the law.

'If a gang member was shot dead, I saw that as a positive,' he says.

Having left the police, Stevens has become a self-taught expert on street gangs and discovered that cops and crooks share characteristics.

He joined the force in 1982 and spent years working in the cauldron that was Kings Cross, dealing with gangs, drug dealers and victims before moving to the Tactical Response Group, the team called in to deal with dangerous offenders.

'It wasn't a great leap from Kings Cross to the TRG because they were both areas of high-adrenaline activity.'

Within two years of his joining, the TRG was disbanded after a suspect was accidentally shot in the face during a raid. 'It played to the view that the TRG was full of thugs,' he says. 'We were dealing with violent offenders who did what they wanted until they were stopped. Someone had to say no to them.'

Disbanding the TRG left a void. Within months, a 33-year-old man stabbed a teenage girl to death in the Strathfield Plaza then pulled out a semi-automatic rifle to kill six people and wound eight, before attempting to abduct a woman and then taking his own life when he heard police sirens.

It was that sort of nightmare scenario, Stevens argues, that the TRG was assigned to patrol as a first response unit.

Sometimes, he says, that void was filled by gangs. In Cronulla, there was a period of street bashings and stabbings. 'Then the Rebels [bikie gang] rolled in and guess what? The violence stopped and the fear disappeared.'

It was a commercial decision, he says. They ran the nightclubs and the drugs and, in return, they pulled the street gangs into line. 'Certain gangs can be given the green light if they can stop the violence,' he says.

Stevens says in Tijuana – one of the most dangerous cities in the world – the tourist area is relatively safe because the cartels understand that shooting foreign visitors is bad for business.

As a cop-turned-author, Stevens has travelled the world, embedding himself both with police and gangs, publishing his experiences in the book *The Rise of Street Gangs*.

With his US-born wife, Pam, he would travel to America on leave and take the opportunity to patrol as an observer with local police in Los Angeles, Texas and New York.

After 13 years in policing, he resigned. 'My wife wanted to go home, and I thought it was her turn. The death outside our house left her deeply traumatised.'

He took to freelance writing, reporting in Thailand, Australia, the US and South America. He saw how in the Philippines police went out and shot drug dealers, resulting in crime dropping by 78 per cent but turning the streets into a war zone.

Mexican police ignored drug trafficking because taking on the cartels could prove fatal without achieving anything. As if to remind everyone where the real power lay, the drug syndicates shot dead seven local police, just to show they could.

'In Mexico, police said to me that America started the war on drugs, but it is the Americans who buy the drugs. They just don't want to get in the way. There are plenty of other ways they can do good, dealing with violent crimes,' he says.

Why should local police, paid a pittance, try to stop a tsunami with a bucket?

These days, Stevens feels ashamed that he didn't show compassion for drug addicts in Kings Cross – 'they were someone's son or daughter' – and questions the consequences of drug law enforcement.

'According to the UN, 266 million people take drugs and about one in 10 become addicted. If taking drugs was an Olympic event, Australia would be in the finals in every single category. You can order coke in Sydney and have it delivered quicker than you can get McDonald's.

'When the cartels need someone to move the drugs, they have the bikie gangs to distribute, but the bikies aren't standing on street corners, so they use lower-tier gangs.'

He lived and worked on a Native American reservation in California and saw how gangs gave unemployed teenagers an identity.

'I thought [gang members] were lazy slobs, but they were disciplined. They prepared their clothing as if it was a dress uniform. The clothing was impeccable.'

He found the gangs bonded when they had been in dangerous conflicts in the way police did, shared the same type of black humour and valued loyalty and courage above everything: 'I had more in common with them than [with] normal people.'

It is not just poverty that creates the opportunity for gang recruitment but relative poverty. 'Poverty is when you don't have enough to eat, and relative poverty is when the guy next door has a better car than you. Statistics show that societies that are considered poor but have a balanced wealth distribution almost have no crime, and if you go to places where everyone is wealthy, there is also close to no crime.

'If you go to a place with poor people, moderately well-off people and rich people, and the distribution is steep, then the rate of aggressive behaviour among young men starts to skyrocket.

'The more aggressive young men who are unlikely to climb to a dominant position while playing by society's rules turn to aggression to make their mark on the world.'

Gang teens still in school take public transport to suburbs to bash kids from the private schools they will never attend or steal luxury cars they could never afford or rob houses where they couldn't get a job as a pool cleaner.

For a period, Stevens worked as a supervisor in a juvenile justice complex in a remote Californian forest, where the Los Angeles hoods were more likely to be killed or injured by a knife or gun than in a car crash.

One of the inmates, Rascal, had been involved in 20 shootings. Another, J-Rue, told Stevens 'that the high school dance he'd been allowed to attend was the best night of his life'. They were outlaws who craved acceptance.

'Being gangsters . . . empowers them and gives them a family. It is a way to status and money. They say: "I want the car, the bling and the hot women."'

The young gang members model themselves on the Hollywood image, holding their guns with the inefficient horizontal grip. It may be inaccurate, but it looks cool.

Stevens says the hoods are looking for validation using the only currency they have – physical strength and courage. But most of their efforts are not about gaining wealth but beating rivals. 'They would rather get $50 a day as a gangster than $100 working at McDonald's because they have the status.'

But there is a way out. He says many reach a point where they conclude 'I don't want to keep doing this.'

That's when the authorities need to have options in place that include education and employment providing the status they desperately desire.

Just like the young gang members, Brett Stevens came to a point where he thought violence on the street was just part of life. Now he knows there are better ways. We just have to find them.

GOING TO WAR WITH THE HELLS ANGELS

Maybe if the private schoolboy from Melbourne had not rented such a flash car on his fact-finding trip to the US, he wouldn't have been noticed – but a gleaming silver Thunderbird is a head-turner even in laid-back San Francisco.

And maybe if he hadn't given the rental company an address in Oakland's Foothill Boulevard, which happened to be the headquarters of the Hells Angels' mother chapter, Peter John Hill could have slipped in and out as just another Aussie tourist looking for a Californian adventure.

When the Diamond Jubilee T-Bird was seen on a Hells Angels run in Lake County, it was duly recorded and the driver became a person of curiosity. Issued a speeding ticket, he gave a dodgy address – next door to the mother chapter. When he failed to pay the ticket, an arrest warrant was issued. Now he was a person of interest.

Nearly three weeks later, the car was seen at Golf Links Road, Oakland, outside the home of Hells Angels hitman James 'Jim Jim' Brandes. He was also known as The Assassin – with good reason.

Hill was 24 and had joined the Melbourne chapter of the Hells

Angels, a group of toughies living on the fringes of the law. Hill's visits to the US would change all that. From the time Hill returned to Australia, he would help turn the local gang into an organised crime group – and change the face of the national drug culture forever.

It turned out Hill flew to the US four times to link up with the Hells Angels, and was taken into a maximum-security prison to meet Oakland chapter president, Sergey Walton. It was no social call, as Walton whispered to Hill the recipe to make methamphetamine, a drug hardly seen in Australia at that time.

Hill was more than able to return the favour, becoming a smuggler of a key ingredient in the manufacture of speed – the liquid chemical P2P, illegal in the US but legal in Australia.

Hill poured the chemical into three-litre Golden Circle pineapple juice tins and resealed them using a machine stolen from a Queensland canning company, sending six litres a time in the post. He sent more than 200 litres that helped the Hells Angels make $30 million in drugs which in turn funded their defence in organised crime trials.

Meanwhile, Hill was experimenting with the amphetamine recipe and, through trial and error, improved the yield to commercial standards.

It was January 1982 when Detective Sergeant Steele Waterman returned for another stint in the Drug Squad. The summer cannabis crops had hit the street while the greatest challenge was an epidemic of heroin overdoses. No one was looking for speed labs and no one would have – except for an observant grandmother called Mrs Brown, who lived on a farm known as Greenslopes on the outskirts of Melbourne, near Hurstbridge. It was dead quiet out there, which is why Mrs Brown always heard the hotted-up cars and Harley-Davidsons turning up at the rented property across the road.

She contacted the Heidelberg police, who put her onto Bob Armstrong from the Bureau of Criminal Intelligence. Armstrong asked her to jot down a few car numbers, which duly came up as owned by members of the Hells Angels.

Armstrong snuck out with a bureau locksmith and broke in to find a working chemical lab plus gelignite, detonators, a machine gun, and an unhealthy number of handguns. And so the first anti-bikie taskforce – Omega – was formed. Armstrong and Waterman were the operational leaders and effectively went to war with the Angels.

'Peter had an infectious personality. He fell in love with bikes. He joined them when they were just a bunch of baggy-arsed kids hanging out the front of a hamburger shop,' says Waterman.

Hill recruited key members of the gang to help him cook and distribute the drugs, including Roger Biddlestone, Raymond Hamment and John Paul Madden.

Hamment, Waterman says, was the money man, funding the first drug 'cooks' from safe-crackings. 'Roger was not a bad guy, I didn't mind him. He was Hilly's best mate. Madden had the personality of a dead rat. I didn't like him and he didn't like us. He was an imposing figure and if he came to you with a pound of product and said you owed $30,000 you'd pay.'

When they were up and running, they were producing $300,000 worth of speed per week, supplemented by a first-division Tattslotto win of $280,000.

On 10 March 1982, all four suspects were arrested at Greenslopes, but it was only the start of a battle that would take five years, four trials, a mysterious death, a corrupted jury and an international murder plot.

There were many more raids. The bikies took a particular dislike to Armstrong, referring to him as 'Noddy' and 'Benny Hill' (due to his purported resemblance to the British comic).

'Bob was pretty sharp. Bob used to pepper them all the time. He chased them and when a guy drove into the headquarters he followed them. He didn't take a backward step. He would have their bikes pulled over and declared unroadworthy to get them off the road,' says Waterman. Once when they went to Sydney, Armstrong tipped off local detectives who raided the hotel. 'He told the detectives up there to say "Bob says hello".'

With 175 witnesses, listening devices, 640 exhibits including a machine gun, two pistols, cash, 16 sticks of gelignite, 32 electric detonators and a large amount of liquid speed, police were confident of a guilty verdict – but the four bikies looked cocky, and with good reason.

Another bikie arrested in a follow-up raid was Anton Kenny. 'His wrists were so huge you couldn't get handcuffs around them,' says Waterman. Much later, he was murdered and dismembered with a chainsaw.

After a monster trial, one juror wouldn't budge and the jury could not reach a verdict. Much later, Hill would tell police the jury had been nobbled. Waterman says the Angels paid $10,000 to the one juror, who 'was a friend of a friend of one of the bikies'.

'Hilly admitted that they got to one of the jurors. He was coy about it, but he said they paid him,' Waterman says.

(As an aside, when I wrote that a jury had been nobbled but couldn't name the case because of the retrial, Supreme Court Justice Norman O'Bryan huffed and puffed claiming that I had fabricated the allegation and was just looking for headlines. It was his jury.)

For the Hells Angels, a new jury needed a new plan.

According to Waterman: 'One late afternoon, I got a phone call from a lady. She said: "Mr Waterman, Peter and his friends have been here discussing something. They are getting someone from America to come out to kill you and Mr Armstrong. He is from the Hells Angels." It was Audrey, Peter Hill's mother. She was a lovely lady.

'I thought: "Gee, that's a bit savage."

'I went to BCI and got all the names of the Oakland chapter and had 28 put on alert. Next morning, I got a phone call from immigration saying they had someone with one of those names here and he was in the cell [at Melbourne Airport].'

It was 'Sleepy Jim' Brandes who, along with killing bikie associates, had bombed and seriously injured US policeman Bill Zerby in January 1978.

'When we walked in, he looked at Bob and said: "Jesus, you do look like Benny Hill."'

But it was no joke. A search of Brandes' luggage showed he had instructions on how to build a car bomb, the names of jurors in a US trial, a Treasury investigation handbook and a set of thumb cuffs. Immigration refused him entry and he was sent back on the same plane later that day.

Madden died in what was declared a car accident. On a bikie run, the enforcer was run over by the club's own backup van. 'Madden had run out of money and he was starting to give indications that he might cut a deal. He was about to talk turkey,' Waterman says. 'He was dead and buried before we knew about it. They tidied that one up nicely.'

Waterman says there was a falling-out over the money and drugs. 'All of a sudden, Roger Biddlestone turns up in a roll of carpet having had the absolute crap beaten out of him. He'd been hit with a baseball bat to within an inch of his life.

'Hilly was out on a limb. Bob and I went to see him and thrashed out a deal in an hour-and-a-half over burgers and fries. Hilly could out-eat both of us. He just kept ordering more fries.'

He wanted a reduced sentence and to do his time well away from the others. After three trials – a hung jury and two aborted hearings – the prosecutors jumped at the deal. Faced with Hill's statements taken at the Sofitel Hotel ('We had a few bourbons at the Piano Bar to warm him up'), the others pleaded guilty.

Hill did his time and has kept out of trouble, first as a truck driver and later as a block owner up around Mildura. It is said that to stick it up the Hells Angels, he sold his speed recipe to the head of the rival Black Uhlans, a bloke called John William Samuel Higgs who became Australia's most prodigious drug manufacturer.

All because Peter Hill was curious enough to visit the mother chapter in Oakland.

Bob Armstrong would spend many years hunting bikies and was one of the architects of the undercover sting Operation Barkly. More than 30 years after the Omega operation, detectives raided a Hells Angel clubhouse to find on the wall a fake wild boar head with a police cap. Underneath was the inscription: *Bob Armstrong is a cunt.*

The raiding cops texted him the photo.

He was delighted.

THE BLIND ALLEY IN A STRAIGHT STREET

Retired butcher John Magill has helped crack some of Australia's most baffling crimes, but the one that drives him – the murder of his daughter – remains agonisingly out of reach.

The murder of Jane Thurgood-Dove, gunned down in the driveway of her Niddrie home in November 1997, is a crime that could have been solved if not for a series of blind alleys and dead ends.

From day one, the answer was literally up the road, although it would take five long years before detectives concentrated in that direction. This was not a case of incompetence, rather of strong circumstantial evidence pointing to a different (and innocent) suspect and leading police down the wrong path.

First, the crime.

On Oaks Day, 6 November 1997, Jane Thurgood-Dove, 35, pulled into the driveway of her Muriel Street home, having picked up her three children aged 11, six and three from school and preschool. As she was getting out of her Toyota LandCruiser, a stolen Commodore pulled up behind to block her escape and a pot-bellied gunman stepped out.

He chased her around her car until she slipped, then shot her twice. It had all the hallmarks of a gangland hit – except Thurgood-Dove was no gangster.

Her parents, John and Helen Magill, at home after watching the races, were settling in for an early dinner when there was a knock at the door. It was a detective who, according to Helen, said: 'You have a daughter, Jane?'

'We said yes and he said: "Well she's been shot and she is now dead."'

They were told, as was Thurgood-Dove's husband, Mark, that they would be treated as suspects. As they were eliminated, the investigation would widen in ever-increasing circles.

While checking Jane Thurgood-Dove's private life, they found she had links to a policeman, who knew the family and employed her to clean his house. Investigations showed he was obsessed, had a 'shrine' to her in his house, his computer password was her date of birth and he had tried to buy a cemetery plot next to hers.

Two witnesses gave police a description that fitted the senior constable and he invoked his rights to refuse to answer questions, provide a DNA sample or participate in a line-up.

He did agree to a lie-detector test. When asked: 'Are you responsible for the death of Jane Thurgood-Dove?', he answered: 'No.' The machine suggested otherwise. It looked like he was the guy.

Except he wasn't.

While he became the prime suspect, there was another theory that remained largely unexplored.

A few days after the murder, my phone rang at work. It was 'Joe', a former butcher who had fallen in with corrupt ex-solicitor Philip Peters.

Peters, known as 'Mr Laundry', wanted to drug, abduct and murder underworld figure Peter Kypri, whom he blamed for a $200,000 insurance fraud rip-off. The plot was to take Kypri to a St Arnaud farm where he would be tortured and murdered. 'Joe' would then use his butchery skills to dispose of the body.

Joe went to the police who set up a sting operation codenamed Soli. Using a borrowed human dummy from a TV show, police planted it in a car boot, allowing Joe to show Peters what he claimed was the abducted Kypri.

As he shut the boot, police swooped in, placing them both in a bugged police car where Peters made damning admissions.

It was April 1994 and Peters was charged with conspiracy to murder; he pleaded guilty to attempted abduction, perjury and cultivating marijuana. He was sentenced to three years and was released a few months before Thurgood-Dove's murder.

Joe said to me: 'When I saw her [Jane Thurgood-Dove] on *Australia's Most Wanted*, the hairs on the back of my neck stood up.' He said she looked like Kypri's wife, Carmel – the same build, hairstyle and age.

I told Joe I didn't understand the connection. He said: 'Don't you know the Kypris live in Muriel Street?'

Not only did they live in the same street, they both lived three houses from a corner in light-coloured weatherboard homes on the same side of the street with a light pole at the front, had school-aged kids and drove four-wheel-drives.

By the time Peters was released from prison, the Kypris had fortified their home and stopped their children playing in the street.

Carmel told my colleague Andrew Rule she had considered the possibility she might have been the real target of Thurgood-Dove's killer. 'If it wasn't meant for her, it makes you wonder,' she said. Within weeks, the Kypris moved.

Less than three weeks after the murder, we published a story raising the possibility that Carmel Kypri was the real target and Thurgood-Dove was the victim of mistaken identity. We had no idea about the growing body of evidence pointing to the policeman.

John Magill thinks police should have investigated the connection to the Kypris back then.

I kept in touch with John and Helen, two decent people dealing with grief. Five years had passed when John contacted me because he wanted the government to offer a $1 million reward for information, an unprecedented sum. I said I didn't think they would do it for just one case, no matter how tragic. But what about a special category for murders, where the victims were seemingly random victims of violence and police believed they were close to laying charges?

I took the suggestion to one of then premier Steve Bracks' advisers Jane Wilson, a respected colleague when she was an on-the-road reporter.

To his credit, Bracks ran with the idea. In 2003, the reward was announced. It would result in breakthroughs in several cases, such as that of Mersina Halvagis, who was murdered tending her grandmother's grave, and James Russouw, ambushed in Nunawading in 2008. (The scheme has since been broadened to include cold case murders and another is on the verge of a breakthrough.)

But what about Jane Thurgood-Dove? 'When the reward was posted, within 48 hours they had the names of those involved,' says John Magill.

The mistaken identity theory quickly grew stronger.

The theory is that bikies, led by Steven John Mordy, were hired to kill Carmel Kypri. For four days, they followed Jane Thurgood-Dove, believing she was Carmel.

The pot-bellied gunman was Mordy, who the year before had been acquitted of a NSW murder, and the man who stole the getaway car was his mate Jamie Reynolds. After the reward was announced, a witness told police that a week after the murder, Reynolds had said: 'We got the wrong sheila.'

Mordy became a recluse and rarely ventured outside for the next 18 months, police say, because he feared being identified as the gunman. Two people witnessed Thurgood-Dove's murder. At least one picked Mordy as the killer from a series of photos.

By the time of the reward breakthrough, it was already too late. Mordy had died from drug abuse in September 2001.

Attention turned to Reynolds. The plan was to question him, offering a deal to turn on the person who put out the contract on Carmel Kypri.

This is where the Magills question the priorities of the criminal justice system. Many investigations, including Thurgood-Dove's, were put on hold as investigative resources were assigned to the Purana Taskforce, looking at gangland murders.

In April 2004, Homicide investigators were ready, but days before they were to grab Reynolds, he drowned in a boating accident at Barwon Heads. With the deaths of Mordy and Reynolds, the mistaken identity theory could not stand up in court. Peters has been interviewed twice and has not been charged. Presumably he denies any involvement (he could not be tracked down to ask), and we don't suggest he was involved.

So what about the policeman who failed the lie-detector test? He was asked: 'Are you responsible for the death of Jane Thurgood-Dove?' As he mistakenly believed that Jane's husband, Mark, had killed her out of jealousy, he did feel 'responsible' – although he wasn't the killer.

If he truly cared for Jane, he should have answered police questions in the first place, allowing himself to be cleared and preventing officers from wasting years on the wrong track.

Yet there are others who know the truth, and there is $1 million and an indemnity on offer for anyone who can lead police to the person willing to pay a hit team to 'kill the sheila in Muriel Street'.

As John Magill says: 'There is no crime that can't be solved.'

TURNING KILLERS, BUT AT WHAT PRICE?

From the day the former army tank crew member walked into his first station as a freshly graduated police constable, he was a marked man.

Just 21 years old, well-built and easy on the eye, Shayne Kerley was not targeted by local St Kilda crooks but by four female senior constables, who put a $50 bounty on his head. The first to score a date takes the pool.

Senior Constable Michelle Carey fronted the new cop in the privacy of the station stairwell. If he just said they had done the business, they would split the $200 reward.

It showed many of Michelle's traits that served her well – a sense of mischief, a capacity to find lateral solutions and a gift to persuade people to her point of view.

Not that much later, they moved in together.

For a time, Shayne and Michelle were a power police couple. Shayne would join the elite Special Operations Group (SOG) while Michelle became a respected detective, a member of the Purana Taskforce and helped to turn three notorious killers into police witnesses.

He would win a Valour Award for being part of the team that risked their lives to save a woman and her children from a gunman who had already killed two people, attempted to kill a dozen more, and remained armed with a carbine and 100 rounds of ammunition.

She was the inspiration behind the character Detective Jacqui James, superbly played by Caroline Craig in the original *Underbelly* TV series. Her Purana crew boss, Stuart Bateson became Detective Steve Owen, played by Rodger Corser.

Shayne joined because he saw a greater future in policing than the army. Michelle, from Newcastle, was set on being a police officer but because there was a temporary recruitment freeze in NSW, she joined the Victoria Police in 1986, the only female to graduate from her squad.

Squadmate Paul Robson says while other recruits went home at the weekend, she would stay in at the academy. They would go on to share rented accommodation when both were stationed at St Kilda, once deciding to give her shaggy cat a mohawk haircut as a point of difference.

'She was a great person and a great detective,' he says,

The early days were hectic for the now married Kerleys. Shayne was getting smashed by SOG selection and training while Michelle was doing the demanding 12-week Detective Training School course.

'She had study notes taped all over the house, on the fridge, in the shower and in the toilet. I think I could have passed the course, I read the notes that often,' says Shayne.

They had two children, Tyson and Bronte (and became guardians for a third, Bethany) and Michelle decided that when the kids were young, having both parents on call wouldn't work. At a time when there was no job sharing or part-time options, she resigned in 1997, rejoining four years later.

Back in The Job, they both stayed in the fast lanes, Shayne in the SOG for more than 10 years while Michelle was picked for what was the hottest job in policing. On 17 October 2003, then a senior detective, she was selected for the Purana Taskforce with one instruction: stop the underworld war.

Bateson's crew were assigned the June 2000 murder of Mark Moran, the June 2003 murders of Jason Moran and Pasquale Barbaro and the killing of Michael Marshall just a week after Kerley joined Purana.

According to Shayne, it was the murder of Marshall in front of his five-year-old son, which drove her on. Bateson says she often spoke of the child, standing there watching the shooting, frozen to the spot because he knew it was wrong to cross the road without holding his father's hand.

The crew had a plan. Build overwhelming cases against the shooters so they would do deals to give up the organisers – particularly drug boss Carl Williams.

Bateson says it was one thing to get statements from the killers, but another to manage them until they gave truthful evidence in court.

'That's where Michelle was at her best,' he says.

Using humour, a warm personality, the knack to deal with people and a dogged persistence, she kept three ruthless killers onside. It was the tipping point.

Shayne came home to find a bag of an unknown man's washing in the laundry. It was the clothes of a multiple killer who was at a secret location making multiple statements against Williams and others. Michelle volunteered to wash the underworld underpants. Anything to help the investigation.

The killer cannot be named other than by the nickname the Runner. Suspected of the murders of Jason Moran and Pasquale Barbaro, police had a bug and tracking device in his car when he started patrolling South Yarra. Too late they realised he was planning another murder, running from the car to shoot Marshall.

He later rang Williams with a coded message the hit had been conducted. 'That horse you like, it has been scratched.'

Williams was making more than $100,000 a month through drugs but when it came to contract killings, he liked to cut corners. And so the dominoes began to fall, with key allies turning on him. There was the Lieutenant, the Driver, the Veteran, and even a relative, but the real star was one police at first didn't even try to turn, for he was a career armed robber who had always refused to talk: the Runner.

When the Runner was arrested for the October 2003 murder of Michael Marshall, Williams tried to distance himself, urging his hitman to plead guilty so they would have separate hearings. In jail, the Runner was visited by barrister and informer Nicola Gobbo, telling her his elderly mother needed help and rubbing his fingers together to indicate he wanted his mum paid in exchange for his silence. Gobbo wrote a note to say she would be seeing drug boss Tony Mokbel and Williams later that day.

Williams eventually sent the mother just $1500. It was a false economy.

He had promised the Runner $100,000 to kill rival Jason Moran – which he duly did, during an Auskick morning in Essendon North. But in June 2003 Williams short-changed him, producing only $2500.

The Runner contacted police, asking to meet. He was secretly moved from prison and over 30 days made a series of statements implicating Williams and Tony Mokbel in several murders. After he signed up, police asked what he wanted and he replied he had a craving for a vanilla slice.

It was Michelle who was vital to keeping him on track to the point where he would give evidence.

Not that Michelle was always assigned the Good Cop role. When seven-time killer Andrew Veniamin was on the verge of losing his cool, it was Kerley who marched up to restrain him. Asked if she was concerned, she laughed. 'I just wanted to feel his abs. They were pretty good too.'

Even though she was pivotal in charging Carl Williams with

murder, he would send her chatty notes from his jail division, while the Runner sent her artwork he painted in prison.

Bateson says Michelle's sense of irreverence helped Purana in the dark days, remembering a morale-boosting dinner attended by then Assistant Commissioner Simon Overland.

Michelle said to the assistant commissioner: 'You are a good-looking man, but you are going bald, and it's time you shaved it off.' According to Bateson: 'Two days later, I was not surprised to see he had done just that.'

When the murder toll kept mounting and the pressure ramped up, it would be a wisecrack from Michelle that would keep them grounded.

When the killers became witnesses, Williams was charged with multiple murders. Bateson and Kerley sat together in court when the jury returned the Marshall murder case. 'When the jury said guilty Michelle grabbed my hand and gave it a squeeze. It was perhaps my favourite moment.'

It is a lovely story. The tragedy is that Bateson told it as part of his eulogy at Michelle's funeral held at the Police Academy. She died on 18 June 2023, aged 55.

At the funeral were loads of friends and family, rows of police brass and *Underbelly* actor Caroline Craig.

As is the way at a police funeral, the service record is read. She received multiple awards including a Chief Commissioner's Certificate for her Purana work that highlighted: 'Exemplary service, outstanding commitment to duty, dedication, teamwork, patience, perseverance, and investigative skills.'

Her Purana reputation should have set her up with a successful career as a police leader. She was a great investigator, fun, hardworking with a sincere interest in the welfare of fellow workers. But it didn't happen. One boss outrageously blocked her from a key job because she was married with children, which could make her 'unreliable'.

I showed her kids, now grown up, a draft of this story and they thought that while it captured her professionalism, it maybe didn't highlight her sense of fun. Well, here it is: she was always up for a good time. The cops who do the grim jobs usually have the capacity to laugh. When you socialise with them, they would always rather talk about the stuff-ups than the big arrests. Their best stories rarely make the headlines.

She became a much-loved law instructor at the Police Academy, teaching students the law but also inspiring them with Purana war stories. Many cops went on to become detectives because of Michelle.

The only way she could get the promotion to senior sergeant that she deserved was to take a country posting to Swan Hill. (She and Shayne had separated by then.)

At the station she was seen as a 'people person', looking after the welfare of others but, behind the scenes, she was struggling, managing PTSD. Diagnosed with diabetes (one) and troubled by a back injury, she was found unconscious and airlifted to Melbourne in a serious condition. She wanted help but didn't want to be declared unfit for duty. Her medical support team wrote a letter saying it was urgent she be transferred to Melbourne.

This is where it gets messy. The police transfer system works by applying for a vacant job and choosing the preferred candidate. Under a welfare application, the police officer is shoe-horned into a position ahead of others who may be equally qualified, but that requires the good will of the bosses in that area.

If you take on someone with mental or physical health issues and they require extensive sick leave, that area is left shorthanded. Police have a term for someone in that position – a broken biscuit.

There is no doubt some colleagues who knew Michelle and her outstanding work should have stepped up sooner. Life is not always about the future but respecting the past.

Her children drove to Swan Hill, packed her, along with the cats and dogs, to bring her back to Melbourne while her supporters tried to find Michelle a position as part of the road back.

Eventually, a compassionate transfer was approved. Too late.

Michelle was found slumped on a kitchen bench of a friend's house in Geelong. She was dead.

> Her boss at Purana, retired Detective Inspector Gavan Ryan, wrote in a tribute: Michelle was pivotal to the success of the Purana Taskforce.
>
> Her unseen role in the 'rolling' of multiple hardened criminals will never be forgotten by taskforce members. She was a genuine person who gave it all during that difficult period in Victoria's history.
>
> Her legacy is one of displaying incredible courage under relentless pressure to stop the shootings. A kind soul who loved her family, loved her team members, and provided stability in a difficult time.

We sit with Shayne at the Broadmeadows Police Station. Downstairs, uniformed cops deal with dozens of queries from citizens at the watch-house counter looking for help. In the acting inspector's office is a deconstructed bomb, his Valour Award certificate and mementos from a glittering career. On the desk are jars of lolly snakes and M&Ms as rewards for cops doing the job.

He smiles when he talks of the early days with Michelle and his eyes glisten when he talks of the latter years, reflecting on the police force they served with distinction. 'If we do anything well, it is a funeral.'

My father was a traditional police officer who could forgive anything except disloyalty. I remember when one of his most experienced officers went on long-term sick leave for cancer treatment. I asked him if he had selected a replacement.

He looked through me (those who remember Fred will know that look) and said: 'We carry our wounded.' It was the end of any discussion.

Someone should remember that before they need to make the trip to the academy for another funeral.

PART 4

THE GOOD GUYS

It is hard to imagine anyone more positive than Jimi Kelly who, as a two year old, was so badly burned he died three times before being revived. He refused to accept he was a victim, was subjected to countless operations before joining the Australian Federal Police where he works as a front-line dog handler. It is a story sure to put a smile on your face.

Speaking of dogs, we look at the Feds hi-tech labradors that can sniff out a USB stick in a bowl of garlic.

Sam Russell is a Victorian detective who made a silent vow to find the body of her missing murder victim. She found her buried in a tip and was able to return her to her family.

Sometimes investigations are more than getting a conviction.

A DETERMINATION FORGED IN FIRE

Even as a two-year-old, Jimi Kelly showed the trait that has been his guiding light through an incredibly rich life: a determination to prove people wrong. It was then, as a toddler, that he proved too stubborn to die.

Having watched someone fill the mower with petrol before cutting the lawn preparing for Jimi's second birthday, the curious kid managed to get into the shed, climb a shelf and accidentally spill the contents of the fuel can over himself.

'I walked back inside and Mum was cooking. The open flame ignited the fumes,' he says. She was preparing party food for later that day.

His mother and a neighbour smothered the flames but not before Jimi suffered burns that should have been fatal.

'He died three times – once in the house, in the ambulance and in the hospital – and was revived each time,' his wife, Emma, says.

It was not just the skin that was destroyed by the burns that went down to the bone and damaged muscle. What skin was left was used for multiple grafts, meaning no part of his body was unaffected.

It was 1979 and for the surgeons of the day, there was no complete playbook for treating a child so young with wounds so severe. When it looked as if he could lose a thumb, a surgeon had a go at saving it. When the medic removed the bandages, he said: 'Well, that seems to have worked.'

But this story is not a tragic one. When you meet Kelly, you soon realise he is comfortable in his skin, even if the strangers who stare at him are not.

He says some people stare so hard at him that they walk into stationary objects, with one the other day almost overturning a supermarket display. 'It's hard not to laugh.'

Kelly enjoys proving people wrong. He was told he may never walk again. He eventually ran a marathon. They said he may never talk, now he goes at a million miles an hour, with his wife saying the slightly husky tone hits a certain attractive note.

He was told his injuries would cruel his ambition to be a police officer. He is now an acting sergeant in the Federal Police.

He was told he would not regain the use of all his digits. Now he is a qualified police firearms instructor.

The girl he wanted to date immediately rebuffed him. Now they are married.

Jimi and Emma have two daughters. They are a fun, loving couple who share a passion for life and for finishing each other's sentences. They sit together, tell each other's stories and tease the other with affection. To put it simply, they are fun to be with.

When Jimi was stationed in Canberra as a Protective Service Officer and Emma was a public servant, a mutual friend suggested they share a house.

'Within three months, James confessed his undying love for me,' she says. Rather than seeing it as romantic, she was spooked at the intensity, so much so that she immediately sought alternate accommodation. 'I was young and silly, so I ran.'

But if you believe in sliding doors, this was one. The former housemates were both raised in Geelong, and they ran into each other while visiting their respective families six months later. One thing led to another, and they were soon dating.

'He has the most wicked sense of humour,' she says. 'Even on our first conversation on the phone he had me in hysterics.'

Emma, who now works for the Federal Police in corporate support, admits occasionally it takes her a little time to pick his deadpan jokes.

'Sometimes I think I've wasted my best lines,' he says with theatrical exasperation.

He says receiving his injuries at such a young age was a blessing in one way, as he has no recollection of being any different. It is who he is.

But on the physical side, the earlier age left many medical challenges. His repaired skin lacked elasticity, which meant as he grew, he needed regular running repairs. 'For 27 years he was in and out of hospital,' Emma says.

'He has a beautiful group of mates that went through primary and secondary school with him who were really protective,' she says.

'Sometimes overprotective,' he adds with a smile. He now knows they would get in fights if they heard a snide remark that Jimi either didn't hear or chose to ignore.

While his friends enjoyed the beach and sports during the summer school holidays, Jimi would be booked into hospital as doctors dealt with his annual growth, replacing and patching grafts.

As an adult, it has proved to be a great diet incentive – put on weight, and you may need more grafts. As a young adult touring Britain, he confesses he was attracted to the tourist diet of 'curry and Guinness' that could have had serious consequences.

'My plastic surgeon put it pretty simply: "If you are driving and you see the Golden Arches, keep driving."'

Kelly joined the AFP in 2007, working in the Diplomatic Protection Unit, retrained as a sworn police officer and began general duties in 2010.

He was not particularly attracted to the traditional police role or long-term criminal investigations. 'I've always been an active person and love to run around,' he says, so he gravitated to action-based specialist squads.

He worked in targeted operations, including in the Solomons and Christmas Island, counterterrorism based at airports, as a sky marshal and undercover support.

He says his appearance can be an asset. 'I don't look much like a copper.' His wife says she was aghast when he returned from one long-term job wearing some sort of lumberjack shirt, missing buttons, a tracksuit bottom about three sizes too big and having allowed his sparse hair to grow until he looked like Sideshow Bob.

When asked by a colleague if he had purchased his disguise from an op shop, he said: 'No, from my wardrobe.'

He trained for a year to try out for Tactical Response, a unit that requires elite fitness and the capacity to swim under duress. The trouble was Kelly swam about as well as Ned Kelly in his armour.

'He is a sinker,' says Emma.

This was partially due to the tightness of his skin, which restricts arm movements, and partially because his running repairs make him heavier in the water.

'The first time I saw him try to swim, I thought he was joking. He left more water out of the pool than was left in it,' she says.

And so night after night he went to the pool to practise. As part of the training course, he had to swim wearing heavy boots and overalls. He passed, although he was ultimately not selected for the unit.

In 2020, he joined the Canine Unit. 'It looked like a fun role.'

He now has two dogs – Quixie, whose job is to discover hidden explosives, and Kylo, who is a drug, cash and firearms specialist, recently finding 300 grams of cocaine overlooked by human searchers.

The dogs are devoted to him and can pick his gait when he arrives at the kennels.

Asked if having suffered from burns made the search for bombs more stressful, he pauses, then says: 'I haven't really given it much thought.'

Jimi says working in specialist areas has an added bonus because you are part of close-knit units where members are judged on personality, attitude and performance, not superficial appearance.

Emma then makes an interesting point. 'Australians are not very good with things that are different.'

In America, it is different but occasionally embarrassing, as some people jump to the conclusion that Kelly is a wounded war hero.

'People come up and shake my hand, saying "Thank you for your service." I don't know what to say.'

Kids, they both say, are just honest. Emma says a little girl walked over to Jimi and asked: 'Why do you look like that? You look weird.'

'He smiled and explained that it was just him.'

The girl was satisfied with the answer and the conversation moved on.

Another suggested he looked like Deadpool, the immortal, scarred, wisecracking superhero of comics and films.

Emma is happy with that. 'I'll take Ryan Reynolds [the impossibly handsome actor who plays Deadpool] any time.'

TWO RODS AIMING FOR ONE SHOOTER

Constable Rod McDonald was lying on the ground, wounded, frightened, bewildered and bloodied. Only gut instinct and reflexes had saved his life, but this was hardly a moment for reflection. He felt anger towards the man who had ambushed him and was now attempting to escape.

It was just after 9 pm on 12 October 1982. More than 40 years later, he feels he remains Victoria Police's forgotten victim, with the investigation into his shooting allowed to lapse and the offender never formally identified.

A series of minor but annoying factory burglaries in Oakleigh meant the local afternoon divisional van crew was briefed to check likely targets. McDonald was walking along Winterton Road, shining his police-issue torch at factory windows to look for breaks, when a passer-by yelled to look behind.

'As I turned, I saw a person crouched under some bushes . . . I saw him bring a handgun up pointing directly at my face. He just fired, and I simultaneously threw my hands instinctively in front of my face.' Effectively he caught the bullet before it smashed into his skull.

'The impact knocked me from my feet and back against the factory wall, and then I fell to the ground, both my hands searching for the bullet hole I knew was in me but didn't know where.'

The wounded usually try to crawl to safety, but McDonald chose a different option. 'I heard him get up and run – my anger took over from my fear. I drew my .38 Smith & Wesson and fired two instinctive shots in his direction. I chased him to the end of the building, where he disappeared into the dark bushes.

'Then I saw my firearm was glistening bright red in the streetlight, and I saw my right thumb shredded, pieces hanging over the hammer and blood spraying like a spray gun.'

The bullet had hit his right thumb, smashed the torch he was carrying, entered his left wrist and travelled along his arm, lodging just under the skin near his elbow. When his partner, who had been searching nearby factories, found him, the laconic McDonald said: 'That's stuffed my piano playing.'

The gun was a 9 mm Browning pistol, not the sort of weapon usually carried by a factory burglar. But this was no average burglar, although it would take police nearly three years and several casualties to grasp the dangers. An informer gave one of the investigators the name of a possible suspect: factory worker named Pavel 'Mad Max' Marinof.

When police searched his house, they found a shooting range in the basement, but Marinof had disappeared. He was a Bulgarian army deserter, a gun nut and, in all probability, an underworld firearms dealer. And he would return with a bloody vengeance.

After McDonald was shot, the burglaries stopped for 18 months and then began again. The burglar would hit up to 12 factories a night, beginning around 10 pm, to pilfer petty cash and small items. His patch was an industrial triangle including Oakleigh, Clayton and Moorabbin, and although McDonald was shot in that zone, police seemed reluctant to link these burglaries with the earlier ones. Which is why, when Cheltenham police decided to stake out likely targets, they didn't know the offender would almost certainly shoot to avoid capture. They were setting themselves up to be ambushed.

McDonald was told his best option for recovery was to have his thumb replaced with the big toe from his right foot. Even as he was about to be wheeled into surgery, he thought about getting up and walking out. But it was too late.

Presented with the prestigious Victoria Police Valour Award, he returned to work around the time the burglar returned to his line of business.

'I was never the same. I fought the nerves and the fear that crept into certain situations and eventually succumbed to it,' he says. He took medical retirement. Then, after physical and psychiatric treatment, he returned to policing for a further 12 years, although the dark cloud of the shooting refused to lift.

In late May 1985 local police started their operation to trap the burglar. Rather than patrol his beat, giving him the chance to hide, they would wait in likely spots for him to show his head.

On 18 June, Sergeant Brian Stooke and Senior Constable Peter Steele decided to pull over a yellow Ford Cortina. It was in the factory area of Keys Road, Cheltenham, just before midnight – the right time and the right place for their man. While they searched the car, the driver bolted and when the police gave chase, he started firing, hitting Stooke and then Steele in the shoulder. He returned to Stooke, lying on the wet road, and shot him three more times, leaving him a paraplegic.

In the immediate search for the gunman, two more police – Sergeant Ray Kirkwood and Constable Graham Sayce – were shot. Sayce was lucky to survive after a bullet grazed his head. Soon after, Senior Constable Gary Morrell, a dog handler, was shot in the hand. The bullet would have entered his chest if not for his ballistic vest.

Again Marinof disappeared, this time for eight months, until the search centred on a property at Wallan.

Two Major Crime Squad detectives, John Kapetanovski and another Rod MacDonald, followed a panel van that left the property and headed along the Hume Highway. They were not certain the driver (who was wearing a wig) was Mad Max. As he was heading into Melbourne, where they might lose him, they decided to pull him over.

Armed with shotguns, they approached cautiously, barrels facing down as a safety precaution. They ordered him to place his hands outside the door and just as he seemed to be complying, he dragged his concealed gun and started firing, hitting Kapetanovski in the shoulder and hand and MacDonald in the chest.

In a replay of the shooting of our first Rod, Kapetanovski threw up his arms to shield himself. The first bullet passed through his chest into the bone of the right upper arm, while the second was aimed directly between his eyes.

That shot hit the left hand and travelled from the top of the palm through the inside of the middle finger, smashing three bones and destroying the top joint. It was enough to deflect the bullet, which only creased his right eyebrow. If not for the deflection 'Kappa' would have been hit between the eyes and been dead before he hit the ground.

Badly wounded, second Rod fired his shotgun through the rear windscreen as Marinof drove to escape. The car slowed, veered into a paddock and stopped; the gunman was dead.

The investigation into the 1982 shooting of Rod McDonald stopped with the death of Marinof because everyone knew he was the gunman. The trouble was that no one actually finished the file.

McDonald remains angry that his case remains unresolved. 'They have failed me,' he says. Every time the victims of Mad Max are listed without him, he feels like the forgotten footnote in a terrible chapter of policing history.

Now in his late 70s, he wanted to leave his dark memories behind and is living a simple life in Siem Reap, Cambodia.

Former colleague Wayne Rotherham lobbied for a review. One of the key pieces of evidence was the 9 mm bullet that hit Rod One. If it could be matched with the gun used to shoot Rod Two and

Kapetanovski, it would prove the case. But the Rod One bullet had been turned into a necklace for McDonald's daughter and the years had worn away ballistic marks needed for comparison.

After the review, Detective Superintendent Peter Brigham wrote to McDonald: 'It is not possible to prove "beyond doubt" Marinof was the offender . . . Considering the nature of the crime you were attending, and Marinof's MO and firearms proficiency, I believe it is "highly likely" that he was the offender.'

Rod Two believes Rod One was shot by Marinof: 'The stance and accuracy [of the offender] is identical. He shot in the same way. It would mean so much to him [Rod One] for it to be formally acknowledged.'

In 2021, undercover operative Rob Robertson was presented with a Valour Award for an operation 43 years earlier, where he persuaded a gunman not to shoot three police forced into a dumpster at the Victoria Market.

The award identifies the gunman as the notorious armed robber and escapee Russell 'Mad Dog' Cox, although Cox was never arrested, questioned or charged with the offence.

McDonald's citation ends with the words: 'Despite an intensive search, the offender was never located.'

Would it really be too hard to insert 'believed to be Pavel Marinof'? It would make the world of difference to a police hero who gave so much and just wants history to reflect the truth.

ON THE TRAIL OF FAKES AND FORGERS

It seems entirely appropriate that the man who has uncovered thousands of forgeries began as a fake himself.

David Black was 'bored rigid' working in a packaging and printing business when a mate working with Victoria Police's forensic science laboratory suggested he put in for a job at an organisation filled with boffins.

While Black had a science degree in chemistry, he had no forensics experience, but that did not deter him. He was invited to Victoria Police's new forensic services complex at Macleod in Melbourne's north-eastern suburbs.

'It was 1986 and Forensic Drive wasn't even in the Melway [street directory]. I pulled over at a phone box and rang to ask: "Where the hell are you?"'

After a few relaxed interviews over a series of months (that he thought were going nowhere), Black was offered a job in early 1987. Because he had rudimentary knowledge of the printing business, he was selected for a position in the document examination unit, which led him into a career of finding clues in the ashes and exposing a forger from a tiny tic in a signature, including one producing cheques valued at $US500 million.

'I had no idea at the beginning,' he says. By learning on the job, Black is now one of Australia's most respected forgery hunters, finding everyone from scammers to would-be killers.

His area is the sometimes-controversial cognitive forensics that rely heavily on the opinion of experts rather than the black-and-white results from a chemical test such as blood alcohol or drug analysis. 'We are the black box,' he says.

This means he and his colleagues have to fight against context bias that can lead scientists up the garden path to an outdoor toilet. There are five experts in the document examination unit, and they do so much more than look for dodgy signatures on rubbery cheques.

The most chilling was over the border in South Australia – the terrible Snowtown multiple murder case. Between 1992 and 1999, three men killed 12 people, putting their remains in barrels later found in the town of Snowtown. While the murders could be described as 'thrill kills', the killers accessed social security accounts of at least eight victims, stealing an estimated $95,000. Life is cheap to psychopaths.

'Handwriting examination by our South Australian colleagues showed exactly when the signatures changed from the originals, which pointed to the time when the victims were murdered,' says Black.

Not all cases are so grim, and Black has had his fair share of the bizarre.

The Case of the Strange Grange

In 1998, a man turned up at Langtons, the specialist wine auction house, with a box of 1990 vintage Penfolds Grange Hermitage that he wanted to sell.

All looked legitimate, down to the branded wooden crate, the grey-coloured packing paper and the unique foil cap cover. Yet to the experts, it was obviously a fake.

'The barcode was black, but Penfolds had changed it to red,' says Black.

The classic was the written advice on the label to pour the wine into a decanter, but in the forgery the advice was to 'poor'. All that effort and not a dictionary in sight.

'When the bloke was confronted, he panicked and ran off,' says Black. But he left one bottle.

It turned out he was sold the box at a pub by a bloke who said it was his Christmas bonus, with the scammer declaring he was not a wine drinker.

Black believes the wine was sold locally because the 1998 stock market crash and world recession temporarily dried up the Asian market. 'One small bottle shop in Footscray claimed to have 10 boxes.'

The breakthrough came not through high-tech forensic study, but by accident. Because of lack of room, Black stored a bottle in the exhibit fridge and, when he took it out, the condensation showed a serial number imprinted into the glass.

The 1990 Grange was bottled in 1991. The bottle in Black's hands was bottled on the 312th day of 1995 at 8.32 am.

A call to Penfolds showed it was from a pallet of stolen Penfolds 389 Shiraz, known as the 'Baby Grange'. Only an expert was likely to taste the difference. It is estimated 60 boxes made it to the market.

The world's most notorious wine forger was Rudy Kurniawan, who sold more than $30 million in counterfeit wine to collectors all over the world. He produced 12,000 bottles of high-end fakes and was finally caught when some of the wines were labelled with vintages that didn't exist.

Ashes to ashes

The elderly woman was old-school, insisting on doing her banking at her local branch using the same teller.

'The middle-aged female teller thought the little old lady would never notice if she skimmed off the account, but she was wrong,' says Black.

Noticing the discrepancy, the customer went to the bank, reporting the theft to her favourite teller.

'The teller told her to go home and collect all the paperwork, and she would meet her there,' Black recalls.

Sure enough, after collecting the paperwork, the teller left and burnt the evidence in her wood heater. Realising she would eventually be identified, the fraudster returned to stab her victim with a filleting knife.

'The elderly lady rolled over and played dead.'

Black was called to the scene, but police had already removed the ashes from the heater, turning most to black dust. Only a tiny scrap remained legible.

'It was the account number from the victim,' Black says.

Our Don Bradman

There is a lucrative market in fake Bradman memorabilia, and The Don was generous with his signature. 'Don Bradman would sign anything put in front of him, using anything from a pen to a texta,' says Black.

The size of the industry was shown when he was asked to go to the Moonee Ponds Police Station. 'There was an interview room that was filled, floor to ceiling, with signed Bradman memorabilia . . . mini-bats, posters and expensive glass display cabinets.'

The best evidence was elsewhere: an exercise book filled with copies of Bradman's signature as the offender practised forging the cricketer's brand.

In another case, a detective wanted Black's expert opinion on forged Bradman signatures, having one legitimate copy for comparison.

When Black told the cop he needed more than one real example, the enterprising detective took it upon himself to turn up at the great man's door in Adelaide as part of his inquiries.

'It was just an excuse. He was a cricket nut and ended up with a photo of himself with Bradman, plus plenty of genuine signatures.'

Here is the cricket nut's version of events.

Work in the fraud squad is often important but hardly likely to create a TV mini-series but for the sports-happy young detective the case of the fake signatures would lead him to meet some of the greats – and none greater than the greatest cricketer of all time – Sir Don Bradman.

It began in 1999 when the manager of motorcycle champion Mick Doohan spotted some signed pictures of his client for sale online. The scrawl looked a little strange and when he showed Doohan, the champion said they were fakes.

Turned out a photographer had taken snaps of Doohan during a race at Phillip Island and was wandering around trying to run into the motorbike rider to ask for them to be autographed.

An enterprising American, who claimed to have a friend in the Doohan team, said he could get them signed in exchange for a slab of beer. Best guess is he went around the corner, scrawled the fake signatures, then scored 24 cans of beer for the trickery.

The fakes were traced to a sports collectable shop. Soon, newly minted detective Paul Maher was part of a raiding party. Faced with signed sporting goods and photos, Maher's boss made an on-the-spot decision – seize the lot, including boxing gloves allegedly signed by Mike Tyson and Mohammed Ali.

There was another point that could lead a suspicious detective to believe all was not quite right with the store. There was a hydroponic cannabis crop growing upstairs.

So how could they work out what was real and what was fake? He was told to go to the source, which was slightly difficult in the case of Ali Tyson, Tiger Woods and Formula One driver Ayrton Senna.

But he was able to track down the locals, such as legendary race car driver Peter Brock, basketballer Andrew Gaze and larrikin AFL star Billy Brownless. But the biggest of them all was Bradman, living on his own at the age of 91 following the death of his wife, Lady Jessie.

Maher contacted the Bradman Foundation in Bowral and explained that he would like to speak to Sir Don on official business. Sure enough, he was provided with a phone number.

The cop made the call and the thin voice of The Don replied and a meeting was set up. Maher and his offsider headed off, stopping at a Horsham sports store to buy a couple of cricket bats. They were not looking for batting tips from the former Australian captain but a couple of sneaky signatures.

On the assigned day, they turned up at the red brick double-storey house the Bradmans had built in 1935. 'In the garage was a battered old Toyota Corolla,' says Maher.

They sat and chatted. The detective produced some signed memorabilia and Bradman said it could be his. This meant it would not be part of the prosecution, but it did not mean the trip would be wasted.

The cops asked him to sign two bats and two photos. Bradman agreed as long as they were not to be sold on the open market.

'In the room there was only one photo of another sports person. It was a picture of Bradman with Pele, taken in front of Sir Don's portrait.'

Even in his last few years, Bradman would go to his writing room and reply to any letters he received from fans around the world.

The owner of the sports store was acquitted of theft by deception charges and Maher still has the signed bat and the photo to prove his unlikely meeting with The Don.

The devil is in the detail

Often, Black says, the forger goes to great effort to get it right then fails through the simplest mistake.

In 1999, Caroline Reed Robertson, 19, strangled Rachel Barber, 15, a girl she used to babysit. With little forensic evidence, Black was given an exercise book seized from the suspect's home that had pages missing.

Using an 8000-volt electrostatic detection apparatus, he lifted the indentations left in the book that showed a step-by-step murder plan and a plot to take over Barber's identity.

Robertson was convicted and served 15 years.

When the experts get it wrong, the consequences can be horrendous.

In March 2004, terrorists launched attacks on the Madrid train network, killing 193 people and leaving more than 1800 wounded.

The Spanish National Police found two fingerprints on an abandoned bag of detonators and sent the images to Interpol.

The FBI ran them through the system and returned 20 possible matches to one of the prints. One of those 20 was to Braydon Mayfield, a former army lieutenant who was then a lawyer in Portland. His prints were on the system from his army days.

Although he had not travelled to Spain and had no history of sympathy for terror, the FBI decided he was the guy and put him under intense investigation as the prime suspect. Mayfield had converted to Islam after marrying his Egyptian wife. Meanwhile, the Spanish authorities were telling the Americans they were wrong. Despite the fact the prints were not identical, FBI experts refused to reverse their decision because they wanted Mayfield to be guilty.

Eventually, the print was confirmed to have come from an Algerian suspect. The US government apologised to Mayfield and paid him $US2 million in compensation.

It is, Black says, the best-known case of context bias – the big case that everyone wants to be solved.

To fight against it in Victoria, when evidence comes in, it is examined by an expert and then all details of the case are removed from the file so the next set of examiners do a 'blind analysis'.

They want to detune the examination so the forensic investigators don't feel pressure to crack high profile cases.

'You don't want the investigator telling you that your evidence is vital,' says Black. 'We aren't on anyone's side. We are here to examine the evidence.'

LOST LONG WEEKENDS ON THE DRINK

Members of the younger generation, it seems, are self(ie)-obsessed Instagram influencers who insist on spreading COVID-19 by attending dance parties to take drugs while coughing over each other, leaving scientists to conclude the mosh pit is the petri dish of the pandemic.

Members of the older generation mutter through their masks from their living room La-Z-Boy armchairs that it was never like that in their day.

But memories fade, and we all rewrite history to suit ourselves.

Frankly, there is ample proof that the generation who today chip the young spent most of their younger days totally off their chops.

In the battle to get Victoria moving again, there is a host of regional events planned that include visiting museums, food tastings and the occasional visit to a winery. For example, the Tastes of Rutherglen event, devoted to the finer things of life. It is delightful, well run and always worth a visit. But it was not always so.

More than 50 years ago, they had a similar idea and came up with the Moomba Rutherglen Wine Festival, encouraging Melburnians to head up the highway for a sophisticated long weekend.

While the older generation look back at the Woodstock and Sunbury music festivals as times of peace and love, few talk of Rutherglen – probably because most of those who were there were too drunk to remember the details. This lot makes the anti-vax mob look like the Vienna Boys Choir.

The festival was held in 1967, 1968, 1970, 1972 and 1975. The original was planned to raise funds to build a local swimming pool, and it was considered such a success the city fathers decided to make it a regular event.

The first festival was cutting-edge stuff. After all, the 'six o'clock swill' (pubs closing at 6 pm, leading drinkers to binge before they were thrown out) had only been relaxed the year before. Even under the new laws, Melbourne pubs closed at 10 pm.

Takeaway Chinese food was collected in saucepans, fish and chips in newspapers, and unless you were a polar bear, the idea of eating raw fish would be greeted with revulsion. If you went to a cafe and tried to order smashed avocado on sourdough for brunch, you would have been smashed in the face with a lamington and served a cheese sandwich with the crusts cut off.

In an attempt to modify drinking, the MCG introduced a limit of two dozen cans that each patron could bring into the ground. Some brought coolers the size of coffins. During a five-day Ashes Test in Sydney, it was reported the crowd drank 460,000 cans.

In many ways, Melbourne was slowly emerging from a culture stuck in the 1950s. On Sunday, people went to church for salvation, not Bunnings for a sausage, and pubs and shops were banned from opening. This meant you couldn't order a screwdriver to drink or buy one to fix a dodgy door hinge.

Red wine was for migrants, artistic types and homeless people, sherry for elderly aunts and vodka for communists. Most Australians thought muscat was a gun, merlot a magician, tokay a fungal infection and cabernet a French cupboard.

The first two festivals were attended by the few who appreciated wine, but by 1970 the word was out, spread by young men and women tired of weekends dominated by family Sunday roasts and Channel Seven's *World of Sport*. They were the baby boomers – the first generation not scarred by war, brought up on TV that proved the world didn't end at the Murray River, optimistic from years of economic growth and confident enough to challenge accepted norms. They would take to the streets to protest against conscription and apartheid, wear their hair long and listen to music their parents thought would cause frothing at the mouth and the collapse of society.

Not that it was all culture-changing conversations. Many, like generations before, loved getting on the grog. And so thousands headed up the Hume Highway for a long weekend on the drink. The town of 1200 swelled to 20,000, and most of the visitors were very thirsty.

The revered newspaper columnist Keith Dunstan, writing for *The Age* 'Epicure' section in 1997, recalled:

> Rutherglen had seen nothing like it since the Gold Rush. The battered Holdens, the Falcons, the MGs and the endless Kawasakis streamed up the highway . . .
>
> Perhaps my most vivid memory of the [1970] Rutherglen Wine Festival was the day the yobs moved in at the Starlight Barbecue on the football ground. It was Saturday night, the barbecue was over, the yobs had consumed a drop or two, noted the hay bales where the crowds had been sitting and set them ablaze.
>
> There wasn't time to call the fire brigade. George Sutherland Smith Junior, the festival president, made an instant decision. He had a tanker full of wine and gave the order to use it at once. It tore at the heartstrings of a wine lover to see good Rutherglen shiraz being used for such a purpose.

The Age reported that at the 1970 festival 2500 gallons (more than 11,000 litres and well over 100,000 standard drinks) were consumed. This is without attempting to calculate the beer intake as all local pubs were packed with braver (and drunker) revellers taking to the roofs to watch the passing parade. The report said up to 17 prisoners at a time were held in the police station's two tiny tin-roofed cells. The police ran out of bail forms and most of the inmates were bailed for $2 or $4 following 111 arrests.

The town's publicans said thousands of glasses were stolen in the festival.

According to *The Age*: 'Camping hippies showered under a water tower in the main street on Sunday. More than 2500 gallons of red and white wine were drunk – some from flagons in the street.

'Drunken revellers lit fires at a pop concert, broke into a shop, and tried to steal the town's fire engine during the four-day festival.'

Wine, pumped from plastic hoses, was sold at 10 cents a glass. 'Police had to break up wild street dancing.'

To skirt strict liquor laws that banned selling takeaway booze on a Sunday, organisers 'gave away' 3000 pint bottles of wine on the understanding the revellers would buy a program to cover the costs. A group of soldiers tired of queuing at a winery scaled a giant barrel and using straws managed to construct a rudimentary syphoning system.

Town elders advised that having fun with wine did not mean 'pouring it down your throats until it comes out your ears'. Few listened, with many finding the impressive gutters in the main street the perfect position to recline between tastings.

The real tragedy was that drink-driving seemed acceptable. The road toll peaked at 1061 in 1970. During the festival there were eight car smashes and four fatalities in the highways around Rutherglen. In March, 106 deaths were recorded on the roads. Seat belts, random breath testing and a change of culture has resulted in the road toll declining since.

Now retired after a long and successful career in the Commonwealth public service, Peter Barrett recalls that as a young Monash University economics student, he headed to the Rutherglen wine festival in 1970 and 1972.

In those days, he says, students drank beer and wine was the domain of toffs, which is why, on that first trip, they came armed with two car fridges for cold ones. He was 19 and, along with his friends 'up to no good', although in reality they were looking for harmless fun. They managed to secure a site at the local camping ground, a strategic point to launch forays on the town pubs and 15 local wineries. 'It was wall-to-wall tents with other people sleeping in their cars.

'The Rutherglen main street was awash with drunken youths by warm late afternoon or early evening,' he recalls. 'The focus of activity was near the magnificent old two-storey Star Hotel. Many of the yobs stationed themselves on the pub's first-floor balconies overlooking all the action. How those landings didn't collapse, I'll never know.'

In 1972, he, his mates and girlfriends were more organised, renting a bigger tent and a powerful hurricane lamp. Fortified by the local fortified product, when he saw the lamp's flame dangerously close to the flammable tent's ceiling, he grabbed it without hesitation. His motivation was not to save fellow campers, but to save the bond money outlaid for the camping equipment.

The resulting burns required a quick trip to the hospital, where he joined the queue of the self-inflicted wounded. He was soon patched up and declared fit to party.

Today he may occasionally sip a smooth red at his favourite Italian bistro and, if the mood strikes, partake in an occasional Rutherglen muscat. 'Just a small drop these days.'

Who said youth is wasted on the young?

PASSING THE HIGH-TECH SNIFF TEST

If the greatest asset of an investigator is the capacity to sniff out key evidence, then Georgia the black Labrador may be Australia's greatest detective.

We all know police dogs have been trained to follow trails, sniff out drugs and find explosives, but Georgia is the star of her class for the Australian Federal Police as a technical detection expert.

The feds are increasingly turning to traditional canines to do what humans can't: find tiny plastic devices, such as SIM cards and USB sticks, that can be hidden in the strangest places.

In a world filled with plastics, finding that one piece of evidence requires genetic skill, an enthusiastic work ethic and a truckload of training. It is not finding a needle in a haystack but finding the needle in a stack of needles.

From January 2021 to November 2022, the AFP tech dogs did 160 searches and found 691 hidden items including a USB stick in a bowl of garlic cloves, a hard drive stashed in an Esky of food, a buried electronic ankle bracelet, phones hidden in shoes and a SIM card in a wall cavity.

Georgia, with her handler, Leading Senior Constable Scott Lewis, went on 14 searches over four months, finding 83 devices including mobile phones, USBs, SIM cards, SD cards, hard drives and smartwatches. She could open her own PAWn shop.

In December 2020 Georgia succeeded where police had failed. Brisbane terror suspect Raghe Abdi had cut off his electronic ankle monitoring device, allegedly murdered two people – Maurice Antill, 87, and Zoe Antill, 86 – and was later shot dead by police.

Georgia and Lewis were called in to search for the bracelet. They were assigned 1.6 hectares of heavily treed land dotted with running tracks where the tamper GPS on the bracelet had been activated.

When local police and Georgia found nothing, Lewis decided to broaden the search area and let the dog roam. As the sun began to set, Georgia stopped at a giant tree trunk, circled and began to dig. She had found the bracelet that was later downloaded as part of the double homicide investigation.

Such was her success that the program was rapidly expanded to 13 dogs around Australia. The initial funding came from assets of crime, which means the crooks paid for the dogs that would catch them. When the program was expanded, funds came from $31.6 million provided to the AFP for child protection investigations.

Sadly, that makes up a depressingly large part of their work, as the offenders try to conceal evidence on external memory platforms. But the dogs are also used in cases such as counterterrorism and transnational serious and organised crime. Like the rest of us, crooks are reliant on technology, which always leaves a footprint.

Senior Constable Paul Ioannou is a cop with an engaging smile, a salt-and-pepper beard and a love of his job. He has worked in many areas of policing, but you feel he will be with the dogs for the rest of his career.

He has Bondi, a drug, firearms and cash specialist and Doris, a specialist tech-detector. Among the 100 federal dogs there are also specialist explosive hunters. It stands to reason they are the most laid-back, as you don't want an excited dog jumping on a bomb.

For just over 12 months, Ioannou and his Victorian-based Labrador Doris have been on the hunt for hidden data devices often missed by human searches. These are the top-end dogs and are used on federal jobs and increasingly to support state police operations.

Ioannou explains that dogs process smells differently to us. 'Think of a pizza with the lot. We smell the pizza and a dog identifies every topping.' An example was Doris finding a USB hidden in a plastic sleeve buried among stamp collection albums.

Team leader Sergeant Craig Kersten says dogs on the trail sniff between five and 10 times a second, inhaling through one nostril and exhaling through the other. Their smell processing capacity is 40 times stronger, and they can find a scent as faint as one part per million.

'Dogs smell on a molecular level, processing individual scents,' he says.

Puppy training, from eight to 14 weeks, is the critical development period, he says, to tap into instinctive urges. 'It allows them to fulfil their biological potential to hunt.'

The tech dogs have to reach another level, as the scent of electronic memory devices is tiny. If there is time and handlers are briefed before a raid, the dog can have a quick refresher on the exact scent of the devices that need to be found.

The dogs begin full-time training aged around 12 months and retire to their handlers' homes or a foster family at six to eight years.

In training, they are sent to recently vacated public housing to replicate the hundreds of scents that would be picked up in a real search.

The role of dogs in policing is expanding. They can bring down suspects, fly in helicopters, find evidence, lead raids, support victims giving evidence, lift morale in offices and care for officers suffering from PTSD.

'We are pushing the limit [of what dogs can do] and haven't found it yet,' Kersten says.

Dogs and handlers are matched through personality traits. Kersten says the best advice is for the humans to get out of the way and let the dogs do their thing. He says human searches miss items because of preconceptions. We see a coffee machine, smell coffee and believe it is what it seems. A trained dog sees a potential hiding space. 'Dogs don't lie,' says Kersten.

(Although they can cheat. A dog's handler can't be used to plant an object to be found in training, as the dog shortcuts the process by following the familiar human scent to the hiding spot. They can also read their handler's body language, which can hint at an outcome.)

For the dog, success doesn't result in a kill but a reward. 'Some dogs love hugs, others a ball or a game of tug of war,' says Ioannou.

The dogs are housed at the AFP kennel in outer Melbourne, clearly a Club Med for pups. There is a creche for 12 puppies that includes chew toys and play units; down the back is a pool, exercise track and an obstacle course. They will be sent to foster families before returning to the program. About half will make it through the selection and training process.

If a dog slips out, they can usually be found near their favourite activity, hanging around the pool or the exercise track. They are not encouraged to play together, as they wear each other out and they need all their energy for work. The mature dogs have individual runs, sleeping quarters and meals professionally planned and measured to the gram.

When the dogs see handlers walk by, they bark and run – a 'pick me, pick me' routine, as each wants to be chosen for the next job. Clearly, they love their work.

Doris and Ioannou, who have trained together for a year, arrive at a building that can be configured as different styles of house for training drills. As soon as the dog is dressed in an AFP harness, she knows it is time to go to work. Both handler and dog are full of energy and enthusiasm.

Doris is sniffing walls and furniture, tail wagging furiously. Then she sits at a spot, satisfied she has done her job. A quick search finds a phone hidden in a shoe. She finds a USB in a heater and a micro-SD card in a cupboard. They are then told they are on call for a raid search expected to be conducted in the next 24 hours.

The AFP started the tech-dog program in 2019 after seeing its successes in the United States. Seven years ago, Connecticut police started experimenting with the use of dogs to find electronic storage devices and the FBI became involved.

According to the *Australian Police Journal*, one of the early dogs, Bear, was used to search Subway frontman Jared Fogle's home, finding a flash drive filled with child pornography images. Fogle was later sentenced to 15 years' jail.

There can be no greater example of how traditional sniffer dogs assist in the high-tech world than Operation Ironside, the police sting that saw them intercept 27 million organised crime messages from an encrypted app.

The dogs were sent to 12 Ironside targets in Australia and recovered 80 mobile phones, USBs, SIM cards and SD cards.

As Kersten says, you can't trick them.

Postscript

I was having a routine medical procedure the other day (OK, it was a colonoscopy – proving it is not only reporters who want to get to the bottom of important matters) when I was ushered into a side room by the surgeon and his anaesthetist.

Not sure if this would be grim news or a pep talk, I slowly wandered in. It was neither. After briefly discussing the procedure that many criminals (and one police crime commander) have threatened to conduct on me over the years, we got down to brass tacks.

'What's the latest in the Leongatha mushroom case?' one asked. Turns out, one of the medicos had just returned from London where the case was a matter of endless fascination, which may be why

The New York Times and *The Times* reported the arrest of Erin Patterson on three counts of murder and five of attempted murder.

Patterson was the host of a July 2023 luncheon where three people died and one became perilously ill in what police allege was a case of death cap mushroom poisoning.

It has produced worldwide interest. Type in Erin Patterson and mushrooms and you'll get more than 10 million Google hits in just over three months. Prime Minister Anthony Albanese comes in at a lifelong figure of 8.690 million, Richmond footballer Dustin Martin at 6 million and Eddie McGuire at 5.78 million. Dancing Martians comes in with a somewhat disappointing 1.78 million.

My phone went nuts with radio and TV interview requests from producers looking for a talking head (or, in my case, an aged mumbling one) to discuss the latest. There was even one from Irish TV, which may have been even more excited if it was potato rather than mushroom poisoning.

Veteran Homicide investigators – some who investigated the Underbelly War – have never seen anything like it. As a consequence, they have kept their cards close to their chest.

Police who raided Patterson's sprawling Leongatha home came with a dog, but not any dog. Georgia – the Australian Federal Police first specialist technology dog – was flown down from Brisbane for the search.

At Patterson's court hearing, police said they needed time to download a laptop found at her home during the search.

There are dozens of unfunny mushroom memes and posts ignoring the fact Patterson is now before the courts. For the people of Leongatha, the fascination with the case seems to ignore the human tragedy – a point reinforced by the head of the Homicide Squad, Detective Inspector Dean Thomas.

Three people died: Heather Wilkinson, her sister, Gail Patterson and brother-in-law, Don Patterson, while Heather's husband, Reverend Ian Wilkinson survived against all odds.

One resident said of the four victims: 'You will not meet better people. Intelligent, humorous, generous and with integrity in spades. You could search forever in South Gippsland to look for an enemy for them, but you would not find one.'

Meanwhile, Erin Patterson is in a cell waiting for a chance to tell her story. One thing is certain – the world is waiting to hear it.

'SEXY LEXY' BEATS DRUM FOR JUSTICE

When the very talented but slightly lazy star recruit Darren 'Jars' Jarman finally turned up at Hawthorn for preseason training, his new teammates wondered what all the fuss was about. He was slow, uninterested and looked like a high-priced dud – that is, until the footy came out and he turned from mug to magician.

Justice Lex Lasry is the judicial version of Jars – not much good at training but elite at the real stuff. He was, he cheerfully admits, a mediocre high school scholar who became 'an appalling student who was lazy and disinterested' during his Monash law years.

At the end of third year, he failed two out of four subjects, forcing him to waste valuable summer beach time sitting supplementary exams that left a professor asking: 'Do you really think the law is for you?'

'It was an entirely reasonable question,' Justice Lasry acknowledges. The following year, he studied criminal law, which sparked some degree of interest, but it was only when he entered a real court while doing his Articles that he thought: 'I like the feel of this.'

If he wanted to see the difference between the university law library and the cut and thrust of the courtroom floor, he found it in spades when acting as a junior barrister for the prosecution of three men charged with the murder of Melbourne businessman Roger Wilson, who went missing in 1980.

During a legal argument in the absence of the jury, one of the accused – hitman Christopher Dale Flannery – discarded the usual practice of allowing his lawyers to object. Instead, he went bananas, yelling from the dock he intended to kill all the prosecutors. 'That was a sobering moment,' Lasry recalls. Welcome to the real world.

'Rent-a-kill' Flannery and the other two were acquitted while Debbie Boundy, a potential prosecution witness, was murdered and her body never found. Her killer was almost certainly Alphonse Gangitano, who was later murdered in Melbourne's underworld war.

In 1985 Flannery was murdered and, like Wilson and Boundy, his body was not located. Which means it is much safer to sit at the prosecutor's table than in the dock behind.

After 46 years in the law, the last 11 in the Supreme Court, Lasry is retiring from a career that began modestly and grew prodigiously.

He is no ivory tower judge. His carefully crafted deadpan appearance masks a man of social conscience and self-deprecating humour.

Called 'Sexy Lexy' (behind his back) by some court reporters, for decades he has raced vintage Porsches. At 70 years of age, he still drives his GT3 996 left-hand drive, six-speed manual cup car at around 240 km/h on the straight at Sandown. The trick, he says, is not to look at the speedo when the foot hits the floor.

It is a passion that goes back to university days, when he raced MGs. 'I wasn't much good,' he says. This is trademark Lex, saying he isn't much good at anything, yet he became an outstanding judge, a competent race car driver and a musician of some note.

For 20 years, he has played drums for the Lex Pistols, which he describes as 'musical therapy for criminal lawyers'. The band is actually not half bad and they are routinely booked for Bar dinners and other legal social functions.

For all his dry wit and exotic hobbies, Lasry is a man with a burning passion for justice – even when he knows the cause is lost from the beginning, such as the case of Melbourne man Van Tuong Nguyen, arrested in 2002 carrying heroin when he was searched during a four-hour stopover in Singapore.

Lasry became part of the defence team shortly after the arrest and, despite a three-year battle, says 'it was obvious from the start' that Nguyen would hang. 'You could feel the futility.'

On 1 December 2005, Lasry and other defence lawyers went to Changi Prison to say goodbye to their client, who remained composed and courageous although only having hours to live. On the way to prison, Lasry asked one of the local lawyers what to expect. 'He said the lawyers normally fall apart and the client spends the time comforting them.'

He fought a losing battle for Andrew Chan and Myuran Sukumaran, two of the Bali Nine arrested for drug trafficking in 2005. This time there were moments of hope that were finally dashed when they were executed on 29 April 2015.

Lasry has a 'game face', as do all judges. Just as the figure of Lady Justice is blindfolded, judges cannot show any emotion in front of a jury as it can be seen to add weight to damning testimony. One we know left the court stone-faced to collapse and cry in the rear stairs.

Lasry says he has presided over 'far too many' murder trials where the victims are children, such as that of Robert Farquharson, who in 2005 murdered his three sons by driving them into a Winchelsea dam, and Akon Guode, who killed three of her seven children in a similar way.

'I have mastered the art of shutting off [emotions]. You have to if you are to do this job effectively.' He says it has come at a cost, as he can be seen as 'relatively unsympathetic' in his private life.

But if you want to make Lasry cry, there is a simple way. Put on the iconic Al Pacino speech in *Scent of a Woman*, the final scene in

Dead Poets Society or the climax of *Twelve Angry Men*. 'No matter how many times I see [them], they always get me.'

Is it any surprise each movie is about the battle for justice against the odds?

Lasry is one of many judges who feels frustrated at allegations they are soft, out of step with community expectations and put the interests of the convicted criminals before the rights of victims.

Several federal cabinet ministers have been scathing of Victoria's Supreme Court, culminating with former Home Affairs Minister Peter Dutton asserting that Melburnians were 'scared to go out to restaurants of a night time because they're followed home by these [African] gangs . . . You look at some of the jokes of sentences that are being handed down'.

The debate on sentencing tends to polarise, but in the heat, there is little light. To over-inflate the issue for political gain is simply wicked, while trying to suggest there isn't a problem is simply stupid.

The suggestion that sentences are lighter now for serious crimes is just wrong. In the early 1980s, the true length of incarceration was deliberately fudged. A convicted murderer may have received a life sentence but the minimum term would be set around 18 years. Then there was a further discount within the prison system of about one-third and with a few further incentives, the killer could expect to be out in 10 years.

Take the case of Kai 'Matty' Korhonen, who in 1984 fired more than 130 shots, killing security guard Peter Poole, critically wounding policeman Ron Fenton and injuring another two. He was sentenced to life plus 88 years, and was out in 15.

Today, the actual bare minimum for Korhonen would be 35 years. We now have truth in sentencing, where the earliest release date is published, a much tougher parole system and stronger supervision on release.

'Politicians say crime is out of control but the statistics don't support that,' Lasry says, although he agrees that 'people are genuinely frightened by [home invasion and carjacking] crimes'.

He says too many people have come to conclusions about the courts without knowing how the system works. 'We have to get out there and explain instead of judges making speeches to other judges.'

Like all judges, he opposes mandatory sentencing. 'If you take away judges' discretion, there is a risk of unintended consequences.'

He says that when the official punishment for murder was a mandatory death sentence – nearly always commuted by cabinet – juries often only convicted on the lesser charge of manslaughter.

'Offenders don't think of sentences when they commit a crime. Young people doing a home invasion don't think of the consequences.

'We need an insightful discussion on deterrence and to examine why certain crimes are happening. Sentencing alone is not the whole answer.'

Lasry is conflicted by his mandatory retirement. He thinks the time is right but worries about the future. 'I don't think I am defined by being a judge.'

He will head to France for a holiday and a bike ride along the Tour de France route, but with his desire to defend the court system and with the shackles of being a serving Supreme Court judge gone, you get the feeling we haven't heard the last of Sexy Lexy.

From now on, he will be beating more than just the drum of the Lex Pistols.

STEALTHY GUARDIANS OF MELBOURNE'S FRIENDLY GAMES

This is a world exclusive: the true story behind the secret security strategies used to keep an Olympic Games safe. It is about how a young orchardist from Templestowe became a key Olympic security strategist and the personal bodyguard for the Duke of Edinburgh. Sadly, it has taken us just a little time to chase it down – 56 years to be exact.

It was a world unimaginable to today's security-conscious world. The MCG has 485 cameras covering every inch, entrance, exit and even garbage disposal spots. The cameras are so precise they can read the print in your footy record.

Back in the 1950s, however, young David Chivers had his own concerns. He looked to be heading to the Scottish Regiment in Surrey Hills to do his national service – except he didn't fancy wearing a kilt. Instead, he joined the Australian Intelligence Corp and became friendly with Frank Douglas, a young man with big ideas and the gift of the gab.

Douglas found himself at a social function where the chairman of the Melbourne Olympic Organising Committee, Sir Wilfred Selwyn

Kent Hughes, was complaining loudly that everything was behind schedule and police couldn't even protect building sites, let alone the Games proper.

'Frank was full of bluff and he told him that he would be able to do the job,' recalls Chivers, still clearly amused 56 years on.

But Hughes, a former military man, was impressed enough to draft the sergeant into his inner hub. Douglas was 23 years old and Chivers just 21 when they became chief and deputy chief of the Olympic Security Division.

For the 2012 London Games, the security operation took eight years to plan. The London Games had a security force of 37,000, more than two guards for every athlete. There were security cameras everywhere, missiles hidden on buildings and main roads covered by a numberplate recognition system known as the 'ring of steel'.

In Melbourne, two part-time intelligence officers had less than a month.

Of course, it must have been so much simpler back when Melbourne hosted the 1956 Olympics, now remembered as the Friendly Games. Or was it?

In fact, the build-up was anything but. The Korean War was still front of mind, the Cold War was yet to defrost, anti-Japanese sentiment was strong and the White Australia policy was still in force.

Egypt, Iraq and Lebanon boycotted the Games over the Suez Crisis while the Netherlands, Spain and Switzerland were no-shows because of the crisis in Hungary. The Chinese also refused to attend because Taiwan turned up. And to top it off, Russia invaded Hungary weeks before the opening ceremony.

So you would imagine ASIO, the Commonwealth Police and local authorities would have been up to warp speed.

Apparently not.

Chivers says they set up headquarters at the Olympic swimming centre, recruited a few dozen others to help, and began 24-hour patrols about three weeks before the opening ceremony.

It did not begin well. One guard 'must have been asleep' and failed to make an hourly check on the western wall of the freshly constructed pool. When he finally arrived, he found, written in huge letters in blood red paint, the decidedly unfriendly message *BAN RUSSIAN MURDERERS*.

'Frank got some scaffolding and 44-gallon drums and stacked them high enough to hide it,' says Chivers. Better to leave the area looking like a scruffy building site than to insult a humourless nuclear superpower.

It became a pattern. The young intelligence officers thought on their feet – and, on one occasion, their bottoms.

So popular were the main events that many had bought tickets just to see the athletes train. When Chivers arrived at the Olympic Park velodrome one day, the new stand was already full. He was, therefore, slightly surprised to see Douglas not in his customary suit but fully decked out in cycling gear. There had been a mix-up and the teams were all training down at Geelong. 'Quick,' said Douglas, 'get a bike, we'd better put on a show.'

David Chivers could grow a mean nectarine but hadn't been on a bike since his school days. But in matters of national security, an order is an order and he soon managed to find a racing bike in a shed. More Chesty Bond than James Bond, he removed his shirt to ride in his singlet. 'I then tucked my pants into my socks and was ready.

Douglas led the way, which wasn't a good move as he wasn't aware the bike didn't have brakes – until he crashed into the first wall. Finally, they made their way onto the track to 'an enormous cheer from the full grandstand'.

The crowd's good humour began to evaporate when the two peddled sedately around the flat bottom of the track. Chivers recalls cries of 'Get up on the wall, ya' mug.' They sped up. 'I found the trick to riding at 45 degrees was just to keep peddling fast, but after four laps, I said to Frank: "I'm done."'

To keep up the impression that they were international stars, the two bunged on fake French accents (Bazza McKenzie meets the Tour de France) and signed autographs for the crowd. And who said the spy business was tough?

Fast-forward to London 2012. The British criminal justice system, upon which ours is based, has traditionally held that a person is innocent until proven guilty. But this concept has been compromised in the wake of the 2005 London Tube bombings. Sixty-two groups have been banned as terrorist organisations, and suspects could be held for 14 days without charges.

Battle hardened through their bloody experience with the IRA, the British are more matter-of-fact than many about the possibility of terror attacks. And their intelligence networks are considered among the best in the world. In the seven years after 2005, police and intelligence agencies disrupted 21 out of 22 realistic terrorist plots. (They missed the 2007 Glasgow airport attack as the offenders rarely communicated and were unknown outside their own peculiar world.)

The contrast could not be greater. Back in Melbourne 1956, Chivers was assigned to protect the Duke of Edinburgh and shadowed him to the soccer. 'I was happy with that because I had never been to a soccer game.' He sat three rows behind the Duke. 'But I didn't spend too much time watching him because I was too busy watching the game.'

When authorities received intelligence that the Duke could be in danger at the MCG, the security team launched a sophisticated operation. Chivers slept the night in the room where Prince Philip was scheduled to appear the following day. And to make doubly sure, he wedged a chair under the doorknob, Wild West fashion.

Meanwhile, the tensions between the Soviets and Hungarians spilled over at the water polo in the famous 'Blood in the Water' match. 'Let's say they were not on speaking terms and there was plenty of claret left in the pool,' Chivers remembers.

In between security scares, our agent would pop back to the family orchards to check the crops, while Douglas involved himself in counter-espionage. At night, Douglas would drive out in a dark sedan to the Olympic Village in Heidelberg for clandestine meetings with

Hungarian athletes, trying to persuade them to defect. Many did. 'He was very enthusiastic, a real character who had an answer for everything,' Chivers says of his former boss.

After the Games, Douglas (who died a few years back) used his contacts to build a successful security business now run by his son, Craig. And Chivers went back to the Templestowe orchards before moving to the Yarra Valley and then to Queensland, eventually building a golf course at Bundaberg.

Now aged 76, he can still be found on the fairways most days on a tractor. But never a bicycle – unless, of course, it is a matter of national security.

CYBER COPS

Very few people have heard of Detective Sergeant Dion Achtypis, but there may well be no more important investigator in Australia.

You won't see him holding a media conference at a murder scene, and he doesn't command a squad of detectives. He doesn't use a sledgehammer during raids, for he gains access in a much more subtle way. He is part of a three-person team working in the present while exploring the future.

What Achtypis and his team have discovered in 12 months has changed the very nature of investigations in Victoria, and will become the template for how serious crimes are tackled.

We are talking about so-called new technology – which is anything but, as online crime is now the main game. One senior officer observed: 'Organised crime bosses must laugh when they see headlines that we have seized a couple of motorbikes and a few million in cash when they are moving hundreds of millions around the world.'

Let's look at a notorious 'traditional' crime. On 22 June 1994, five men set up fake roadworks at the Richmond freeway entrance, stopped an Armaguard van that had just left the Reserve Bank and stole $2.3 million.

The gang trained for months, set up warehouses to store gear, carried out dry runs, recruited insiders and used a corrupt solicitor to launder the funds. Only one of the gang, Percy 'No Mercy' Lanciana, was convicted, after he was linked to money from the job being exchanged at three banks – undone not by the crime but the cash.

Less than 30 years later, in 2022, there was an equally well-planned theft from a Victoria-based cryptocurrency exchange that didn't dominate the headlines. 'It was instantaneous,' says Achtypis. Without entering a building, pointing a gun or driving a getaway car, the crooks escaped with $135 million. None of the money has been recovered.

'Over several months, there has been a spiderweb of thousands of transactions to international exchanges – everywhere except Australia,' Achtypis says.

Usually police respond to a crisis: if street gang crime is on the rise, form a special unit; if there is a spike in the road toll, send more cars onto the road. But the Cryptocurrency Operations Team was formed in 2022 on guesswork. There were no reliable figures on the extent of the crimes and no comparable unit in Australia to act as a model.

Police work under the *Crimes Act* which came into operation in 1958, two years after black-and-white television was introduced in Australia. So the question is, how do you investigate a crime when the offender is in an office in Moscow and the victim is sitting on their couch in Footscray? And how do you seize the assets of crime when there is no cash and the profits are moved offshore with the touch of a button?

Achtypis says the investigator has had to throw away the old rule book not once but again and again.

'It is not about just re-honing the same old tools, but going to the drawing board and designing entirely new ones, with the very real understanding that many of these will likely be useful for only a short time before they themselves are rendered obsolete,' he says.

The crooks are constantly looking for a weakness to exploit while the cops are searching for a weakness in the criminal organisations' defences.

This means just about every police breakthrough will be redundant. Like the flu vaccine, what works this year will be obsolete the next.

The Cryptocurrency Operations Team discovered a local money-laundering operation that turned over nearly $500 million in six months.

Achtypis says the money, from South-East Asia (original source unknown), was used to buy real estate in Australia and around the world. 'They bought every flavour available – land, commercial properties and residential at both ends of the market. This means home buyers are indirectly competing against criminals at auctions.'

Crooks have embraced cyber laundering because, he says: 'it is more secure than having a pile of cash, you don't have to trust a middleman, and you can transfer money anywhere in the world without using a bank'.

How did Achtypis end up an international cyber cop? After graduating from Monash University in sociology and psychology, he felt he lacked life experience and decided to join the police for a few years to gain it. Twenty-seven years on, he's still there.

A point of indulgence here: Dion says after reading crime books such as the critically acclaimed (again, surely not) *Underbelly* series co-authored by this writer, he decided to become a crook catcher.

A self-confessed computer nerd, he joined the E-Crime squad in 2012. The following year, a suburban detective with misgivings about returning information to a suspect from a seized computer called the squad.

Achtypis says an examination showed drug trafficking through the Dark Web and 24,500 Bitcoins, then valued at $3.4 million. 'At its peak, it was valued at $2.4 billion.'

From a standing start, the Cryptocurrency Operations Team of three discovered a local money-laundering operation, assisted in

44 virtual currency seizures totalling $13 million, uncovered serious corruption and assisted in more than 200 major crime investigations. Not bad for a unit that could hold its Christmas party in a phone booth (or perhaps a small internet cafe).

Dion loves his job and increasingly so do his colleagues. 'They have taken to it like ducks to water. It is a shiny new investigative tool.'

These six facts, he says, speak for themselves:

- Australia has the second-highest concentration of Dark Net drug traffickers in the world, just behind the Netherlands;
- A staggering $50 billion of Bitcoins changed hands in the past 24 hours;
- The World Economic Forum lists both cyberattack and data theft in its top 10 risks, between extreme weather events and armed conflict;
- Sixty per cent of human communication is data-based;
- Fake identity technology that a few years ago was only used by high-end hackers is now available through off-the-shelf apps; and
- Data-based businesses have replaced oil as the most valuable industry in the world.

The twist is that new-world policing can turn the computer weapons used by crooks against them. Operation Ironside is the perfect example of the new rules. Using a former syndicate insider, the Australian Federal Police and FBI built the phone app An0m, sold as a rock-solid encrypted phone system for crooks.

It grew to 12,000 phones connecting 300 criminals around the world. The organisers had a help desk for IT problems and answered queries promptly – it is unwise to leave psychopaths on hold. But there was a back door, and 27 million messages sent over three years were automatically downloaded to a police-friendly server.

Cryptocurrency movements, Achtypis says, leave a trail. You only need to find the tools to follow the money. The Cryptocurrency

Operations Team has developed a cold case capacity to look back at cryptocurrency movements, which means an offender who thought he had successfully tiptoed with the crypto worth millions some time ago has recently been arrested. There will be more.

Achtypis says while the technology has changed, the motive is the same: make money illegally and hide it. They are modern-day pirates who use the Dark Web rather than shovels to bury their treasure.

Take the Nigerian Scam, where thousands of emails are sent by someone who says they have millions locked away unfairly and, with just a little financial help, the fortune is there to be shared. Before it was the Nigerian Scam (or 419 Fraud, as it is also known), it was called the Spanish Prisoner. It was a letter with a Barcelona postmark from a jail inmate with two cheques valued at £75,000 ($140,000) pleading that if the recipient helped retrieve the money, they would be rewarded with £25,000.

That sting started in 1807.

'We started with gold, then notes and coins and now cryptocurrency. There was snail mail, then faxes and now social media,' says Achtypis.

'It is the same old scams really. Nothing has changed.'

TRADITIONALIST LAWMAN'S LONG BEAT

The difference between a satisfying career and a police funeral can sometimes be measured in millimetres, milliseconds or milligrams. So it is with Victoria's longest-serving policeman, who could have ended up dead on a bathroom floor when he was still just a young cop.

Richard 'Dick' Quigg was a constable when he was called to what appeared to be a routine domestic argument at a house in the Geelong suburb of Norlane. The mother and a child were slumped on the front fence and when Quigg and his partner approached, the distressed woman said her husband was inside and 'very sick'.

Quigg believed the dispute was alcohol-related and the man in question was probably in the bathroom 'driving the porcelain bus'. But when he walked in, the suspect was sitting with a rifle pointed under his chin.

Quigg tried to talk him out of pulling the trigger, saying he had a wife and son outside who relied on him. Eventually the man asked: 'You don't want me to shoot myself?' and the policeman-turned-counsellor said he didn't because the paperwork would be a nightmare.

With that the man said: 'Well then, I'll shoot you.'

'He stuck the barrel in my guts and went click but it didn't go off.' Quigg ripped the gun from him and wrestled him to the ground. The gunman was charged with attempted murder but was found unfit to plead and released after six weeks. It was 1968 and Quigg was presented with the prestigious Chief Commissioner's Certificate for devotion to duty and was lucky it wasn't posthumous as tests showed the loaded gun worked, and while the hammer had left an indentation on the bullet, it hadn't detonated.

Quigg was four when he decided to be a policeman, largely because he was impressed by the bobby-style hat won by a relative who was already a serving cop. 'I told my mother I would be wearing that uniform one day.'

It was in June 1963 when he walked into the old Police Depot to begin a career that has lasted more than 54 years. Sir Robert Menzies was prime minister, decimal currency was three years away and there was no Westgate Bridge, with cars crossing the Yarra on a slow-moving ferry. Pubs closed at 6 pm, there were no nightclubs and sweet and sour pork and chop suey masqueraded as exotic ethnic food.

There were 4402 police of which 58 were women. There were 2831 assaults (compared to at the time of writing 43,478), 219 robberies (3200) and 17 armed robberies. In 1963 triple-0 received 7232 calls for police assistance. That number now exceeds 1.3 million. Although even then there were concerns about juvenile crime and speeding, according to the 1963 Police Annual Report:

> Of the other happenings, possibly the most serious, were an outbreak of hooliganism in the Moonee Ponds and Essendon districts, and acts of lawlessness on trains, particularly at night and during week-ends.
>
> Special teams of police were organised and detailed to patrol the areas where hooligans were congregating and the presence of these teams and the apprehension of several undesirable types

> of larrikins eventually eased the problem, and few incidents of this nature are now being reported.
>
> Reports have been received that several young girls disembarking from late trains are being molested and no stone is being left unturned nor efforts spared to stamp out this type of offence.

As to speeding on our roads, the 1963 report said: 'A mechanical speed-testing machine now in use on some highways has proved to be a most successful adjunct in the control of traffic. It records the time a vehicle takes to pass over two points, defined by rubber tubes fixed on the roadway, and the readings obtained as vehicles pass over these tubes have all been accepted by the Courts without question.

'It is proposed to develop and use these machines to their fullest possible capacity.'

In a career where 60 used to mean mandatory retirement, Quigg, now 72, continued because he has always loved the job and is pulling up now only because of ill-health. Given the choice, he would still be wearing the uniform rather than sitting in his living room, dealing with cancer.

'I always wanted to be a policeman. I had no aspirations to do anything else.' And when his generation and the one after that retired, he kept going 'because I still enjoy it'.

He has worked under 11 chief commissioners, 10 premiers and has seen massive cultural shifts that have changed the face of policing.

When he started as a 19-year-old recruit, one of his first duties was to chop the wood for the inspector's fire and one of his first acts of disobedience was to sneak out at night with other students to get a hamburger at Ma's Caravan just down the road. 'We worked so hard and there wasn't enough food. We were starving.'

After graduation, like all new police, he moved into the Russell Street Police Headquarters where he was used as part of a dawn raiding party on the Queen Victoria Market in the investigation into a series of Mafia-related murders.

It was a time when police patrolled on their own, were rarely armed, didn't carry a radio and were expected to check every city laneway at night. Police were so rarely required to carry guns, they were not issued with holsters and in patrol cars, the very unreliable pistol was usually just stuffed in the glove box.

By 1965, his closest police mate suggested they put in for posts in Geelong.

Dick got the job, and he has spent most of his career in the district, seeing it grow from a big country town to a regional centre facing the same drug and crime problems as Melbourne.

When he started in Geelong, the most serious volume crime was breaking and entering, usually committed by a handful of professional thieves. 'You usually could work out who did what.'

But by the early 1970s, drugs were changing the crime scene. The first wave of heroin addiction arrived, and users started committing house burglaries to pay for their drugs. 'That's when the rot first set in.'

Sergeant Quigg is an old-school copper (which is not a cute code for a hard-nosed bash artist). Once when he brought a crook in for questioning, the suspect slipped his false teeth into his handkerchief. When Quigg asked why, the crook said he didn't want them broken in the subsequent flogging. The policeman told him he could pop them back in his mouth as the only thing that would pass his lips was a cup of coffee.

The grateful suspect was then happy to make a full confession.

It is a message the veteran gives to generations of police. 'There is no need to be nasty to people even if they are nasty to you.'

When a group of prisoners kept in poor conditions in a police watchhouse became restless, instead of trying to bully them into submission, he popped out and bought them fish and chips, reasoning that battered flake would be a better look than battered crooks.

In court he took some pleasure when a big city lawyer tried to question his evidence. His client, a former private schoolboy, had thrown a champagne bottle at police during Lorne riots, injuring one.

The barrister asked with so many people there, how could he be sure it was this particular fellow.

Quigg said he was wearing a distinctive Hawaiian shirt – the same one, in fact, he was wearing in court that day. He was found guilty and fined $1000.

He is a traditionalist, saying a strong visible police presence is the best way to deter crime. When there was a spike in violence and criminal damage around Geelong nightclubs after 3 am, a police brawler van was dispatched to patrol hotspots. The impact was immediate and the crime rate dropped. 'Touchy-feely methods just don't work in policing.'

In recent years, Quigg has been in charge of the Geelong Operational Tactics and Safety Training that has become popular not only with local police but many stationed in Melbourne.

The veteran has seen many tragic deaths, such as the little boy who drowned in a flooded gully trap trying to rescue a toy car, the man who threw himself off a building over the most minor tax issue, and the 16-year-old stabbed to death over an adolescent tiff.

He says you have to control your emotions to help the grief-stricken. 'You just have to switch on and do the job. You have to try and look after people when they are falling to bits.'

ONE LAST FIGHT FOR THE UNDERDOG

They buried Bernard 'Barney' Cooney in February 2019. The service celebrated the life of a good bloke, a man with a social conscience who always wanted to help the disadvantaged.

Mourners were told of a long life, of a loving husband and father of five who built a career in the law, helped fashion fairer work rules, provided pro bono legal advice for the disadvantaged and spent nearly 18 years in the Senate, one of the few politicians who refused to become a tribal warrior.

The eulogies did not dwell on the end – slow, miserable and dehumanising as it was. But as he physically decayed and was unable to move, former senator Cooney was still determined to make a contribution.

Before his body betrayed him, he worked for those who didn't have a voice. In one speech to the Senate, he said: 'We all want to see that justice is done to everyone in our society so that those who would seem to be at the periphery, those who are on the edge, become the brothers and sisters of those at the centre.'

The mark of a politician is often not what their team says of them but what their opponents think of them. When he retired in 2002 as an ALP senator, Liberal opponent Senator Robert Hill said: 'Barney sets a standard to which most of us seek to aspire, but rarely reach, in terms of his personal demeanour, his commitment and his values . . . He is always fighting for the underdog.'

Days after his death, former Liberal senator Amanda Vanstone wrote in *The Age*: 'Colleagues of all persuasions come and go but rarely ones like Barney. If you want an example of what a decent, hard-working, committed parliamentarian looks like, you couldn't do better than him.'

He was banned from taking the lead during question time because he sought constructive answers rather than cheap political points. Formerly a handy amateur boxer, he refused to land a low blow.

In his final chapter, the ex-senator became one of those he had once championed – someone virtually helpless. A little while ago, as he lay in his reclining chair-bed that had become his prison, he gathered his strength to whisper his final legal submission to the Royal Commission into Aged Care Quality and Safety, for he knew he would not last until its first sitting date.

His faithful transcriber, leaning forward to catch each husky word, was former Supreme Court judge Frank Vincent. They have been great friends for six decades.

'When I came from Tasmania to Melbourne University, I knew no one. I mated up with Barney and we were close friends ever since,' says Vincent.

Barney had cancer in a leg. They didn't get it all, came back for another attempt and eventually had to amputate. Still it didn't stop and for the last few years, he has been in care.

'As he physically deteriorated, his mind remained incredibly active,' says Vincent. His wife, Lillian, was in the same care facility but they were too ill to meet.

Vincent would visit his old mate once a week. After the royal commission was announced, Barney said he wanted to make a submission. He was in one of Melbourne's best facilities and was not mistreated – his family stress that the staff were diligent and committed – but he wanted the commission to know that the very process stripped the elderly of their dignity and left them to die miserably.

Here is Senator Bernard Cooney's final submission:

'Here is your coffee.'

There was no greeting or even mention of my name as the staff member placed the cup on a stand well beyond my reach. She did not inquire as to how I would reach it or assist me to do so or indicate that she would arrange for another staff member to help me, although I was clearly incapable of moving the bed-like chair to which I am confined.

There was a straw in the cup that had been placed there, because it was understood that I would experience difficulty in holding it and drinking the coffee. In fact, this would have been impossible without assistance even if it had been within reach, as I am unable to move my head sufficiently and have a very limited range of hand movement and control.

The responsibility of the particular kitchen staff member was only to deliver the afternoon coffee to my room, and she had done that. I do not criticise her for her performance of this limited role and she was not a carer, but rather want to draw attention to the deeper issues with which residents like myself are confronted. These can be manifested by something as simple as the drinking of a cup of coffee but they are evident in almost every interaction with staff.

The operators of the aged care facility could truthfully assert that afternoon tea was available and provided to all residents. If challenged about the practical impossibility of drinking the coffee when it was placed beyond my reach, they undoubtedly would have responded that I could have simply pressed the call button placed on my chair and assistance would be provided.

The absurdity of this statement arises from the fact that, as those responsible for my care are well aware, I simply do not have the strength to press it. It also assumes, of course, that my call would be answered some time before my coffee had become stone cold. However, in my experience, even when it is pressed by visitors on my behalf for one reason or another, there is often a considerable delay.

I do not hold the staff members responsible for their frequent failure to respond within a reasonable time to such calls. There are often insufficient numbers on duty to attend to the needs of residents.

Unsurprisingly, I often experience considerable discomfort and require repositioning in my chair to secure relief. Unless I have a visitor at the time, I will have no means of communication. Staff assistance is irregular and lengthy periods will elapse before anyone comes to check on me. My voice is very weak and I cannot call out. I experience such times as a form of torture.

I make no complaint about the physical conditions in the facility, which are fine, nor generally in relation to what could be described as compliance with the required formal standards. My concerns arise from the essential depersonalisation of very vulnerable residents.

The systems and structures are clearly designed for their cost-effective management and handling rather than the provision of personalised care. The staff members at my facility try their hardest to fill this gap, but they lack adequate training and the support required to enable them to do more than quickly attend to the resident's specific requests when time permits. From whatever perspective this situation is viewed, it is clearly very unsatisfactory.

I am not being overdramatic when I state that I sit here slowly dying. It is a process that is neither physically comfortable nor emotionally easy to cope with. But I am not dead yet and I have not given up on life. I am not alone in this experience, as there are others in this home and thousands across the country who share it. I want our position understood.

Inevitably, as our physical and mental situations deteriorate, our universe becomes smaller and smaller, until it is eventually confined to a few rooms in a single building. Slowly, for many, our circle of visitors who bring the outside world to us declines the longer we remain here, until finally there are family members and a few long-term faithful friends.

Fortunately, I am not in the position of many who are largely isolated in this way. Mentally we may be quite alert but are still infantilised when spoken to by some staff. There are some programs and residents welcome them to help pass the time, but few provide any stimulation. They are generally tired and unimaginative.

The obvious and continuing failure of our system to address seriously the mental and emotional wellbeing of our aged population shames our community. Neglect at this level can be as destructive as physical abuse and contribute to great distress.

As I understand the situation generally across the country, there are few social workers or other trained personnel to assist residents who are often experiencing a powerful sense of separation and loss of their homes, associations and social and other activities.

This type of support and assistance has not been given anything approaching sufficient significance. It should be integral to all such services and not treated as a kind of add-on and its provision generally left to some good-hearted community groups and limited chaplain services.

There must be recognition and support to assist us at this level as we struggle to maintain our human dignity and involvement in life when, in consequence of our physical circumstances and diminishing personal autonomy, it is constantly being stripped from us.

Barney died on 9 February 2019. He was 84. For God's sake, let's not bury his final message with him.

THE COP THEY COULDN'T CRUSH

On the ground floor of the Victoria Police Centre is the Honour Board For Courage that lists the names of nearly 500 police who risked their lives in the line of duty.

But in policing there are two types of courage; there is the instinctive act of physical bravery and the moral type that requires the strength of character to uphold the law when pressured to compromise. Former policeman Denis Ryan knew his name would never appear on the honour board, although he is a hero who was prepared to sacrifice his career on a point of principle.

He refused to buckle when his bosses wanted him to ignore a paedophile priest. He was then hounded from the job in a conspiracy that many believe went all the way to the Chief Commissioner's office.

Now, 44 years after he was forced to resign because he cared more for children than his professional future, he has been vindicated. It was only a few words and a handshake, but when Victorian police commissioner Graham Ashton formally apologised on behalf of the police force, it was a victory for a man who refused to be crushed by two powerful institutions. 'Denis wouldn't look the other way.

He acted with propriety and courage and it is a testament to his character. We can't right the wrongs of history, but we can acknowledge and learn from them,' Ashton says.

So why was an honest cop hounded from office for trying to do his job? First, we must look back to a time where the police force was poisoned by secular interests and some cops put church before duty. These men were hypocrites, having sworn on the Bible to uphold the law, they conspired to protect paedophile priests without a thought for the kids whose lives were ruined. They didn't just look the other way but built escape tunnels for these rats of the cloth.

Senior Detective Ryan was a staunch Catholic who was determined to uphold the oath he swore on the Bible. Melbourne-trained, he transferred to Mildura after a doctor advised his son's asthma would improve in a drier climate.

In 1971, St Joseph's College vice-principal John Howden contacted Ryan to tell him that Monsignor John Day had molested a young female student, adding that Ryan shouldn't tell his immediate boss, Detective Sergeant Jim Barritt.

Barritt was Catholic, a mate of Day's, a control freak and a member of a loose cartel of cops known as the 'Catholic Mafia' who protected priests accused of crimes.

In Melbourne, Ryan had been approached by a senior officer and asked to join the group that made allegations against the church disappear. Ryan stared him down. In Mildura, he began his investigation and easily found a dozen boys and girls who had been molested. Day was so arrogant, he hardly bothered to cover his tracks, believing he was a protected species. Ryan soon had formal statements from the victims and it was clear the monsignor was a monster.

Ryan hoped that when he presented his evidence to Barritt's superiors, they would have no choice but to support Day's prosecution, naively believing duty, honour and evidence would defeat the white-anting by the Catholic Mafia. He was wrong. It was Ryan rather than Barritt and Day who was attacked, with the detective told he had breached the chain of command. He was then ordered to drop the case.

Protocol rather than protecting victims was the priority.

It would have been easy for Ryan to just follow orders, but he thought of the victims and knew that if Day was not stopped, the offending would continue. 'It was all swept under the carpet. I took 12 statements and I could have taken 100,' he recalled.

When Ryan refused to stop, senior police begrudgingly conducted an investigation that had Barritt's fingerprints all over it and although he was Day's close mate, he sat in on the priest's interview in what was a clear conflict of interest.

The final report was so inept, it had to be fixed. It concluded that there was 'insufficient evidence' to prosecute Day, yet found he'd 'misconducted himself'.

Nobody mentioned that Day would tell Barritt secrets from the confessional about local crimes and the compliant cop would organise offenders to work at the church and school rather than take them before the courts.

Everyone in the inner circle in Mildura knew the truth. When one boy was appointed altar boy, his father, a senior officer in the Shire, made sure the decision was revoked.

Day was at first defended by Bishop Ronald Mulkearns, then finally moved when the allegations threatened to become public. In 2016, Mulkearns died in disgrace after he was found to have protected paedophile priests, including the notorious Father Gerald Ridsdale.

Even though the doctored police report effectively backed Ryan, his career was doomed from the moment he refused to join the conspiracy. Senior police, right to the office of then Chief Commissioner Reg Jackson, declared that this was a personality clash between two headstrong detectives.

And so in 1972, Barritt was transferred to Echuca, which was no big deal, while Ryan was ordered back to Melbourne – a move senior police knew he could not make because of his son's health. He was effectively forced to resign, which meant they rid themselves of the honest cop and protected the cover-up artist.

Over the years, there were attempts to have Ryan's case reviewed but each time, senior police supported the bogus 'clash between colleagues' line.

Then Ryan found an ally in former Chief Commissioner Mick Miller, who had been a senior officer at the time of the case. Miller (who was overseas at the time of the transfer decision) was assured by senior colleagues he considered his friends that it was a simple conflict that had been managed correctly. 'You can only be betrayed by the people you trust,' he said in 2016.

Long after he retired, Miller read Ryan's account in the book *Unholy Trinity* and realised he had been kept in the dark while the Mildura detective's career was destroyed.

In 2015, he told the Royal Commission into Institutional Responses to Child Sexual Abuse there had been 'misconduct by senior Victoria Police officers, including dereliction of duty, conspiracy to pervert the course of justice and inciting other members of the police force to join the conspiracy against Denis Ryan in order to conceal the crimes committed by Day'.

Ryan told the hearing: 'I knew that if I resigned from the force I would lose my police and emergency services pension, which was significant, and all my benefits. I would also lose a job that had previously been my life. However, I knew that if I resigned and stayed in Mildura, my voice would still be heard. In the early days, I had nightmares of Monsignor Day raping kids and the way the police force had condoned these offences.'

Ashton had also read *Unholy Trinity*, but it was at Miller's urging he decided to call for the files and see for himself. With no skin in the game, he could see the obvious: that a decent policeman had been railroaded for doing his duty.

It would have been easy for Ashton to consign the story to history. Instead, to his credit, he took action. To do anything less would have been hypocritical as he has been publicly scathing of institutions that supported a cover-up culture, once telling a state parliamentary inquiry: 'The processes of the Catholic Church are designed to put the reputation of the church first and the victims second.'

'If you call out other organisations then you have to call out your own. Society's greatest duty is to care for our children,' he said.

At a private morning tea attended by senior police, Mick Miller, and a group of men who lobbied for Ryan over the years, Ashton turned to the retired detective and said: 'Denis, you were right and your commitment has been outstanding.'

Police Association Assistant Secretary Bruce McKenzie also apologised, acknowledging they should have done more to defend Ryan. The meeting with Ryan was more than a cup of tea and an apology: the very admission means the force will pay the former detective some form of compensation for the past wrong.

Two years later in a confidential settlement, Ryan was awarded sufficient compensation to live for the remainder of his life in comfort.

Ryan, 84, read from a prepared statement, thanking Ashton for being 'forthright and frank', adding:

> In my day as a detective, I became aware and indeed had my career roughly ended by some of the most senior members of the force who had a distorted sense of loyalty to other institutions.
>
> That failure led to what I have described as an epidemic of clerical child sex abuse in Victoria. That the Catholic Church covered up and engaged in criminal conspiracies brings great shame on that institution.
>
> But the failures of policing in pursuit of that distorted sense of loyalty led one victim to become two, to become ten and awfully and finally for the number of victims to become too large to count. My own circumstances have been distinctly grim since I left the force but as dark as some of those days have been,

> they have no parallel with those forced to endure the pain and suffering of sexual abuse.
>
> What makes it worse and haunts my dreams to this day is that if we as a police force did what we were supposed to do, what we were charged to do, what we took an oath to do, so much of that pain and suffering would not exist today.

Out of this dark episode, there is a shard of light. Ryan has agreed to video his story so serving police will see that courage can come from sticking to your guns as much as using one in times of physical danger.

'I'M NOT LEAVING UNTIL WE FIND HER.'

Detective Senior Constable Samantha Russell, dressed in a pure white forensic suit in contrast to the wet, stinking, rubbish dump she is searching, stops to confirm what she suspects, slumps with her hands on her knees with relief and then waves her arms wildly to get the attention of her colleagues. They have found her.

She had been dead for months, murdered by a wannabe boyfriend, but for Missing Persons Squad investigators, arresting the offender is secondary.

The head of the squad, Detective Acting Inspector Tony Combridge, says: 'Our priority is to return the victim to their family.'

One reason, he says, is that no matter the evidence, families will hold on to a shred of belief that the missing will defy the odds and be found alive.

'One of our jobs is to extinguish that last piece of hope, so they can grieve properly.'

In the case of Ju 'Kelly' Zhang, police knew what had happened, had arrested the offender and were confident they had the evidence to convict. But they were not going to stop until they found her.

Police budgeted to spend $1 million in a 12-week search of a 40-metre deep, 300-metre by 200-metre channel in the giant Wollert tip. But this was no needle-in-a-haystack job – with the help of the refuse management experts onsite and GPS and altitude monitors on the collection trucks, they had pinpointed the near exact area. The search took four days.

At first, dozens of police raked through scoops dug up by the excavator. Then the operator began to use his digger as a sifter, gently shaking each scoop, like a gold prospector in a river.

Kelly Zhang, 33, was stabbed to death in her Epping home on 1 February 2021, with her eight-year-old son, Jack, in the next room.

Joon Seong Tan, who had met Zhang through an online dating site only one month earlier, stabbed her to death when she wished to move on.

The following day, he declared her missing, claiming she had walked out the front door in her pink dressing gown and disappeared. 'The locals [police] were not happy with the story and came to us [missing persons],' says lead investigator Sam Russell.

Russell is everything you want to see in a modern cop. Smart, dedicated and committed to her job and the victims she represents. The former emergency nurse took to policing in 2011 and soon knew she wanted to work on complex cases such as Zhang's. Ten years later, she won the Mick Miller Detective of the Year Award for her work on this case. 'I've told her, I'll be working for her one day,' says Combridge, her squad boss.

Identifying the prime suspect was not the challenge; Tan had lied about Zhang's disappearance and behaved as someone hiding a guilty secret.

'Within days, he was trying to hide. He changed his phone number, hid at a female friend's house and had left his car at a reserve. He was arrested on Sunday, the 7th, in a Doncaster street, waiting to be picked up and driven to Perth,' says Russell. He was carrying $3500 and his passport.

When he was interviewed, they didn't have enough but only days later, they did.

His phone showed he had conducted online searches, including 'How many years for killing a person in Australia?'; 'How is stinky garbage disposed of in Australia' and 'Garbage disposal in Australia'.

Nine days after the murder, he was arrested at Melbourne Airport about to fly to Perth (without his passport, which had been seized by police), where he had planned to find a boat to return to Malaysia.

Zhang's parents flew in from mainland China, hoping their daughter had been kidnapped. They checked the letterbox every day, hoping for the ransom demand. Despite having spent their life savings, they were determined to pay. It was Russell's job to care for them, and to manage their expectations while gathering evidence on Tan.

Using statements and electronic evidence, Russell concluded Tan had disposed of Zhang in the Heidelberg area. Police searched parks and creeks and checked dozens of industrial bins but came up empty.

Later, police would find that on the night of the murder, Tan drove through Heidelberg and saw it was bin night. He drove back to Zhang's house, where he had hidden her in a cupboard, wrapped her in a blanket, then put her body in her own rubbish wheelie bin and took it to Heidelberg to be collected. The following morning, he took the bin back to Zhang's Epping home and cleaned it.

After breaking Tan's friend's alibi, Russell worked out what had happened, concluding the bin would have been collected and its contents dumped in the Wollert tip. Months had elapsed when Combridge made his pitch to his bosses: we need up to $1 million to find her.

He was asked how confident he was that they would find the body. He put his reputation on the line, saying he was 85 per cent sure. Those who signed the cheques liked the odds.

'We were told: "If it needs to be spent, spend it,"' Combridge says. (They ended up spending only $36,000.)

We should all pause here. The offender was in custody, a conviction was likely and the family would hear in court what had happened.

Yet the search was authorised. There are few jurisdictions in the world where an operation like this would have been conducted. As long as we are prepared to respect the dead and care for the living in this way, we remain a civilised society.

A massive 250,000 tonnes of refuse had been deposited since Zhang disappeared, but luck was on the investigators' side. The day after she was murdered, the tip operators moved to a new channel to dump rubbish.

From here, it was the tip workers rather than investigators who took the lead. Using GPS readings, they identified the specific area in the giant channel. So, rather than looking for a needle in a haystack, they were looking for a needle in a hay bale.

When Russell arrived at the tip, she had one thought: 'I'm not leaving here until we find her.'

After four days of searching, workers told police they were close and thought they would find her in a few days. 'Forty-five minutes later, she was found,' says Combridge.

Russell was standing near the excavator. 'Steve [Anderson] operated it like a third hand, gently lifting scoops. He said he was thinking with every scoop: "Please be her",' she says.

Russell looked in the hole and saw something wrapped in a blanket. 'I called out to Steve: "I think I can see her hand."

'He gently scooped her up and put her down next to me. Then I could see her blue stripey pyjamas and pink dressing gown.'

Russell said she felt a wave of emotions. 'There was happiness, shock, and I was sad she had been left in that environment.'

It was, she says, 'pissing rain', and the detective, perhaps instinctively, used a tarp to protect the victim.

But she didn't have time to dwell. She and Combridge headed out to tell the family before the news broke.

They spoke to Jack, the only family member who spoke English. They told him they had found his mother. He asked: 'Is she alive?'

'He was devastated,' says Combridge.

As were her parents, but there was another emotion – relief. 'It is hard to reconcile how grateful they were that we had found her.'

Tan was convicted of murder, sentenced to a minimum of 23 years and will face deportation at the end of his sentence.

Justice Amanda Fox praised Russell for her thorough investigation. At the sentencing, the tip team who worked with police were there, all dressed in pink, Zhang's favourite colour.

'They were brilliant. I didn't know when this started that I would end up making friends with the 70-year-old tip manager,' says Russell.

Harry Taylor did much of the heavy lifting, helping find the spot where Zhang was left, and, with another worker and two police, carrying her body out in knee-deep mud.

Taylor's victim impact statement illustrated perfectly the commitment shown by the police and the Wollert workers. 'Although I never met Ms Zhang when she was alive, it seemed to me, in a strange way, that she and I, who had never met, were on a journey together. I attended her funeral at Springvale, contributed to the limits of my capacity in an appeal to support her destitute parents. My wife and I put together and delivered a hamper for her mum and dad and Jack for Christmas.

'On behalf of all the landfill team, Kelly, we did our best for you, and it turned out that our best was good enough.'

Yes it was, Harry.

SEEING THE LIGHT (IN MORE WAYS THAN ONE)

The chap heading to clean the pit toilets at the isolated camping grounds was only slightly miffed when he heard one boy say to his mate: 'Yuck, here comes the dunny man,' before crossing the road to stay upwind of the self-styled sanitation engineer.

'I thought: "I've done a fair bit of uni to get here,"' says Australia's newest lighthouse keeper, who doubles as an associate professor of forensic medicine.

As far as sea changes go, this is a beauty. He and his mates have leased a remote lighthouse with a public campsite to boot.

Dr David Wells is reflecting on his career thus far as he retires as a head of clinical forensic medicine to split his time between the Point Hicks lighthouse and a series of United Nations and World Health Organisation projects.

For the past 25 years, first as a police surgeon and then as the head of the clinical section of the Victorian Institute of Forensic Medicine, Wells has dealt with the victims of violent crime on nearly a daily basis. He has seen people who have been bashed, raped, stabbed or shot. And he has seen those whose lives have been irrevocably altered by car accidents.

And yet in this world of horror, he has seen countless cases of heroic recovery. People who have refused to be defined as crime victims.

'We often see people at the worst moment of their lives. It can be exhilarating to see the resilience of those who never give up and turn their life around.'

Such as Kelly who, at the age of nine, was the victim of repeated sexual assault by her father. At the court hearing, the little girl collapsed in a sobbing fit, unable to give evidence. And little wonder: the man who stole her innocence was sitting in the dock, staring straight at her.

Called as a last resort by police, Wells spoke to the victim during a court break. 'I said: "I can't tell you what to say but I will stay in the court. Just look at me and don't worry about anyone else."'

She managed to get through her evidence; the accused was committed, convicted and jailed.

It may have been the end of the prosecution, but only the beginning for this little girl. After her family moved, the new owners of the house heard suspicious noises and called the police. Kelly was hiding in the dirt under the house, cuddling her dog, directly under her old bed.

The demons refused to be silenced – she descended into a life of drugs, prostitution and self-harm. 'I certified her many times. She hated me with a vengeance.'

Her partner took his own life in front of her with a shotgun, leaving Kelly to bring up their two children as a single mother.

Wells and two police who had known her since she was that confused little girl refused to let go. Through remarkable self-will, she dragged herself back to a form of normality. Both children are in the top of their classes and have won academic awards.

Not so long ago, Wells' wife, Jill, wanted to meet this remarkable woman. When the doctor returned to the park with some food, both were crying as the children played on nearby swings. 'When I was that age,' the survivor told Mrs Wells, 'I was already having sex and taking drugs.'

Jill Wells is confined to a wheelchair these days, due to multiple sclerosis, which is why as near newlyweds in 1980, the couple took off overseas to backpack soon after she was diagnosed.

'We did then what we thought we may not be able to do now. It was the best thing we ever did,' he says.

It was while working in a Middlesex hospital that he started to examine rape victims and saw how badly they were treated.

'They would be in a thin cubicle next to other patients, dealing with the most intimate issues, surrounded by horrible disinterest.'

It sparked an interest in victims' rights. When he returned to Melbourne, he completed a master's degree on the way children were expected to give evidence. 'They were brought into a court and treated as adults. It was embarrassing.'

And he knows that for every Kelly, there are many others who never find their way back.

He was part of a study that tried to track child victims from the 1980s and early 90s. The grim results showed they were at greater risk of suffering psychiatric illnesses and premature death from drug overdoses and suicide.

While working as a GP, he became a part-time police surgeon and in 1987 took over the role full-time. Too often under the old system, police doctors were seen as part of the prosecution team and were pressured to provide slanted evidence. Wells often found himself in conflict with senior police when he refused to parrot the company line.

After a spectacular fallout, he returned when the process of medical examination was taken away from the police in 1995 and assigned to the independent Victorian Institute of Forensic Medicine.

The institute now sees up to 3500 patients a year and examines about 500 alleged victims of sexual assault.

He is, perhaps, Australia's most impressive expert, viewing cases from a medical, legal, prosecutorial, evidentiary and welfare perspective, and his views carry great gravitas.

And after seeing thousands of sexual assault victims, his verdict is damning. The criminal justice system has failed them dismally and some involved in the process have an entrenched reluctance to embrace change.

'There is something fundamentally wrong with the way we treat the majority of rape victims. Most never get their day in court and never get to hear the words: "Guilty as charged."'

Dr Wells says that in most cases, the investigation comes down to one person's word against another. 'In the vast majority of cases, the victim knows the accused and the prosecution goes nowhere. We take these people through a traumatic examination and have them share intimate details with almost certain knowledge it will go nowhere. It is almost a fraud.'

He says the intellectually and psychologically vulnerable are often victims of sex crimes and yet 'I have never been called to give evidence in such cases [as none ended up in court].'

Most disturbing of all is that Wells conducted a straw poll of female doctors, lawyers and police, asking them if they would report their own rape. 'Not one said they would.'

He believes there is no serious debate on alternative resolutions because those involved in the present system are protecting their patch.

He favours a conciliation process, where the parties meet in a non-adversarial environment. 'Often the victim just wants the crime acknowledged.'

On the road toll, he is a strong law-and-order man. He says while the drink-driving message has resonated with most, 'there remains a small group of sociopaths who don't give a stuff about anyone else'.

He remains baffled at the general tolerance to motorists who continue to drive after their licences are cancelled. 'On losing their licence, their vehicle should be seized. When you lose a firearms licence, the weapon is removed. Why is it not the same with a car?'

He remains frustrated that 'Mr Cruel', the serial child molester (and the suspect in the murder of Karmein Chan, who was abducted from her Templestowe home in April 1991), was never caught. 'There was so much good work done in the case but no closure.'

But even in such a dark case, there were moments of light.

He spoke to the parents of one victim, telling them that he would help their young girl when she was found. 'They said they knew they would never see her again.'

But they did. She was found and Wells treated her and gathered evidence in hospital for three hours before opening the doors to allow the parents to see the daughter they thought they had lost forever.

'They were in each other's arms sobbing. There were tears glistening on the cheeks of everyone there, including mine. Even the most hardened detectives were crying.'

Still emotional, he left the hospital to find a news photographer waiting to take a picture of the victim. A robust discussion ensued. 'I might have given the camera a little tap. I got a please explain for that one.'

The good doctor learnt to handle himself when he worked in Melbourne pubs while a university student. On the first day he saw the publican march two patrons out by holding broken glasses at their necks. It was not the sort of place that would be awarded five stars on Google reviews.

Soon he learnt that an after-hours knock on the back door would be the local coppers after a slab, no questions asked.

Wells worked at several tough pubs but drew the line at one notorious city establishment. 'They wanted me to wear ladies' clothing one day a week.'

In the office that he is about to vacate is a black-and-white photo of former prime minister Gough Whitlam. 'He saved my life. My father was a linguist and I was doing languages badly at school. I failed French and reminded my father that Whitlam said it was a dying language.

'He said: "Well, you better be good at sciences then."'

And he was.

He wanted to be a vet and was shattered when his marks only allowed him to study medicine at Monash.

Now he looks back on his career with few regrets. 'This has been a great place to work and I just decided it was time to go. I wanted to leave on my terms.'

He will continue to tend hives as an amateur beekeeper, assist in international forensic medicine projects, watch whales breach off his 123-year-old lighthouse on Bass Strait – and work part-time as Australia's most overqualified lavatory hygienist.

LUCY – WHAT'S NOT TO LOVE ABOUT HER?

I was in a waiting room at the Office of Public Prosecutions when the subject of this story wandered in with a relaxed look on her face and gently gave me her business card. Nothing unusual in that, except Lucy is a three-year-old chocolate Labrador.

The OPP houses more than just stern-faced lawyers who demand the death penalty for speeding tickets. It has a program using dogs to help calm traumatised witnesses giving evidence in court cases.

The court system has slowly realised there is a duty not only to search for justice but to protect victims from being further traumatised. Dogs do more than dig holes, round up sheep and wag their tails. Many breeds help people in need – and we are not talking about St Bernard snow rescue dogs that offer a tot of brandy to warm you up in a blizzard.

(Disclosure: in the view of this reporter, there are only two types of people. Those who like dogs and psychopaths.) Dogs brighten the mood in aged care homes, assist traumatised first responders and ex-service personnel and are welcomed into hospitals for patients receiving end-of-life care.

Victims engagement coordinator Julie Morrison is in charge of the OPP program, and you could not find a more passionate advocate for the use of dogs in the court process. A former teacher and human resources executive, Morrison has a background in training and competing dogs.

'In 2017 we started a pilot program using a dog for half a day a week. It was supposed to go 12 weeks but after six weeks we knew we were on to a winner.'

The feedback from witnesses, lawyers and police is overwhelmingly positive. 'She's a lifesaver. She is amazing. Holding the lead really helped to ground me. I took my shoes off so I could feel her at my feet,' says one witness.

'All of the witnesses commented on how much they loved having her around as a source of comfort during what was a fairly stressful few days for them,' says an OPP social worker.

Assistance Dogs Australia has helped people with restricted mobility, autism and PTSD. The dogs have been sent to schools to lower stress during exams.

At a funeral, an ex-policeman suffering from PTSD was in a pew, clearly distressed. His companion dog stepped up, placing paws on both the man's knees and looking directly into his eyes. The man gained comfort by burying his head in the dog's fur.

The funeral was for Ron Fenton, a policeman shot on duty who later suffered terribly from PTSD. He said he would have taken his own life if not for Yogi, his trauma dog, trained by a Bathurst Prison inmate.

In 2019 Morrison won a Churchill Fellowship to study the use of dogs in the US and Canadian criminal justice systems. She says the dogs in North America have 26 different roles, from the crime scene to the court. 'At the Las Vegas mass shooting [in 2017 a lone gunman killed 60 and wounded 411 people], six dogs were sent to the MGM Casino to assist witnesses. They can go to a crime scene and one dog can help a witness through the whole process.'

She says they are also used at natural disasters such as wildfires, an initiative that could easily be adopted here. Canadian police use them at crime scenes, hospital casualty wards and serious accident spots.

Lucy, the first full-time court dog in Australia, underwent eight months' training at the Southern Queensland Correctional Centre as part of the Pups in Prison program. Her handler was a female inmate serving time for murder.

Morrison says: '[The inmate] is the sweetest, loveliest lady. When Lucy graduated, she said: "I know I have hurt a lot of people and by now helping people it makes me hate myself a little less."'

Such has been Lucy's success that the OPP has expanded its program at Child Witness Services with Kiki, a black Labrador. She was trained by the same inmate. (The assistance dog programs in NSW and Queensland prisons consistently receive rave reviews for aiding the community and lowering recidivism rates. The prisoner who trained Yogi for Ron Fenton is now a successful plumber in Sydney. That a similar program has not been adopted around Australia beggars belief.)

The dogs are truly remarkable. A Canadian handler reports he can walk into a class of kids and the dog will head to the one who has been traumatised.

Labradors are the perfect fit for court work for they like people and are relaxed by nature. Like newspaper reporters, they are highly social, low in energy and love free food.

Lucy has a bag of tricks; she can bow on command, play bowls, and turn the pages of a book. She is so popular she now has her own Instagram page, @courtdoglucy. Cute, but hardly likely to make a huge difference to a traumatised victim of crime. The real work is about trust, companionship and the dog's ability to pick up on the emotions of the witness.

Lucy meets the subject away from the court to establish a relationship. Morrison says the witness is encouraged to hold the lead as if Lucy is their dog and not just a visitor. She will lie quietly, leaning slightly against the person's leg. The victim can lean down to stroke her or take a shoe off to rub her with a foot.

She is more than friendly; she has the capacity to bond quickly and be a friend. For victims of sex crimes, the process of recalling the crime in front of strangers and then to be questioned in excruciating detail can be a raw and bruising experience.

Repeatedly, witnesses say having Lucy means having a friend in their corner. As one young victim said: 'I'm special 'cause I've got a dog.'

Lucy is chilled – sometimes too chilled. More than once during evidence, there has been an unexpected background noise. 'She is a bit of a snorer,' says Morrison. (This is a trait shared by some jurors and the occasional judge during particularly boring tracts of evidence.)

Sometimes a witness, particularly a child, can become engaged with Lucy to the point of distraction. Then the dog is left in the waiting room to act as a companion during court breaks.

In its first four years of the program, the dogs have supported almost 300 witnesses, nearly half of them children. The OPP has made 250 requests to magistrates and judges to allow Lucy and Kiki to accompany a witness giving evidence. There have been only five refusals. Most involve remote video evidence, where the victim is kept apart from the court and the alleged offender.

Lucy is also the first dog allowed into the witness box during testimony. She even bows to the judge. Morrison says all parties in the court see the value in support dogs. Less stress means fewer court breaks and allows trials to proceed more smoothly.

While Lucy's workload is full-time, occasionally during COVID she was able to support frightened child victims who police needed to interview.

In a suburban station, Lucy was sent to support one of three children. When Morrison and the dog were about to leave, a detective approached in desperation. 'She had a five-year-old boy who was totally withdrawn and asked if we could assist,' she says. 'Lucy walked in and within 10 minutes, the little tacker was making a full disclosure.'

The detective said she had never seen such a transformation.

Courts and law offices are intimidating at the best of times and for a victim unaccustomed to the austere nature of the justice system, it can all be too hard.

Gabby, the victim of a serious sexual assault, felt the walls closing in when she sat in the OPP waiting room. 'I felt like I was heading to the principal's office.'

Then she was introduced to Lucy. 'I immediately felt calmer because this majestic, beautiful dog was there for me.'

Sitting in the interview room, Gabby was asked if she was thirsty. 'Lucy went to the fridge and got me a bottle of water. I couldn't believe it.

'I have a strong bond with Lucy and things became a lot easier when I relaxed. She knew when I was anxious and would sit there licking my hand or putting her head on my knee. She could pick up on my emotions.'

Even when she was alone: 'I would look at her business card and talk to it. I thought "We can do this together." If not for the dog, I wouldn't have given evidence.'

Morrison says Lucy and Kiki's job is not just to support witnesses during court, but to minimise ongoing trauma by lowering stress levels. One tactic is to give witnesses a wristband from Lucy saying: *You are pawsome.*

There was one young witness who didn't seem that taken with the dog. Three months after the trial, her parents rang. 'She was beside herself because she had broken her bracelet. We sent her another one.'

And while on the subject of dogs

Wild dogs or a wild man? That is the question sweeping Victoria's high plains after a mysterious attack on a camper that sparked a remote rescue near Jamieson.

First, what we know.

On 10 December 2023, an experienced female camper went to bed in her tent around 8 pm. She woke two hours later to feel something tugging outside her tent, and then again around midnight.

At 1 am, she realised her tent was slashed or torn near the ground and her satchel, containing essential maps, her mobile phone and batteries, was gone.

The 40-year-old bushwalker was deep along the Australian Alpine Track on Mount Magdala on the Howitt Plains.

It's almost dead centre between Mount Buller and the Wonnangatta Valley, where, it has been alleged by prosecutors in that case, campers Russell Hill and Carol Clay were allegedly killed in March 2020.

Alone and far from help, if the female bushwalker panicked, she could have been dead. Being bloody-minded and continuing her journey could have resulted in the same fate. Instead, she weighed up the situation and used her Garmin emergency satellite device to send an alert that included her location.

Leading Senior Constable George Crawford from Jamieson drove three hours while the camper walked two hours to an agreed pick-up point.

'It was an extremely scary situation for her,' he said. 'Without maps and a phone, she made the right decision not to push on.'

Crawford said it also showed the importance of carrying emergency back-up equipment such as a satellite phone, noting the satchel was later recovered about 40 metres away with teeth mark indentations.

'There are packs of wild dogs in the area, and it is a timely reminder to place items in packs inside tents at night,' Crawford said.

Another group of campers reported seeing a dog snout sticking through their tent fly at night and Parks Victoria have at least four reports of wild dogs stealing from camp sites.

But the experienced camper told police she did not believe wild animals had stolen the satchel.

In a social media post, the woman wrote: *I have left the Alps track for now. Around 1 am the night before I left I had a flap cut in my tent mesh and a ziplock bag with valuables and electronics taken.*

I woke to the sound of the bag being pulled out of the flap in my tent. I went out and checked the area around but found nothing.

The image of the tent she posted online seems to show a straight cut in the tent material.

One local wondered why a dog would steal a satchel that didn't contain food and raised the name of a local legend dubbed the 'Button Man', who is always mentioned when there are mysterious goings-on in Victoria's High Country.

Many campers and hunters have stories of the Button Man emerging from the dark at camp sites. He is described as around 70, with short grey hair, wearing dark jackets and 'bloody scary'. Others say he is 'spooky', but no one reports any threats or violence.

He will grill them on why they are there but rarely responds to questions about himself.

The Button Man will gather supplies at a local store and head to the remotest areas, taking with him snares and Indigenous-style spears. He is known as the Button Man as he fashions buttons out of deer antlers. He also wears two as giant ear studs.

They say he moves through the toughest terrain with the competence and stamina of someone half his age.

At least eight experienced bushmen have had encounters, one saying he had a 'thousand-metre stare that made the hairs on the back of your neck stand up'.

They say no one knows he is near until he decides to make himself known. A wildlife photographer spent days taking shots in the area near the Button Man's camp. When he returned home and downloaded his photos, there was one unexplained shot of the photographer asleep inside his tent. No one knows who took the shot.

Bushies who have hidden firewood have found their stash gone. They say someone must have been watching to know the location.

For reasons only known to himself, he builds rock pyramids in random spots and places piles of pebbles on roads, so he knows if a car has passed.

There are many stories of experienced campers and hunters surprised when the Button Man has appeared after apparently silently following them.

When Button Man once wandered into a camp occupied by three military types, he asked what they did for a living. When one said: 'We hunt people', it's claimed the Button Man responded: 'So do I.'

The mystery of the mountains includes the disappearance of several people in the area, ranging from experienced bushwalkers to novices.

In each case, mobile phones or satellite devices were not activated and the bodies were never found.

In 2019, Niels Becker, 39, an experienced bushwalker, went missing on a five-day hike. He left the Upper Jamieson Hut on 24 October and two days later sent a message to his family from Vallejo Gantner Hut that he was heading to his car at Mount Stirling.

The last confirmed sighting was by the Button Man, who told police he saw the well-equipped hiker. The track took him past the Button Man's camp.

There is nothing to link the Button Man to any of these mysteries, but one thing is certain: his name will be whispered around High Country camp sites for many years.

And he may even be listening.

AT LAST, A STAR FOR POLICEMAN'S WIFE

Senior Detective Fred Milne was one of the best crook catchers of his generation – and there were plenty to catch.

It was post-Depression Melbourne and after 13 years as a uniformed policeman, Milne became a detective who specialised in working the slum of Fitzroy – then known as The Narrows – when Squizzy Taylor and his gang ran the district.

In an era when many police were on the take or prepared to look the other way, Milne was tough and honest – and the subject of regular death threats.

The official police record on Milne says: 'He had been part of and on the periphery of some of the biggest investigations of that period, including those of the notorious criminal Squizzy Taylor and had, along with other members, been the subject of threats against his person.'

He arrested gangsters, cracked a forgery racket and disrupted Taylor's blackmail business. A non-drinker, he moved on local sly-grog shops.

According to legendary crime reporter Hugh Buggy, writing in *The Argus*: 'He had a photographic memory for faces and was a shrewd, able and patient investigator. Those talents earned him many of the tougher assignments and pitted him against some of the most arrogant and powerful figures of Melbourne's underworld of the 20s.'

Eventually Fred took his wife, Aimee, and their three children away from Melbourne's underbelly to Geelong to work in the Criminal Investigation Branch where, Buggy suggested, 'he could have reasonably expected a little peace and quietness after years of turbulence'.

Instead, in the predawn darkness, an enemy bombed his house, intending to murder the policeman. Instead, Aimee was killed.

What happened in the early hours of 13 July 1936 involved what today would be considered an act of terrorism, an unsolved murder, an attack on law and order, and a massive oversight that Victoria Police is about to address, 83 years on.

Chief Commissioner Graham Ashton is to honour Aimee Milne by posthumously awarding her the Victoria Police Star – the first non-police recipient to receive the prestigious medal. The submission said: 'Although outside the policy, it is quite clear Aimee Milne's death is intrinsically linked to her relationship to her husband and . . . the Victoria Police force.'

In an official ceremony recognising her sacrifice, a plaque will be unveiled on her East Geelong grave and another will be mounted at the Geelong police station. Her family will be presented with the star.

The plaque reads in part: *She was an innocent victim of an attempt to murder her husband, Detective Sergeant Frederick Milne, a highly respected member of the Criminal Investigation Branch tackling organised crime in Geelong and Melbourne.*

Back then, Victoria's detective force was exclusively male and wives were expected to act as unpaid assistants. Police historian and retired chief inspector Ralph Stavely wrote: 'Police families were much more a part of the community. Security was non-existent and a policeman's home address was widely known. It was common for official queries to be directed to a policeman's wife in the absence of her husband.'

We tend to look back at those days as if the world was a better place; milkies with horses and carts delivered dairy to your home, men wore hats, women wore gloves and the city settled to sleep in the evening. In reality, we had a thriving underworld, prostitution networks, illegal gambling syndicates that survived by paying off police, and a barely concealed appetite for violence.

There were a series of bomb attacks on the private homes of police, one recorded as early as 1906, a number in the 1920s and the bombing of the East St Kilda home of a senior detective in 1931.

On 5 July and again on 7 July, Milne received telephone threats while working at the Geelong Police Station but having stared down Melbourne's worst gangsters, he was hardly worried. His wife, however, took them seriously and was particularly worried by violent local crook Edward George Carr, arrested by Milne at least three times.

She was concerned enough to tell friends she feared something dreadful was about to happen.

Discussing the case with a neighbour, her husband played down the threat. The inquest was told that Aimee Milne said: 'It's all very well for you to laugh, Fred, you do not know what sort of man you have to deal with.'

At 3.20 am on 13 July, Aimee, 40, woke when something sizzling and sparking was thrown through the front bedroom window of their five-room weatherboard home in Manning Street, Newtown. The inquest was told she leapt from her bed and shouted: 'Fred, I think it's a bomb or something.'

Fred looked out the window to see a man with a lighter. Almost certainly he was lighting the fuse to a second device.

According to police reports, Aimee tried to throw the first bomb out of the house when a second was rolled in. Evidence at the inquest indicated she could have been holding that bomb when it detonated.

Such was the force of the blast she was thrown out into the street, the front of the house was destroyed, their garage collapsed on the car, houses within 800 metres shook and the blast was heard three kilometres away. Aimee was killed instantly. Remarkably, Fred survived, shielded by the blankets still wrapped around him.

Thrown through a hole that opened in the floorboards, he was temporarily blinded and partially deafened but the first rescuers heard him call out: 'Get a light – I can't find my wife.'

His face was caked in thick dust. A neighbour said when the policeman's tears ran down his face, they washed gutters through the ghostly mask of white plaster.

Two of the couple's children, Chloris, 14, and Norman, 9, were safe at the back of the house. George, their eldest child, was not at home. (A few years later, in World War II, George was posted as missing, believed dead until Tokyo Rose read his name out on a propaganda broadcast as a POW.)

Police later established that the day before the bombing, someone stole 162 sticks of gelignite from a quarry less than three kilometres from the Milnes' home. The bombs were packed with more than two kilograms of the explosive.

Milne told fellow detectives: 'The man who was responsible for this crime has taken life without gratifying his desire for vengeance by killing me. I have done nothing to deserve this. I have done nothing but my duty. It is dreadful that an innocent woman should be the victim of such a crime and that my two children should have to suffer.'

Milne was convinced the bomber was career criminal Carr, later jailed for shooting another man.

At the inquest, Fred Milne, still partially deaf, had to cup his hand around his ear to hear. The counsel assisting stood next to the witness box to ask him questions. Milne said he had been warned to drop charges against Carr because he was a 'bad man' who might throw a bomb or set fire to his house. He broke down twice as he said that he had seen a man walking away but not his face.

Milne recovered sufficiently from his injuries to return to work for 14 years, retiring as a detective sergeant at the then mandatory age of 60. He died in 1964, aged 75.

Chloris' daughter, Margaret, said her mother rarely spoke of the death but in later years said that she had called out to her mother, who yelled 'Aimee's coming' just as the bomb exploded. Margaret said they moved in to care for Fred when his health started to fail. 'Mother said he never really recovered [from the murder of his wife] – he was a broken man.'

Norman Milne's daughter, Nancy, says her father was moulded by the tragedy. He was sent to board at private schools through donations from 'good citizens'.

'He didn't talk about it much but said they had a fair idea who did it but the perpetrator was never charged. He [Norman] was a very strong and forceful man probably because he had to become resilient at a young age.'

Norman Milne became a journalist at *The Age* and *West Australian*, breaking stories on secret atomic tests in WA, before moving into public relations.

Nancy remembers her grandfather as a teetotaller who was 'a stern and intimidating character'.

Superintendent Peter O'Neill from the Police Memorials Committee said the Victoria Police Star is awarded to police who suffer serious injury or death in connection with their duty. 'Because of Mrs Milne's close links to policing, she certainly qualifies.'

True Stories of Crimes, Cock-ups, Crooks & Cops
NAKED CITY
JOHN SILVESTER
'No journalist has done more to explain the world of crime, the justice system and the politics of law and order.'
Australian Media Hall of Fame
'He brings to life the characters of the good guys, the villains and the victims.'
Graham Perkin Australian Journalist of the Year Award

Naked City by John Silvester

John Silvester has been reporting on crime from the cop stations, courthouses, back alleys and gangster mansions of Melbourne for forty years. His contact book is a who's who of both sides of criminal justice and the shadowy worlds between. He is the trusted confidant of cops, criminals, lawyers and judges. He knows where the cash is stashed and where the bodies are buried.

Naked City is a collection of Silvester's best stories, from sophisticated heists to mindless acts of violence and deeds of pure evil – impeccably sourced, wry, wise and witty.

Travel the dark depths of Australia's criminal underworld with our most formidable crime reporter and an icon of Australian true crime.

'Sometimes I feel I am at war with Silvester, that I am a soldier in the trenches with my bayonet fixed.' Convicted murderer, Judy Moran

'Dear John, may the Yuletide log fall from your fireplace and burn your house down.' Standover man, Mark Brandon 'Chopper' Read